Writing Papers in College
A Brief Guide

Harvey S. Wiener

The City University of New York
LaGuardia Community College

Longman

Boston   Columbus   Indianapolis   New York   San Francisco   Upper Saddle River
Amsterdam   Cape Town   Dubai   London   Madrid   Milan   Munich   Paris   Montréal   Toronto
Delhi   Mexico City   São Paulo   Sydney   Hong Kong   Seoul   Singapore   Taipei   Tokyo

Senior Acquisition Edition: Lauren Finn
Senior Marketing Manager: Sandra McGuire
Production Manager: Denise Phillip
Project Coordination, Text Design, and Electronic Page Makeup:
  Integra
Cover Design Manager: Wendy Ann Fredericks
Cover Designer: Kay Petronio
Photo Researcher: Rona Tuccillo
Senior Manufacturing Buyer: Dennis J. Para
Printer and Binder: R. R. Donnelley & Sons/Crawfordsville
Cover Printer: R. R. Donnelley & Sons/Crawfordsville

Library of Congress Cataloging-in-Publication Data

Wiener, Harvey S.
    Writing papers in college : a brief guide/Harvey S. Wiener.
       p. cm.
    Includes bibliographical references and index.
    ISBN-13: 978-0-205-02906-8 (alk. paper)
    ISBN-10: 0-205-02906-X (alk. paper)
    1. English language—Rhetoric.   2. Report writing.   3. College readers.
I. Title.
    PE1408.W581947 2012
    808'.042—dc22

                                                      2010053143

1 2 3 4 5 6 7 8 9 10—DOC—14 13 12 11

Longman
is an imprint of

www.pearsonhighered.com   ISBN-13: 978-0-205-02906-8
                           ISBN-10:   0-205-02906-X

Contents

Preface *xi*

PART ONE Principles of Reading and Writing

CHAPTER 1 Reading Critically 1

Why Read? 1

Reading for Best Results 2

TIPS FOR READING CRITICALLY 2

Critical Reading in Action 3

   Lawrence Downes, "The Shy, Egg-Stealing Neighbor You Didn't Know
   You Had" [Annotated professional essay] 4

STRATEGY CHECKLIST: READING CRITICALLY 6

CHAPTER 2 Reading Visual Images 8

TIPS FOR UNDERSTANDING VISUALS 8

Reading a Photograph, Drawing, or Advertisement 9

   Examining a Photo 9

   Examining an Advertisement 10

   Nestlé, "Want a 'Lite' Baby Ruth?" [Advertisement] 10

Reading Charts, Graphs, Tables, and Cartoons 11

STRATEGY CHECKLIST: READING AND INTERPRETING VISUALS 13

Reading and Evaluating Web Sites 14

TIPS FOR READING AND EVALUATING WEB SITES 14

   Examining a Web Site 15

STRATEGY CHECKLIST: READING AND EVALUATING WEB SITES 16

Critical Reading on Your Own 16

   Christopher Caldwell, "Intimate Shopping: Should Everyone Know
   What You Bought Today?" [Professional essay] 17

CHAPTER 3 Active Writing 20

Choosing a Topic 20

   Setting Limits on a Topic 20

   Narrowing a Topic in Stages 21

Determining Your Purpose and Audience 22

Prewriting   23

STRATEGY CHECKLIST: PREWRITING   24

Organizing Ideas   25

Writing Drafts   26

TIPS FOR WRITING A ROUGH DRAFT   26

One Student Writing: First Draft   27

First Draft: John Fousek, "My Roommate" [Student essay]   29

STRATEGY CHECKLIST: HOW TO GET STARTED   30

CHAPTER 4 Finding and Supporting a Thesis   32

Understanding the Thesis   32

Elements of a Good Thesis   32

TIPS FOR EVALUATING A THESIS   32

Stating Your Thesis   33

TIPS FOR DEVELOPING A THESIS   34

Supporting Your Thesis: Details   36

Using Sensory Details   36

Using Data: Statistics, Cases, and Expert Testimony   37

STRATEGY CHECKLIST: STATING AND SUPPORTING YOUR THESIS   38

CHAPTER 5 Planning a Paper: Outlining   39

Making a Formal Outline   39

Establishing Main Divisions   39

Adding Supporting Details   40

Formatting a Formal Outline   40

Writing Topic and Sentence Outlines   41

Preparing Your Formal Outline   43

TIPS FOR WRITING A FORMAL OUTLINE   44

STRATEGY CHECKLIST: PREPARING A FORMAL OUTLINE   44

CHAPTER 6 Writing Your Paper   47

Writing Your Introduction   47

Seeing Various Introduction Strategies   47

TIPS FOR WRITING A STRONG INTRODUCTION   49

Writing the Body Paragraphs   49

Writing Topic Sentences   49

Using Transitions   51

Developing Paragraphs: Unity and Coherence   53

TIPS FOR ACHIEVING PARAGRAPH UNITY   55

TIPS FOR ACHIEVING PARAGRAPH COHERENCE   57

Writing a Strong Conclusion   57

TIPS FOR WRITING A STRONG CONCLUSION   59

CHAPTER 7 Revising for Thought, Content, and Structure   60

Revising to Improve Your Thesis   60

PROGRESS REMINDERS: REVISING YOUR THESIS   61

Revising for Appropriate Supporting Details   61

PROGRESS REMINDERS: REVISING FOR SUPPORTING DETAILS   61

Revising for Better Organization   62

PROGRESS REMINDERS: REVISING FOR BETTER ORGANIZATION   62

Revising for Purpose and Audience   62

PROGRESS REMINDERS: REVISING FOR PURPOSE AND AUDIENCE   63

Revising for Suitable Structure: Introduction, Body Paragraphs, Conclusion   63

PROGRESS REMINDERS: REVISING FOR SUITABLE STRUCTURE   65

CHAPTER 8 Revising to Improve Language   67

Revising Your Language   67

Denotation and Connotation   67

Abstract Writing and Concrete Writing   68

CHAPTER 9 Revising and Editing to Improve Style   71

Wordiness and Economy   71

Cutting Deadwood   71

Avoiding Pointless Repetition of Meaning   72

Cutting Wordy Clauses   72

Avoiding Delay of Subject   73

Passive and Active Verbs   73

Correcting Faulty Parallelism   74

What Is Parallelism?   74

Avoiding Faulty Parallelism   75

Faulty Subordination   76

Revising for Sentence Variety   77

Varying Sentence Length   77

Varying Sentence Structure   77

CHAPTER 10 Revising and Editing for Additional Style Problems 79

Triteness 79

Euphemisms 80

Repetition, Good and Bad 81
Repetition for Clarity 81
Repetition for Impact 81
Undesirable Repetition of Meaning 82
Undesirable Repetition of the Same Word 82
Undesirable Repetition of Sounds 82

Slang 83

Sexist Language 83
TIPS FOR AVOIDING AND CORRECTING SEXIST LANGUAGE 84

CHAPTER 11 One Student Writing: Revising and Editing in Action 86

Peer Review: Learning from Other Students 86

Revising and Editing: One Student Writing 87
Intermediate Draft 87
Learning from Your Instructor's Comments 89
Intermediate Draft with Instructor's Comments 90

Proofreading 91
TIPS FOR CAREFUL PROOFREADING 92

Putting It All Together 92
STRATEGY CHECKLIST: REVISING, EDITING, AND PROOFREADING YOUR DRAFTS 92

Final Draft: One Student Writing 94
Final Draft 94

PART TWO Methods of Development

CHAPTER 12 Description 97

Writing Your Descriptive Paper 97
TIPS FOR WRITING A DESCRIPTIVE ESSAY 97
STRATEGY CHECKLIST: WRITING AND REVISING YOUR DESCRIPTIVE PAPER 99

Writing Topics 100

CHAPTER 13 Narration 101

Writing Your Narrative Paper 101
TIPS FOR WRITING A NARRATIVE ESSAY 102

STRATEGY CHECKLIST: WRITING AND REVISING YOUR NARRATIVE PAPER   105

Writing Topics   106

CHAPTER 14 Example   107

Writing Your Example Paper   108

TIPS FOR WRITING AN EXAMPLE ESSAY   108

STRATEGY CHECKLIST: WRITING AND REVISING YOUR EXAMPLE PAPER   110

Writing Topics   111

CHAPTER 15 Process   112

Writing Your Process Paper   112

TIPS FOR WRITING A PROCESS ESSAY   112

STRATEGY CHECKLIST: WRITING AND REVISING YOUR PROCESS PAPER   115

Writing Topics   116

CHAPTER 16 Comparison and Contrast   117

Writing Your Comparison–Contrast Paper   117

TIPS FOR WRITING A COMPARISON–CONTRAST ESSAY   117

Comparison–Contrast Patterns   118

   Subject-by-Subject Pattern   118

   Point-by-Point Pattern   119

   Combined Pattern   119

STRATEGY CHECKLIST: WRITING AND REVISING YOUR COMPARISON–CONTRAST PAPER   120

Writing Topics   121

CHAPTER 17 Classification and Division   122

Classification and Division in Action   122

Using Division (or Analysis)   122

Using Classification   123

How Are Classification and Division Different?   124

Reviewing Division Strategies   125

Writing Your Classification Paper   125

TIPS FOR WRITING A CLASSIFICATION ESSAY   126

STRATEGY CHECKLIST: WRITING AND REVISING YOUR CLASSIFICATION PAPER   127

Writing Topics   128

CHAPTER 18 Cause and Effect   129

Writing Your Cause and Effect Paper   129

TIPS FOR WRITING A CAUSE AND EFFECT ESSAY   129

STRATEGY CHECKLIST: WRITING AND REVISING YOUR CAUSE
AND EFFECT PAPER   130

Writing Topics   131

CHAPTER 19 Definition   133

Writing Your Definition Paper   134
  Beginning a Formal Definition   134
TIPS FOR WRITING ONE-SENTENCE DEFINITIONS   135
  Writing Your Formal Definition Paper   135
  Writing Your Informal Definition Paper   136
STRATEGY CHECKLIST: WRITING AND REVISING YOUR DEFINITION PAPER   137

Writing Topics   138

CHAPTER 20 Argumentation   139

Using Logic   139
  Induction   139
  Deduction   140
  Using Induction and Deduction   141
  Avoiding Logical Fallacies   141
Writing Your Argumentation Paper   147
  Writing a Formal Argument   147
TIPS FOR WRITING A FORMAL ARGUMENT   147
  Developing a Debatable Position   147
STRATEGY CHECKLIST: WRITING AND REVISING YOUR ARGUMENTATION PAPER   148

Writing Topics   150

PART THREE Research and Writing from Sources

CHAPTER 21 Doing Research   151

Choosing Your Subject   151

Developing Your Thesis   151

Doing Preliminary Reading   153

Preparing Your Preliminary Outline   153

Finding Sources and Developing a Working Citations List   154
  Evaluating Your Sources   154
TIPS FOR EVALUATING SOURCES   154
  Keeping Records for Your Sources   155
STRATEGY CHECKLIST: FIRST STEPS IN DOING RESEARCH   159

CHAPTER 22 Selecting, Organizing, and Integrating Source Material in Your Writing   161

Taking Notes   161
   Recording Quotations   161
   Summarizing and Paraphrasing in Your Notes   162
Quoting and Paraphrasing Sources in Your Paper   163
   Quoting an Original Source   163
   Paraphrasing an Original Source   164
   Direct Quotations: How Many?   164
Avoiding Plagiarism   166
Preparing Your Formal Outline   168
STRATEGY CHECKLIST: SELECTING, ORGANIZING, AND INTEGRATING SOURCE MATERIAL   169

CHAPTER 23 Writing Your Research Paper and Citing and Documenting Sources   170

Writing Your Research Paper: An Overview   170
   The First Draft   170
   Subsequent Drafts   170
   Using Explanatory Notes   170
   Toward the Final Copy   171
Documenting Sources in the Humanities: MLA Style   171
   Parenthetical Citations   172
   A List of Works Cited   174
TIPS FOR PREPARING YOUR WORKS CITED LIST   181
Documenting Sources in the Social Sciences: APA Style   181
   Parenthetical Citations   181
   A List of APA References   183
   Preparing Your APA References List   184
TIPS FOR PREPARING YOUR APA REFERENCES LIST   185
Preparing Your Manuscript   185
TIPS FOR PREPARING THE FINAL COPY   185
STRATEGY CHECKLIST: WRITING YOUR RESEARCH PAPER   186
Sample MLA-Style Research Paper   187
   Elizabeth Kessler, "The Banning of the Polygraph" [MLA-style essay]   188

A Minibook of Essential Grammar and Common Errors   197

Credits   236
Index   237

Preface

College writing courses impart important information about rhetoric, reading, research, and grammar; and most textbooks for those courses weigh in with more than 600 pages and eye-popping price tags. About these textbooks we have heard many complaints: too many pages and too high costs. Was it possible then, we wondered, to reduce the length and price for a college writing text without losing the fundamental nature of instruction?

The challenge we set for ourselves was to produce a brief, flexible, and inexpensive textbook that would guide students successfully through the writing process without omitting key elements along the way.

Writing Papers in College is the result of that challenge. We've boiled down important instruction to its essence. We've created concise lists of tips for developing papers. We've presented plentiful checklists as guides through the basic steps of prewriting, drafting, revising, and editing.

You can use this book as the main text of your course or as a handy reference guide. We cover the range of writing assignments usually required in freshman composition, including the conventional rhetorical strategies that have long been the staple of most successful courses.

In Part One, Principles of Reading and Writing, we show the elements of reading critically both in texts and visuals, including graphs, charts, photographs, and advertisements. Then, we move to a full exploration of the writing process from generating ideas and forming and supporting a thesis through outlining and drafting a paper. Further in Part One, we deal in depth with revising for thought, content, and structure and to improve language. We also investigate revising and editing to advance sentence style and word choice. Readers will see how one student moves through the various steps in the writing process—prewriting, drafting, peer review, editing—and also will examine the student's final draft.

In Part Two, Methods of Development, we focus on various rhetorical strategies, such as comparison and contrast, cause and effect, and argumentation, just to name a few. Charts of tips and checklists on how to develop papers in these standard modes provide succinct, step-by-step, easy-to-follow instruction.

We devote Part Three, Research and Writing from Sources, to the all-important research paper. Students will review the elements of doing research, selecting and organizing source material, and integrating source material into their writing. We provide instruction and models for citing and documenting sources according to the latest guidelines from the Modern Language Association (MLA) and the American Psychological Association (APA). And we present a fully documented student research paper with annotations that highlight crucial points.

Finally, in A Minibook of Essential Grammar and Common Errors, students will find an indispensable, no-nonsense guide to correctness arranged alphabetically for easy reference. We show the most typical errors in writing and ways to deal with them so that students can prevent and correct their usual mistakes when they write, revise, and edit their papers.

Readers will find these helpful features in *Writing Papers in College*:

- Clear, readable instruction in all essential stages of the writing process
- Simple organization of chapters, allowing quick reference
- Numerous examples throughout to illustrate key concepts
- Samples of student writing to demonstrate the various stages in the writing process
- Exercises to stimulate discussion and writing
- Succinct yet comprehensive instruction in all aspects of producing a research paper
- A fully executed student research paper with appropriate citations and successful integration of sources as well as annotations to highlight key features
- Easy-to-use charts of tips and pointers throughout the text to bring fundamental instruction to light
- Abundant checklists for self-evaluation throughout the instructional program
- Instruction in critical reading, which includes strategies for reading visuals such as charts, graphs, photographs, cartoons, and advertisements
- A crucial guide to grammar and correctness in the extensive Minibook of Essential Grammar and Common Errors

For additional resources in reading, writing, and research, please visit www.mycomplab.com. For a fuller treatment of elements in this text, along with many more annotated student writing samples as well as comprehensive instruction in grammar and usage and professional essays, articles, short stories, and poems, see *Student's Book of College English: Rhetoric, Reader, Research Guide, and Handbook*, Twelfth Edition, by David Skwire and Harvey S. Wiener.

ACKNOWLEDGMENTS

This book is the brainchild of Lauren A. Finn, Acquisitions Editor at Pearson Education, and profuse thanks go first to her for her thoughtfulness and imagination in guiding the project to its fruition. Other people at Pearson Education threw their support behind this project, such as Joseph Opiela and Roth Wilkofsky, and I thank them for their attention and foresight. Sandra Manzanares helped shepherd the text through its various stages of production, and I would have been lost without her concentration and care. To my wife for putting up with a writer, especially during a long, hot summer, I owe much gratitude and love.

HARVEY S. WIENER

1
Reading Critically

WHY READ?

Even a few decades ago, the question "Why read?" would rarely have crossed anyone's mind. The essential way to wisdom and enlightenment, to understanding issues and reacting wisely to world events, to filling time with pleasurable activity, was to read books, magazines, journals, and newspapers. Reading brought knowledge; reading brought delight; reading brought comfort and self-awareness.

In an age of multimedia, however, the question "Why read?" has urgency. After all, televisions, DVD players, computers, video game consoles, MP3 players, and cell phones all compete to fill our time with exciting visual and auditory presentations. We can watch and listen to an extraordinary range of information without turning a page of paper.

So, why read? One set of responses to this question is obvious, of course. We read traffic signs and warning signs. We read recipes and directions for putting together a toy or installing an air conditioner. We read menus and sales brochures. Furthermore, we also read in various electronic media. Television images frequently include words that we have to read. Text messaging on a cell phone involves reading and writing. E-mail, instant messages, blogs, and Web sites usually require us to decode written language. So, reading skills such as dealing with new vocabulary, figuring out the meaning of a message, and using inference regularly come into play. At the very least, being an attentive reader is important for survival as we go about our daily lives.

But beyond these practical instances, why should you try to improve your reading competence, especially in college, where you can address innumerable topics and questions through nonbook sources? First, the skills involved in reading print material clearly apply to modern media, too. For example, if you're checking the U.S. Fish and Wildlife Service's Web site (http://www.fws.gov/endangered) to write a paper on endangered species, you're going to have to read what the site has to say. You may also have to read magazine articles and scholarly papers online on the subject of endangered species. Technology, reading, and college learning are clearly intertwined.

Much of the world's collected knowledge still resides in print that dwells in non-cyber libraries and bookstores. To maximize your learning experience, you'll have to read books handed down across centuries, do required textbook reading in your courses, and research newspapers and magazines that may not be online. These print media have a permanence that cyberspace often lacks. (How many times have you checked a site you've visited before only to find it no longer exists or has not been updated to address recent incidents and developments?)

Many people are passive readers. They start reading with little advanced thought. They expect the words and sentences on a page to produce meaning without the reader's help. Passive readers do little to build a partnership with the writer and the text in order to understand what the writer says.

Active readers, critical readers, on the other hand, know that they have to work at getting meaning from words and sentences. They take conscious steps to engage what they read. The writer and the reader together create meaning.

READING FOR BEST RESULTS

Critical readers interact with a text. That is, they raise questions about word use and content, consider aspects of style and essay structure, and examine the facts and ideas a selection conveys. They check the writer's observations and conclusions against their own thoughts and experiences. Critical readers use many of the following strategies when reading.

TIPS FOR READING CRITICALLY

- **Have a reason for reading.** You need to think in advance about what you expect to gain from your reading. You can read to learn new concepts and vocabulary, to prepare for a class lecture or discussion, to stimulate your own writing for a required essay, to explore essential scholarship for a research paper, or to examine writing strategies as an aid to honing your own skills. Without a purpose you risk a passive stance as a reader, and that puts you at a disadvantage of never truly interacting with the words before you.
- **Explore what you know about the topic before you read.** Prior knowledge dramatically influences a reader's response to a text, in terms of both understanding and appreciation. Before you read anything below the title, look long and hard at it. Try to connect the title with any related information you may have seen or heard. Look at any subtitles, photographs, illustrations, graphs, charts—and all the accompanying captions—before you begin reading. Think a moment about the author's name and about any information provided about the author.
- **As you read, record your responses.** Write down what the selection makes you think of or what it makes you feel. Write out any questions you have. Copy out phrases that stimulate, challenge, annoy, thrill, puzzle, or ignite you. Make notes in the margins of books you own.
- **Establish the writer's thesis.** All good readers try to determine the main point of a reading. Sometimes the writer will tell you very directly what the thesis is, and before the end of the first few paragraphs—sometimes at the end of the very first

sentence—you'll know exactly what the piece is about. But in other cases, no single statement or statements will tell you the thesis precisely. Here you have to state the writer's thesis in your own words. The various sentences and paragraphs in an essay will contribute information that you must use to define the thesis yourself.

- **Pay attention to the words the writer chooses.** As you know, words are alive with both denotative (the dictionary definition) and connotative (the implied or suggested definition) meanings. Consider for a moment that a writer naming a person of about thirteen years old can use one of these words that, roughly speaking, would do the job: youngster, child, adolescent, teenager, kid, eighth grader, prepubescent, young adult. Critical readers always consider the implications of word choice and think about why a writer selects one word instead of another.

- **Determine the writer's purpose and audience.** Writers have many reasons for writing: to inform, to entertain, to challenge, to complain, to convince, to describe, to tell a story, to call for action—there are others certainly. As you read, you should be able to figure out the intended purpose. Related to the writer's purpose is the audience the writer has in mind for the essay. The intended audience influences the writing markedly. For example, to write about steps for preventing the spread of AIDS, a writer would use wholly different strategies if writing for eighth-grade kids in a suburban classroom, for social workers in Chicago, or for health care workers in Africa.

- **Consider the way that the writer has constructed the essay.** Look at the sentences to see if they relate to the main point. Look at elements like introductions and conclusions, the essay's opening and closing doors, so to speak. Do they achieve their ends? Do they satisfy you? How do the parts of the essay hold together? Do all the ideas seem to relate to the central point? Do the sentences connect smoothly with each other? Attending to the structure of what you read will help you learn strategies for your own writing.

- **Be aware of the writer's tone.** Simply stated, *tone* is the writer's attitude toward the subject. For example, one writer writing about the high incidence of guns in schools could approach the topic with shock and horror; another, with anger; another, analytically, seeking only to understand motives; another, clinically, simply describing or chronicling events; another, sentimentally, longing for the good old school days with no weapons and with well-behaved kids. Thoughtful readers always keep an eye on the tone; like purpose and audience, it influences word choice, sentence structure, and style.

CRITICAL READING IN ACTION

Look at the following selection and note in the margins the questions and comments raised by a critical reader about the piece "The Shy, Egg-Stealing Neighbor You Didn't Know You Had." Note the steady interaction between the student and the essay regarding language and content—the student reader cross-examines the piece, acknowledges important or difficult words, and makes comments on the writing.

Answer the questions after you read.

The Shy, Egg-Stealing Neighbor You Didn't Know You Had

Lawrence Downes

Odd title—whose neighbor steals eggs? And if it's a neighbor, how could you not know you had it?

1   The suburbs, pretty as they may be, are nobody's idea of nature in balance. Sure, they are lush, green places where people and their vehicles get along with flowers, vegetables, songbirds and the littler mammals. But this harmony is enforced with an iron fist. It takes lots of chemicals, artificial irrigation and gas-powered trimming and mowing to keep such an arbitrary ecosystem under control.

True? Nobody's idea?

Fair? Urban "ecosystems" also arbitrary and must be controlled.

2   Leave it to nature to mount an insurgency against the tranquility of the grass-and-pavement grid. Canada geese and white-tail deer are the most brazen intruders, multiplying beyond all reason and refusing to be subdued. The best-equipped predators, people, sidestepped the job, finding it distasteful. Instead they adjust their garden netting, check for ticks and brood about the tendency of their fallen Eden to keep collapsing into chaos.

Nice word! Implies conscious uprising, people on the attack!

People refuse to control the intruders. "Distasteful" because we'd have to kill them somehow.

Writer's view of suburbs. Good image—"grass-and-pavement grid."

Here, "insurgency" is by geese and deer!

3   But what if that didn't always happen? What if Mother Nature decided not to run amok but to tidy up?

Questions raised: Expect writer to answer them.

4   Just such an amazing circumstance appears to be happening on the outskirts of Chicago. Research biologists there announced last month that they had stumbled across a possible answer to the problem of the proliferating suburban goose: the proliferating suburban coyote.

Coyotes are keeping goose population in check. How?

Good image: "Mother" Nature tidying up.

5   The researchers belong to the Cook County Coyote Project, which has spent nearly six years studying the habits of more than 200 coyotes in the northern and western Chicago suburbs. Among other things, they tried to determine what the growing numbers of these beasts might have had to do with another puzzling development: the sudden end of the goose explosion. The local population of Canada geese had soared in the 1980's and 90's, but by 2000 the increase had slowed to about only 1 percent a year. An unknown predator was assumed to be the reason.

Repetition of word "proliferating"— good balancing. One proliferation is a problem, the other a solution.

Sounds responsible. Google this?

Coyotes grow in numbers. Geese stop populating. What's the reason?

6   The coyote was not an obvious suspect, being small and skulky and unlikely to stand up to a wrathful Canada goose. Examinations of coyote scat had seldom found damning traces of eggshell. But then infrared cameras exposed the coyote as a nest robber, one that carefully cracks open a goose egg and licks it clean.

This is how it's done! Coyote cracks egg and sucks out insides—leaves no evidence.

Canada geese have mean tempers.

7   Evidence like this bolsters the conclusion that coyotes, in their own wily way, have become keystone predators in a

Wily means cunning.

Expert testimony—professor knows the issues as project head.

Resourceful creatures!

land long emptied of wolves and mountain lions. The Cook County project's principal investigator, Prof. Stanley Gehrt of Ohio State University, speaks admiringly of his subjects, who have withstood more than 200 years of hunting, trapping and poisoning and are more entrenched in North America than ever. Every state but Hawaii has them. They have spread into suburbs and cities, forcing biologists to revise their definition of coyote habitat to this. Basically anywhere.

No wolves or mountain lions left to do the job.

Check on coyotes here in this state. Goes back to title "Shy, Egg-Stealing Neighbors."

8   Here is what is really strange: Humans have barely noticed. Egg-rustling, night-howling varmints are raising litters in storm drains, golf courses, parks and cemeteries. They are sometimes heard but seldom seen. In cities, they keep to themselves and work nights. There are coyotes, Professor Gehrt says, living in the Chicago Loop.

Transition refers to previous paragraph.

"Sneaky" and "discreet"—words for human activity contribute to coherence of essay.

9   You could call that sneaky. Or you could call it discreet. Professor Gehrt said that one surprising discovery of the study was how little danger the coyote poses to his unwitting human neighbors. "The risk is quite low, as long as we don't monkey with their behavior," he said. If you assert yourself when you see one—by yelling, cursing and throwing sticks—it will respect your space and lie low. The coyote's tendency to avoid people—and more importantly, raccoons—has made rabies a nonissue, Professor Gehrt said, with only one case of coyote-to-human transmission ever recorded.

Shih Tzu is a small dog, once a favorite of the Imperial Chinese court, now a favorite of wealthy suburbanites.

10   Coyotes will behave, he said, as long as people do not feed them. Leave nothing tasty outside in an open trash can or food dish, and definitely nothing small and fluffy at the end of a leash. Professor Gehrt says with confidence that the sensible suburban toddler has little to fear from the suburban coyote, but he will not say the same for the suburban Shih Tzu.

Obviously a cat or dog—coyotes will go after them.

A little humor here. More use of "people" words ("well-mannered," "responsible").

11   The Cook County Coyote Project is the largest and most comprehensive of its kind, but it is just one study. It is probably not the time to call for coyote subsidies and captive-breeding programs for goose-plagued subdivisions. But any effort to learn more about these creatures—like a four-year coyote study being done in Westchester County by New York State and Cornell University—is highly welcome. It is intriguing to consider the possibility that such a shunned, maligned animal may be a misunderstood hero. The suburbs could use well-mannered, responsible predators, and house cats are clearly not up to the job.

Maligned means badly treated.

Why maligned? What is coyote's history?

For Writing or Discussion

1. What is the main point of Downes' piece?
2. How do the marginal notes demonstrate critical reading?

3. Where does the reader call attention to issues of language? Why does the reader raise these issues?

4. How does the comment about the title show an application of prior knowledge? Now that you've read the selection, how would you answer the question that the reader raised about the title?

5. What additional comments or questions would you raise about this piece?

STRATEGY CHECKLIST: Reading Critically

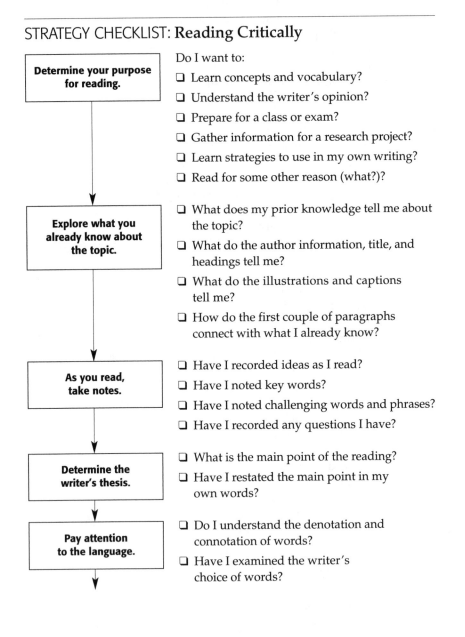

Determine your purpose for reading.

Do I want to:

❑ Learn concepts and vocabulary?

❑ Understand the writer's opinion?

❑ Prepare for a class or exam?

❑ Gather information for a research project?

❑ Learn strategies to use in my own writing?

❑ Read for some other reason (what?)?

Explore what you already know about the topic.

❑ What does my prior knowledge tell me about the topic?

❑ What do the author information, title, and headings tell me?

❑ What do the illustrations and captions tell me?

❑ How do the first couple of paragraphs connect with what I already know?

As you read, take notes.

❑ Have I recorded ideas as I read?

❑ Have I noted key words?

❑ Have I noted challenging words and phrases?

❑ Have I recorded any questions I have?

Determine the writer's thesis.

❑ What is the main point of the reading?

❑ Have I restated the main point in my own words?

Pay attention to the language.

❑ Do I understand the denotation and connotation of words?

❑ Have I examined the writer's choice of words?

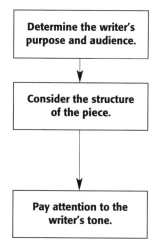

Determine the writer's purpose and audience.

❑ Why has the writer written the piece?
❑ Who is the writer's intended audience?

Consider the structure of the piece.

❑ How do the introduction and conclusion serve the essay?
❑ Do all sentences relate to the main idea?
❑ Do sentences follow one another logically?

Pay attention to the writer's tone.

❑ What is the writer's attitude to the subject?
❑ How does the language contribute to the tone?

2

Reading Visual Images

Not only words and sentences but also visual images fill the pages that we read regularly. Thoughtful readers pay careful attention to visuals.

When you see a visual image—a photograph, a pen-and-ink drawing, a cartoon, an illustration, an advertising promotion—you can't fully understand and appreciate it without language. Always try to put thought into words when you read a visual image. Our powers as thinking, word-using human beings give us the ability to take as much as possible from a pictorial representation.

TIPS FOR UNDERSTANDING VISUALS

- **Translate what you see into language.** Tell yourself what you think the image means. If it has a caption or title, use the words presented as a springboard to interpret what you see.
- **Look at the whole image as well as its parts.** Be sure to examine the parts as well as the whole to get the overall effect of a visual representation. Determine the relations among the people or places or events shown in the picture.
- **Consider the purpose and techniques used by the image creator.** How close is the camera to its subject? What facial expression does the visual aim to capture? Is the scene natural or staged? How does the cartoon exaggerate its subject to produce a positive or negative image? Is the visual a composite, where pieces from several pictures are cut and pasted together to form a new image—and what does it mean if the image is, in fact, a composite?
- **Pay particular attention to advertisements.** Be aware of the elements used in an advertisement. Does the ad appeal to your emotions, fears, goals, dreams, or desires? Who is its intended audience? How does the language in the ad interact with the visual elements? What action does the ad want you to take?
- **Examine carefully all visuals that accompany text.** Look thoughtfully at graphs, charts, statistical tables, photographs, maps, drawings, diagrams, and other illustrations. How do they help you better understand the material you're reading?

READING A PHOTOGRAPH, DRAWING, OR ADVERTISEMENT

Examining a Photo

Look at the picture below. In a sentence explain the point of the picture—that is, what you think the picture is about.

Photo Courtesy: Chris Graythen/Getty Images

You probably said something like, "A young person is carrying three cats in a large plastic container." But certainly there is more to the photograph than that, and only careful observation can help you flesh out other important information. The person is stepping through water with shoes and socks on: That implies some kind of urgent departure, perhaps the result of a flood or a hurricane. Trees immersed in water support that observation. The expression on the person's face is one of worry, even fear; and although you might identify the person as a young male, there is little evidence in the photograph about the gender of the person. The writing on the T-shirt suggests other key elements, or at least helps you raise other questions. Is the word "Jesuit" merely a T-shirt decoration? Or does the word imply a religious or charitable commitment that might explain an apparently selfless act of animal rescue in a dangerous situation?

In the "Strategy Checklist: Reading and Interpreting Visuals" are some questions you should ask when you see a photo.

Examining an Advertisement

Advertisements use images and words to persuade us to buy a product, admire a company, or support a point of view on an issue. Use some of the strategies shown in the "Strategy Checklist: Reading and Interpreting Visuals" on page 13 to answer questions about the following advertisements.

Nestlé, "Want a 'Lite' Baby Ruth?"

For Writing or Discussion

1. Whom does the Baby Ruth ad portray? What kind of job does the man in the ad have? Why does the ad present such a person—an overweight laborer—instead of a teenager or a more glamorous figure? What assertion does the visual image intend?
2. What is the meaning of the words on the man's T-shirt? Why is the word "lite" in quotation marks? Where else have you seen the word "lite" in product

advertisements? What other "lite" product is the man in the picture not apt to use? How do you know?

3. This ad appeared in *Rolling Stone*, a magazine dedicated to music, bands, and recording artists and directed at a young teenage and post-teenage audience. Why would Nestlé, the makers of the candy bar, place an ad in this magazine? And why this particular ad?

4. Would you buy a Baby Ruth as a result of this advertisement? Write an essay in which you analyze the ad and explain its appeal—or lack of appeal—to you.

READING CHARTS, GRAPHS, TABLES, AND CARTOONS

To support their positions on a variety of topics across the disciplines, academic writers are making increasing use of visuals. A writer explaining the inconsistencies in estimating the number of illegal aliens in the United States, for example, would have to provide written evidence. But think about the added impact of the following chart that the writer could insert into the essay:

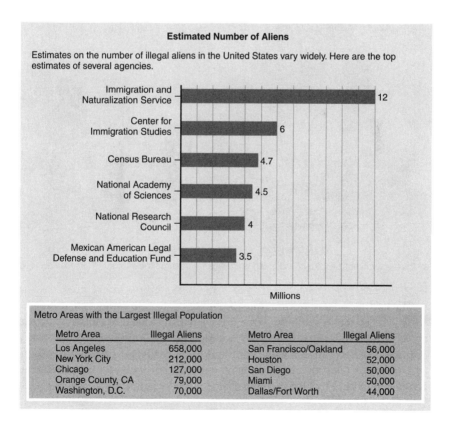

Estimated Number of Aliens

Estimates on the number of illegal aliens in the United States vary widely. Here are the top estimates of several agencies.

Agency	Millions
Immigration and Naturalization Service	12
Center for Immigration Studies	6
Census Bureau	4.7
National Academy of Sciences	4.5
National Research Council	4
Mexican American Legal Defense and Education Fund	3.5

Metro Areas with the Largest Illegal Population

Metro Area	Illegal Aliens	Metro Area	Illegal Aliens
Los Angeles	658,000	San Francisco/Oakland	56,000
New York City	212,000	Houston	52,000
Chicago	127,000	San Diego	50,000
Orange County, CA	79,000	Miami	50,000
Washington, D.C.	70,000	Dallas/Fort Worth	44,000

Note how the graph and the table beneath it put important data in visual and verbal form. The horizontal bars show readers the relations among the various estimates of illegal aliens in our country; the labels to the left of the bars identify the various organizations providing these estimates; and the numbers to the right of the bars indicate the millions of people in each estimate. The table lists in declining order the cities with the largest illegal alien populations and provides the estimated numbers of aliens in each city.

Cartoons too can make important statements in visual terms. Look at this editorial cartoon:

"Well, they look pretty undocumented to me."

© The New Yorker Collection 2006. J. B. Handlesman from cartoonbank.com. All Rights Reserved.

The cartoon makes a humorous point about illegal immigration by using current language to show the arrival of European settlers to our shores when only Native Americans dwelled in America. No one on the *Mayflower* was a documented alien; in this view, the Pilgrims were illegal aliens. The cartoonist's negative view of our documentation demands on immigrants comes across subtly but powerfully in this visual representation.

STRATEGY CHECKLIST: Reading and Interpreting Visuals

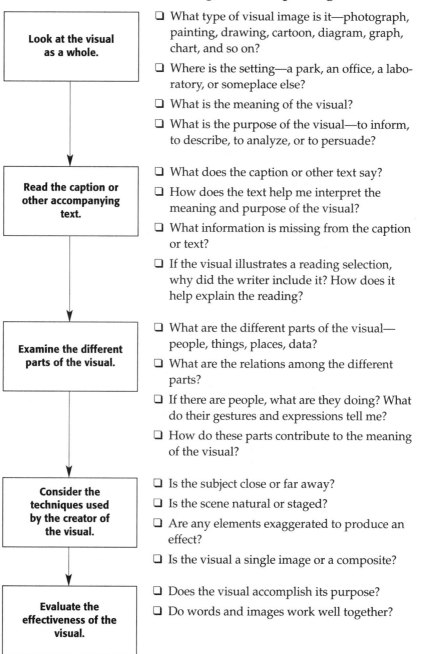

Look at the visual as a whole.

❏ What type of visual image is it—photograph, painting, drawing, cartoon, diagram, graph, chart, and so on?

❏ Where is the setting—a park, an office, a laboratory, or someplace else?

❏ What is the meaning of the visual?

❏ What is the purpose of the visual—to inform, to describe, to analyze, or to persuade?

Read the caption or other accompanying text.

❏ What does the caption or other text say?

❏ How does the text help me interpret the meaning and purpose of the visual?

❏ What information is missing from the caption or text?

❏ If the visual illustrates a reading selection, why did the writer include it? How does it help explain the reading?

Examine the different parts of the visual.

❏ What are the different parts of the visual—people, things, places, data?

❏ What are the relations among the different parts?

❏ If there are people, what are they doing? What do their gestures and expressions tell me?

❏ How do these parts contribute to the meaning of the visual?

Consider the techniques used by the creator of the visual.

❏ Is the subject close or far away?

❏ Is the scene natural or staged?

❏ Are any elements exaggerated to produce an effect?

❏ Is the visual a single image or a composite?

Evaluate the effectiveness of the visual.

❏ Does the visual accomplish its purpose?

❏ Do words and images work well together?

For Writing or Discussion

1. Reexamine the photograph on page 9. Where do you think it was taken? How do you know?
2. What details of the scene best capture the sense of the moment?
3. Write a paragraph or two to tell the story that you think emerges from the picture.

READING AND EVALUATING WEB SITES

Web sites have become important resources for finding information, exploring topics, and doing basic research. Combining vibrant visual images, lively graphics, color reproductions, and sound bytes along with print, Web sites are enticing resources for anyone with a computer. Yet the ease of setting up a site and making it widely available is both the strength and essential weakness of Internet sources. Just how reliable are they? Spammers—those who inundate your e-mail in-box with unwanted messages—no doubt have linked you to many sites of questionable value and authenticity that offer everything from weight-loss programs and cheap prescription medicine to home refinancing and obscene photographs. You already know that suspicious Web sites take up too much space on the Internet.

TIPS FOR READING AND EVALUATING WEB SITES

- **Don't assume that all information found on the Internet is reliable.** Check to see if the information comes from a dependable source. For example, Web site addresses that end with abbreviations like *.gov* (government body), *.org* (non-profit organization), and *.edu* (educational institution) are often reliable and can serve as good starting points for online research. Many *.com* sites are not reliable.
- **Look carefully at the author or sponsor of the Web site.** Check the sponsor's and author's credentials. Identify the author's connection to any organization, lobbying group, or commercial enterprise, or to some association with a political, social, or economic agenda that can influence the site.
- **Examine visual as well as verbal elements.** Web designers integrate words and graphics, so you need to think about how they interact to give you information.
- **Read sidebars, banners, and tabs for more information and related links.** These additional elements can help you find further information on the topic.
- **Use your prior knowledge as a barometer of the information you find on the site.** The online information should seem consistent with your other reading.
- **Determine the purpose of the site and its intended audience and point of view.** If these elements are hidden or not easily accessible, treat the site with skepticism.
- **Look for an indication of the dates the site was prepared and revised.** You want to certify that information is current. Even if the preparation and revision dates seem recent, be sure that the material itself is as well.

- **Be sure that the site indicates its sources of information.** You want to be able to validate the information at similar sources and assure that facts seem reasonable, reliable, and truthful.
- **Check the site for an appropriate level of breadth and range.** Unfortunately, superficial approaches to important topics are abundant on Web sites, and you want to be certain that any site you use shows an understanding of the issues' complexity.
- **Be sure that the site provides adequate evidence to corroborate assertions made.**

Examining a Web Site

Examine the Web site below, paying particular attention to the labels in the margin that point to important features of the site. Then, using the "Tips for Reading and Evaluating Web Sites," answer the questions in the Strategy Checklist (page 16).

STRATEGY CHECKLIST: Reading and Evaluating Web Sites

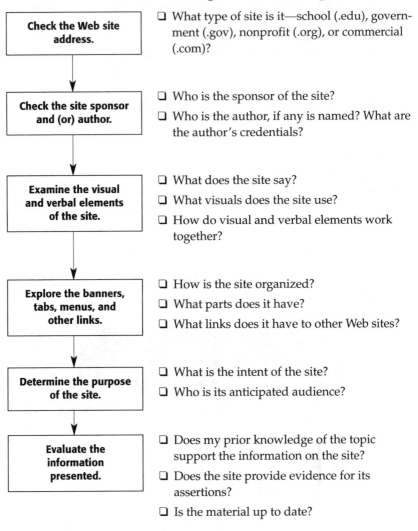

Check the Web site address.

❑ What type of site is it—school (.edu), government (.gov), nonprofit (.org), or commercial (.com)?

Check the site sponsor and (or) author.

❑ Who is the sponsor of the site?
❑ Who is the author, if any is named? What are the author's credentials?

Examine the visual and verbal elements of the site.

❑ What does the site say?
❑ What visuals does the site use?
❑ How do visual and verbal elements work together?

Explore the banners, tabs, menus, and other links.

❑ How is the site organized?
❑ What parts does it have?
❑ What links does it have to other Web sites?

Determine the purpose of the site.

❑ What is the intent of the site?
❑ Who is its anticipated audience?

Evaluate the information presented.

❑ Does my prior knowledge of the topic support the information on the site?
❑ Does the site provide evidence for its assertions?
❑ Is the material up to date?

CRITICAL READING ON YOUR OWN

Read the following selection and, using what you have learned in this chapter, draw on the various skills that will help you understand the piece fully. Take notes as you read. Note the use of visuals and the way that they support the text.

Christopher Caldwell is a senior editor at the *Weekly Standard*. He is a regular contributor to the *Financial Times* and *Slate*. His essays and reviews appear in the *New York Times*, the *Wall Street Journal*, and the *Washington Post*.

Answer the questions after you read.

Intimate Shopping: Should Everyone Know What You Bought Today?

Christopher Caldwell

1   "**Information**," the apostles of cyberspace have been singing for more than a decade, "wants to be free." Well, maybe *your* information does. But in late November, the social networking Web site Facebook discovered that many of its 58 million members don't feel that way. On social networks, people can exchange photos, letters and information with people they know, and "friend" people they don't. Facebook has grown so big, so rich (its market value is estimated at $15 billion) and so addictive because it offers its users new ways to exchange information and intimacies with people they care about. In early November, Facebook's 23-year-old C.E.O., Mark Zuckerberg, rolled out an advertising program called Beacon. It would track users onto the sites of Facebook's commercial partners—Coca-Cola, the N.B.A., *The New York Times* and Verizon, among others—and keep their friends posted about what they were doing and buying there.

2   Did it ever. A Massachusetts man bought a diamond ring for Christmas for his wife from overstock.com and saw his discounted purchase announced to 720 people in his online network. What if it hadn't been for his wife? What if he had been buying acne cream? Pornography? A toupee? You could go on. Researchers at Computer Associates, an information-technology firm, discovered that Beacon was more invasive than announced. MoveOn.org started a petition movement against Beacon that rallied 75,000 Facebook subscribers.

3   Facebook designed Beacon so that members would be able to "opt out" by clicking in a pop-up window. But these windows were hard to see and

Michael Lewis/GalleryStock

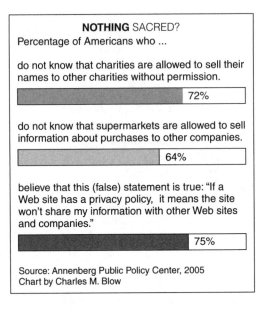

disappeared very fast. If you weren't quick on the draw, your purchases were broadcast to the world, or at least to your network. Since people, too, sometimes want to be free, privacy advocates urged that Beacon be made an "opt in" program, which members would have to explicitly consent to join. In early December, Facebook agreed to this approach.

4   The Beacon fiasco gives a good outline of what future conflicts over the Internet will look like. Whether a system is opt-in or opt-out has an enormous influence on how people use it. He who controls the "default option"—the way a program runs if you don't modify it—writes the rules. Online, it can be tempting to dodge the need to get assent for things that used to require it. This temptation is particularly strong in matters of privacy. For instance, the "default option" of the pre-Internet age was that it was wrong to read others' mail. But Google now skims the letters of its Gmail subscribers, in hopes of better targeting them with ads, and the N.S.A. looks for terrorists not only in the traditional manner—getting warrants for individual wiretaps—but also by mining large telecommunications databases.

5   So it is with Facebook's Beacon. We used to live in a world where if someone secretly followed you from store to store, recording your purchases, it would be considered impolite and even weird. Today, such an option can be redefined as "default" behavior. The question is: Why would it be? The price in reputation for overturning this part of the social contract is bound to be prohibitively high.

6   For the owners of social-networking sites, it may be a price worth paying. Thanks to data-collection technology, your shopping choices and preferences have value. Who owns those choices? Common sense says that you do. If a company wants to use you to advertise its products, it can pay you, just as Nike pays Tiger Woods. But the idea that your preferences (not to

mention your conversations about them) are your property rests on an implicit social contract. And the thing about implicit contracts is that people who can figure out ways to break them can often make a lot of money.

7 The concept of "implicit contracts" was developed in a landmark 1988 paper by the economists Andrei Shleifer and Lawrence Summers. Their subject—hostile corporate takeovers—seems far from cyberprivacy, but it is not. Shleifer and Summers showed that increases in share price following takeovers were not due to gains in efficiency, as the defenders of those buyouts claimed. There often were such gains, but they were not the source of the profits. The profits came from reneging on implicit contracts—like the tradition of overpaying older workers who had been overworked when young on the understanding that things would even out later. These contracts, because implicit, were hard to defend in court. But the assets they protected were real. To profit from them, buyout artists had only to put someone in place who could, with a straight face and a clean conscience, say, "I didn't promise nothin'!"

8 As commerce moves from Main Street to the Web, lots of businessmen are in that position. All bets are off, and entrepreneurs are seeking new ways to make money by trial and error. Sometimes they do so by adding value to the economy. Sometimes they do so by abrogating implicit contracts. Like managers newly seated after a hostile takeover a quarter-century ago, today's online innovators are not always skilled at telling the difference: "Your friendships are your own business? Golly, I wasn't here when they negotiated *that*."

9 Beacon was a clumsy attempt to reset the default on the common-sense understanding of discretion and to profit off the resetting. As in the 1980s, technological sophistication, entrepreneurial genius and gains to efficiency are a part of this story—but a larger part was the attempt to monetize and sell a vulnerable implicit contract. Facebook was thwarted, as the corporate raiders of years past were not, because it aimed not at pension plans and seniority-based pay scales but at something considerably more valuable—the unwritten rules of privacy that make civilized human interaction possible.

For Writing or Discussion

1. What did your prior knowledge contribute to your approach to the selection before reading it? How did the title help? The brief statement about what the essay deals with? The information about the author? The photo? The graph?
2. What is the main point of the selection? State it in your own words.
3. What notes or marginal comments did you write as you read the piece?
4. What was the writer's purpose in writing this piece? Who do you think was his intended reader?
5. How well do the introduction and conclusion serve the selection?
6. What does the photograph add to the selection? The graph? Why did the writer include these visuals with his essay?

3

Active Writing

Writing comes alive when it is the product of active engagement. Getting into the habit of a lively exchange with yourself and others about writing tasks will mean the difference between writing that is vital to you and your readers and writing that is mechanical and tedious, done just to finish an assignment.

CHOOSING A TOPIC

Choosing a subject isn't usually a big problem. If you choose to write about something on your own, you do so because you are interested in it and you want to share your thoughts with others. If you don't actually choose to write but are told to do so, your instructor will usually give you a general subject. For example, your history professor probably won't tell you simply to write a paper; he will assign a paper on the effects of Islamic culture on the Western world. Even when your assignment is an essay based on a personal experience, your instructor will give you a general subject: a memorable journey, an influential person, a goal, a hobby, a favorite magazine or newspaper.

Setting Limits on a Topic

Most subjects need to be limited, and that can create a problem. You need to decide what part of the subject you will write about. Consider the assignment about the effects of Islamic culture on the Western world. The topic is vast, and so you must limit it. Prewriting efforts (see pages 23–25) can help you identify one or two groups of ideas or facts that dominate your early thinking. You could choose one of them as your limited subject.

You can let your special interests determine how you limit the subject. If, for example, you have a good understanding of architecture, you may decide to explain how Islamic culture contributed to modern architecture by exploring geometric forms. Or you might write about the influence on modern sculpture of geometric form as design. If you're a nursing or pre-med student, you could trace the contributions of the Islamic world to medical science. If you're interested in politics, you might discuss the effects on early Islamic cultures of the lack of a centralized government, comparing these cultures with others of the same period that were governed by a pope or emperor. Your interests could lead to other subjects—from military strategies to love poems—and still fulfill the assignment. Any subject, then, can and must be limited before you begin to write, and your personal interests can often determine the way you limit it.

Narrowing a Topic in Stages

Some writers find it useful to narrow a broad topic to a manageable one through a series of three or four steps, each step contracting the topic a little more. By moving from a general topic to more and more specific ones, the writer can shape the subject to suit her interests and meet the requirements of the assignment.

Suppose you wanted to write about the topic *crime in America*. Clearly the topic is too broad. Note how the writer moved progressively to more specific subject matter.

Too General ⟶	More Limited ⟶	Limited Enough
Crime in America	Girls' suburban crime	Shoplifting among teenage girls in an affluent Los Angeles suburb

The topic *crime in America* is much too general to address in an essay; even an expert on crime would have trouble writing an entire book about the topic as stated. The student narrowed the topic further by limiting the issue of crime to crimes committed in the suburbs by girls. That still is too general and raises many questions that the student writer must address before settling on the topic—what age group of girls, what kinds of crimes, in which suburbs? Finally, the writer produced a controllable topic that she could address to meet the terms of her assignment in the time allotted to her for writing. She could produce an essay that dealt effectively with teenage shoplifters in a prosperous Los Angeles suburb. The limited topic allows her to proceed efficiently.

In the following examples you can see how student writers limited their topics in stages.

Too General ⟶	More Limited ⟶	Limited Enough
Sports	High school football	What makes a good high school football coach
Women's fashions	New trends in women's fashions	Body decorations—body paint, body jewelry, removable tattoos—in women rock stars
Politics	The policies of the Democratic party	Why I am a Democrat

---
EXERCISE

Limit the following broad topics, drawn from a wide variety of college courses.

Example

Broad topic	More limited	Still more limited
The Middle East	Peace negotiations in the Middle East	Anwar Sadat's efforts to make peace between Egypt and Israel in the 1970s

1. Rock concerts
2. Hurricanes
3. An embarrassing moment
4. Surgery
5. Domestic violence

DETERMINING YOUR PURPOSE AND AUDIENCE

Once you've limited your subject, you need to set your purpose and determine what audience you will write for, and doing so involves some related choices.

What Is Your Purpose?

You must decide how you will treat your limited subject—that is, being clear about your purpose in writing. What will you do with it? Writing about your summer vacation, will you explain a process—for example, how to pitch a tent? Will you compare two campsites? Will you report an event—what happened when you unwittingly pitched your tent in a cow pasture? Will you argue that one can have an enjoyable yet inexpensive vacation by camping in state parks?

Each of these approaches will help you determine what to include and what to leave out of your essay, and each will produce a different paper.

Who Is Your Audience?

You also must determine what kind of reader you are writing for. In a paper about pitching a tent, just imagine how different the paper would look if you wrote it for Cub Scouts planning to sleep in the backyard, troopers training in unfamiliar terrain, sporting goods sales clerks who have to explain a new product to potential buyers, or out-of-shape senior citizens camping for the first time.

You may now be thinking that any discussion of audience is pointless because you know who your reader is—your English professor. In one sense, that's true, of course. But you'll write better papers if, instead of thinking of your English professor every time you begin to write, you imagine other specific kinds of readers. Define a reader. Are you writing for a group of experts on your subject? for your classmates? for the president of your company? for readers of the editorial page of the morning paper? for readers of *Maxim*? *Vanity Fair*? *People*? for the "general reader"? Defining the reader not only helps you decide the style and exact content of your paper but also makes for livelier reading.

EXERCISE

For each topic listed here, indicate the purposes a writer might have for writing about it. Look at the example. You may wish to limit the topic first.

Example

Topic: Teenage drivers

Possible purposes

1. To describe a harrowing drive with "wild man Bob," my sixteen-year-old cousin.
2. To explain how teenagers can save money on driving costs by following a few simple steps.
3. To compare and contrast male and female teenage drivers.
4. To classify types of sports car drivers I've observed in my job as a gas station attendant.
5. To argue in favor of allowing 14-year-olds to drive under special circumstances.
6. To convince teenagers of the dangers of drinking and driving.

Topics

1. Charities
2. Election reform
3. Job hunting
4. Fever
5. Drug testing for athletes

PREWRITING

Experienced writers use many strategies to limber up, so to speak, well before they start producing the connected sentences and paragraphs that make up a first draft. The convenient label for these warm-up activities— **prewriting**—is a useful term: The prefix *pre-* reminds you that you have a good deal to do in advance of writing your paper. Many inexperienced writers fail because they leap too soon into producing their papers and do not take enough time with the various steps that can lead to successful writing.

By means of prewriting strategies—thinking and talking about your ideas, free association, list-making, brainstorming, keeping a journal, reporters' questions, subject trees or maps—you'll uncover a surprising number of possibilities for your topic. Use the strategies described in the following checklist to get started on ideas for your essay.

STRATEGY CHECKLIST: **Prewriting**

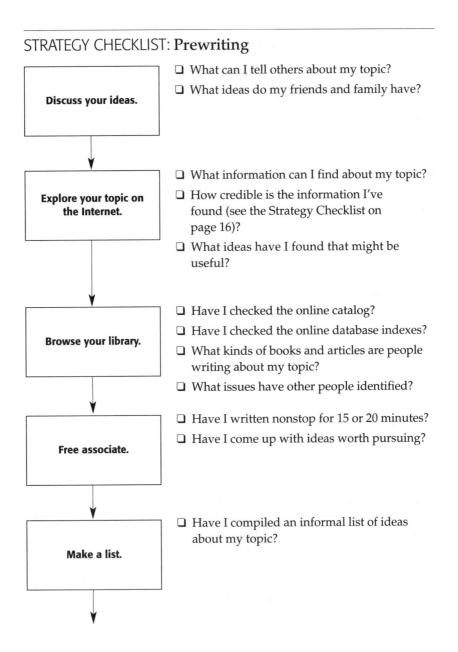

Discuss your ideas.

❏ What can I tell others about my topic?
❏ What ideas do my friends and family have?

Explore your topic on the Internet.

❏ What information can I find about my topic?
❏ How credible is the information I've found (see the Strategy Checklist on page 16)?
❏ What ideas have I found that might be useful?

Browse your library.

❏ Have I checked the online catalog?
❏ Have I checked the online database indexes?
❏ What kinds of books and articles are people writing about my topic?
❏ What issues have other people identified?

Free associate.

❏ Have I written nonstop for 15 or 20 minutes?
❏ Have I come up with ideas worth pursuing?

Make a list.

❏ Have I compiled an informal list of ideas about my topic?

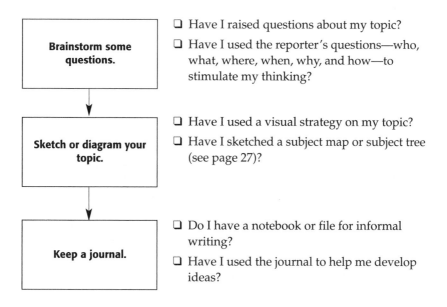

Brainstorm some questions.	❏ Have I raised questions about my topic? ❏ Have I used the reporter's questions—who, what, where, when, why, and how—to stimulate my thinking?
Sketch or diagram your topic.	❏ Have I used a visual strategy on my topic? ❏ Have I sketched a subject map or subject tree (see page 27)?
Keep a journal.	❏ Do I have a notebook or file for informal writing? ❏ Have I used the journal to help me develop ideas?

Organizing Ideas

Try to organize your thinking somewhat. You've identified and limited your topic; and you have considered your *audience* and *purpose*. Now, as you zero in on your central idea (Chapter 4 deals with the all-important thesis statement), look at your written thoughts and eliminate any that seem off target. Cluster the thoughts that seem to go together. You might even try a rough outline of main topics as headings and subtopics numbered beneath them. Or you might draw arrows and make circles to join related ideas, or use scissors and paste to lay connected impressions near each other.

Writing with a computer enables you to move words, sentences, and paragraphs and to keep at hand many versions of your efforts. You can refer to these often and perhaps even salvage thoughts you may have rejected.

Your attempts at grouping related material are important because they can help you develop an outline (Chapter 5), a key organizing strategy for many writers. Outlining is especially important when you deal with complex topics or with lots of research materials. Like a road map, your outline can help you find your way through new territory.

Bear in mind that the prewriting activities described here are not rigid prescriptions. They vary from writer to writer, and they do not necessarily follow each other in an exact sequence. Prewriting is a loosely defined process that you should adapt freely to your own needs as a writer and to the elements of the writing task at hand.

WRITING DRAFTS

Here are some suggestions for writing a rough draft.

TIPS FOR WRITING A ROUGH DRAFT

- **Use your prewriting.** To begin the all-important drafting stage, use your prewriting. Read over your ideas on paper and your efforts at grouping your thoughts.
- **Write a first draft.** Then, without worrying about spelling, grammar, or punctuation, try to get your ideas down. Your first draft is a rough copy that you will revisit later to make changes, additions, and deletions. Delete words and phrases that are dead ends. Insert new thoughts. Don't worry here about being neat or correct. Your goal at this stage is to write clear, connected sentences that address your topic.
- **Show it around.** Once you've produced a draft, show it to a friend, your roommate, or another member of your writing class. Drawing on peer review (see pages 86–87) can provide very useful guidance from fellow writers in your class. Sometimes your instructor will read and comment on an early draft to help you think about possible approaches to your next draft.
- **Revise.** Use the comments made on your papers to help you think about your revision and create your next draft. (Look ahead to Chapter 7.) You don't have to follow all the recommendations you receive or answer all the questions raised—but you must consider them.
- **Write more drafts.** As you revise your paper, change any sentences that are off base, add necessary details to support a point, and fix key errors. Don't concentrate on grammatical errors in early drafts; do address these errors as you move closer to a final copy.
- **Evaluate your writing closely when using the Delete and Move functions on your computer.** After removing words and sentences or shifting text around within your draft, reread your work to be sure the text fits sensibly in its new place.
- **Remember two key words.** Print *and* Save. Before you leave the computer terminal always print out a draft of your work and be sure to save what you have written.
- **Follow your instructor's guidelines about using special word processing features.** Your writing instructor may have strong feelings about computer dictionaries (spell checkers) or thesauruses and grammar or style programs—especially if you're in a course designed to teach spelling, vocabulary, grammar, and style. Be sure that you use only instructor-approved programs.
- **When printing your final document for submission to others, follow the conventions of manuscript preparation.** Remember to leave adequate margins—top, bottom, and sides. Avoid using a variety of typefaces—printing in roman, italic, boldface, small, and large print. Do not justify the right-hand margin.

ONE STUDENT WRITING: FIRST DRAFT

In this chapter and in Chapter 7, you'll see how one student, John Fousek, went about limiting a subject and developing and revising a paper. Having been told to write a short paper on the topic "a friend," John did lots of advance thinking before he wrote. To explore his thoughts, he made a subject map about the topic (see below). As he considered this preliminary effort, he finally chose to write about his roommate, Jim, and began jotting down impressions about him. Because he knew his roommate well, however, John soon found that he would have too much material for a short paper and would have to limit his subject to one of Jim's characteristics. That was easy to do because John had argued with his roommate that morning and, still annoyed, could readily identify his major interest of the day: his roommate's irritating habits.

Next, John began to make a list of any of those habits that happened to occur to him. He ended up with quite a list:

doesn't empty ashtrays	doesn't tighten cap on shampoo
doesn't put out cigarettes	uses my printer paper without replacing
doesn't take out garbage	leaves wet towels on bathroom floor
slams doors on mornings I can sleep	opens bathroom door when I'm showering
doesn't rinse dirty dishes	
uses my after-shave lotion	leaves drawers open
wears my socks	never closes closet door
doesn't write down telephone messages	never hangs up his coat

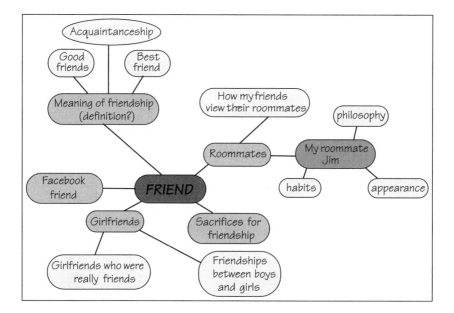

doesn't do his share of cooking	doesn't remove muddy boots
	never empties dishwasher
plays stereo when I'm studying	reads my mail

After studying the list, John saw that he could not develop every point; he had to eliminate some items. He concluded that two of Jim's shortcomings bothered him most: Jim's failure to close things and his failure to dispose of things. He eliminated all items on the list that did not pertain to those two failures and could now group his ideas:

Not closing	Not disposing
doesn't tighten cap on shampoo	doesn't put out cigarettes
doesn't close bathroom door	doesn't empty ashtrays
doesn't close drawers	doesn't empty dishwasher
doesn't close closet door	doesn't rinse dishes

Then John realized that even this limiting left him with too much to cover; finally, he decided to discuss in his paper only his roommate's failure to close things.

As John thought about how to organize his paper, he produced this rough outline:

Intro:

1. how much I like Jim—his personality, sharing, funny, honest

2. what I don't like—never closes things

Drawers

1. kitchen drawer always messy and left open

2. bedroom drawers and closets

3. I'm embarrassed by it all

Bathroom

1. leaves door open—shower area gets freezing cold

2. forgets to close shampoo bottle—shampoo spills all over me, much wasted down drain

Note how the informal outline builds on the preceding grouped list titled "Not closing." The rough outline provides a working plan for the first draft of John's essay.

With his outline and prewriting as resources, John was able to arrange his ideas and write a draft of his paper. His first draft appears on page 29.

John's rough draft is a good start. He states a thesis early in the paper. He presents concrete examples to support his irritation with Jim. He seems to have a good grasp of his topic. The paper has a beginning, a middle, and an end, and its ideas are related to each other. Note how John has raised questions for himself in the margins and spaces between lines.

FIRST DRAFT

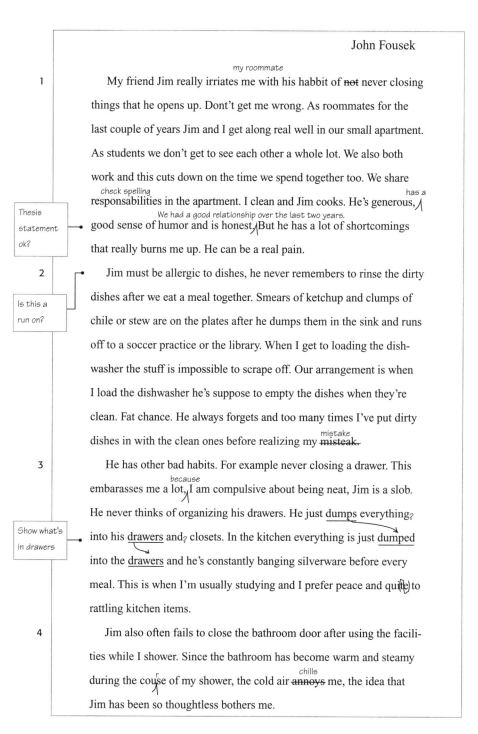

John Fousek

1   My friend Jim really irriates me with his ~~habbit~~ of ~~not~~ never closing
my roommate
things that he opens up. Dont't get me wrong. As roommates for the
last couple of years Jim and I get along real well in our small apartment.
As students we don't get to see each other a whole lot. We also both
work and this cuts down on the time we spend together too. We share
responsabilities in the apartment. I clean and Jim cooks. He's generous, ∧
check spelling   *has a*
good sense of humor and is honest. ∧But he has a lot of shortcomings
We had a good relationship over the last two years.
that really burns me up. He can be a real pain.

Thesis statement ok?

2   Jim must be allergic to dishes, he never remembers to rinse the dirty
dishes after we eat a meal together. Smears of ketchup and clumps of
chile or stew are on the plates after he dumps them in the sink and runs
off to a soccer practice or the library. When I get to loading the dishwasher the stuff is impossible to scrape off. Our arrangement is when
I load the dishwasher he's suppose to empty the dishes when they're
clean. Fat chance. He always forgets and too many times I've put dirty
dishes in with the clean ones before realizing my ~~misteak.~~
mistake

Is this a run on?

3   He has other bad habits. For example never closing a drawer. This
embarasses me a lot, ∧I am compulsive about being neat, Jim is a slob.
because
He never thinks of organizing his drawers. He just dumps everything?
into his drawers and? closets. In the kitchen everything is just dumped
into the drawers and he's constantly banging silverware before every
meal. This is when I'm usually studying and I prefer peace and quite to
rattling kitchen items.

Show what's in drawers

4   Jim also often fails to close the bathroom door after using the facilities while I shower. Since the bathroom has become warm and steamy
during the couse of my shower, the cold air ~~annoys~~ me, the idea that
chills
Jim has been so thoughtless bothers me.

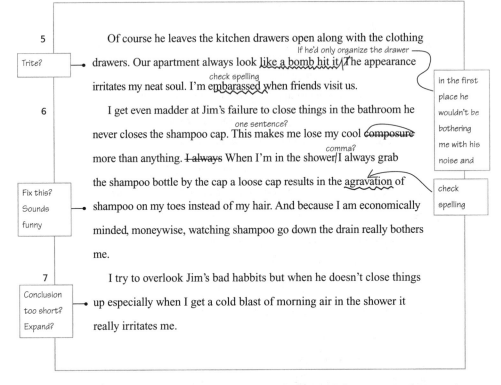

5   Of course he leaves the kitchen drawers open along with the clothing

If he'd only organize the drawer

Trite? → drawers. Our apartment always look like a bomb hit it. The appearance

check spelling

irritates my neat soul. I'm embarassed when friends visit us.

in the first place he wouldn't be bothering me with his noise and

6   I get even madder at Jim's failure to close things in the bathroom he

one sentence?

never closes the shampoo cap. This makes me lose my cool ~~composure~~

comma?

more than anything. ~~I always~~ When I'm in the shower I always grab

check spelling

Fix this?
Sounds
funny → the shampoo bottle by the cap a loose cap results in the agravation of

shampoo on my toes instead of my hair. And because I am economically

minded, moneywise, watching shampoo go down the drain really bothers

me.

7   I try to overlook Jim's bad habbits but when he doesn't close things

Conclusion
too short?
Expand? → up especially when I get a cold blast of morning air in the shower it

really irritates me.

But John's paper still needs revising and editing. John notes in the margin some issues that he wants to think about when he revises, but there are many others he'll have to consider. His sentences are sometimes rambling and repetitive, and the writing is much too informal in spots. The ideas should be more smoothly connected, and some of the paragraphs should be joined—or shifted or perhaps even eliminated. You no doubt noted errors in spelling and sentence structure. John must address all these issues as he develops successive drafts.

STRATEGY CHECKLIST: **How to Get Started**

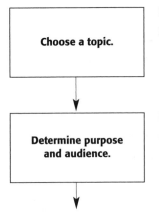

Choose a topic.

❑ Have I picked a topic that interests me?
❑ Have I started to limit the topic so I can manage it in the space and time I have for the assignment?

Determine purpose and audience.

❑ What is the purpose of my paper?
❑ Who is my audience?

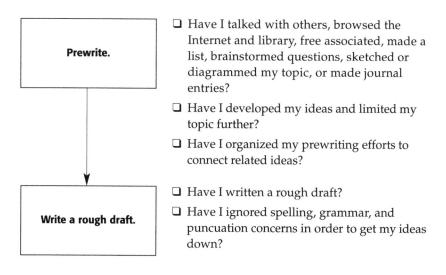

Prewrite.

- ❏ Have I talked with others, browsed the Internet and library, free associated, made a list, brainstormed questions, sketched or diagrammed my topic, or made journal entries?
- ❏ Have I developed my ideas and limited my topic further?
- ❏ Have I organized my prewriting efforts to connect related ideas?

Write a rough draft.

- ❏ Have I written a rough draft?
- ❏ Have I ignored spelling, grammar, and puncuation concerns in order to get my ideas down?

EXERCISE

Examine John Fousek's prewriting activities and his first draft and then answer the following questions.

1. How did John's subject map help him limit his topic?
2. How does John's first list compare and contrast with his second list (see pages 27–28)? What specific features of the first list has John eliminated in the second? Why has he dropped so many details from the first list?
3. How does John's rough outline build on the list that he prepared, "Not closing"?
4. How does John's rough draft compare with his rough outline?

EXERCISE

Use the prewriting techniques explained on pages 23–25 for one of the following topics that interests you. From these warm-up activities, determine how you would limit the subject.

1. Batman films
2. The environment
3. Friendship
4. The homeless
5. Television preachers
6. Volunteer work
7. Elections
8. Cell phones
9. Welfare-to-work programs
10. Being a politician

EXERCISE

Using your prewriting efforts, develop a first draft of your paper.

4

Finding and Supporting a Thesis

UNDERSTANDING THE THESIS

Once you have narrowed your topic and identified your audience and purpose, you have to develop a thesis, a statement of the main point of your essay. Your reader should know as early as possible in your paper just what main point you are trying to make about your topic.

A **thesis** is the position a writer takes on an arguable point—one on which more than one opinion is possible. It is the main idea the paper will support. The writer must convince the reader that this position or idea is valid.

Remember that your topic is not your thesis. Instead, your thesis is what you have to say about your topic. It is an opinion about, or an attitude toward, the topic, which you will attempt to support in your essay. It is a one-sentence summary of the idea the writer will defend. Here are two examples:

Topic	Thesis
Graduation requirements	Technical programs should require students to take some courses in the humanities.
Registration	A few simple changes would improve the registration procedure on our campus.

ELEMENTS OF A GOOD THESIS

There are several characteristics of a good thesis. When you are writing, you can use these tips to evaluate your thesis statements.

TIPS FOR EVALUATING A THESIS

- A good thesis usually can be stated in one complete sentence. Even though you may find that you want to devote a paragraph or more to presenting the idea of your paper, until you can state your main idea in one sentence, you may not have it under control.

- **A good thesis makes a statement—that is, it gives an opinion or attitude about the facts.** To say that in Shakespeare's play *Julius Caesar* Brutus stabbed Caesar on the Ides of March is to state a fact. A thesis, a statement *about* the fact, might read, *Brutus succeeded in killing Caesar on the Ides of March because Caesar had grown too arrogant and proud to protect himself.*
- **A good thesis is limited.** The idea stated must be one that can be clearly explained, supported, and illustrated in the space called for. A long magazine article might have this as its thesis:

  > Although, as a result of a controversial and aggressive promotional campaign, women professional golfers now make more money and receive greater recognition than they did ten years ago, they still do not make as much money, receive as much media coverage, or command as much respect as men professional golfers.

  But this won't do for a thousand-word paper; the writer could not develop the thesis fully in so short a space. A better thesis for a short paper might read, *The promotional campaign for the Women's Professional Golf Association has attracted money and attention for professional female golfers.* An even better thesis would be, *The promotional campaign for the Women's Professional Golf Association will offend members and fans who oppose commercialism in women's athletics.*
- **A good thesis is precise.** It lets the reader and the writer know exactly what the paper will contain. Words such as *good, interesting, impressive,* and *many* are too vague to do the job. They say nothing about the subject: What is interesting or good to one person may appear dull or offensive to another. Don't say, "Agatha Christie's detective stories are good." Say, instead, "Agatha Christie's detective stories appeal to those who enjoy solving puzzles." Don't say, "My history class is interesting." Say, "My professor makes history easy to understand."

STATING YOUR THESIS

Rules for a good thesis are one thing; applying them is another. You may well ask how one arrives at that perfectly stated thesis. The methods may vary according to the circumstances.

Here is the important message: You must have a thesis statement clearly in mind as you plan the rest of the paper.

It should be clear by now that a thesis is different from a topic. A topic is simply the subject of your paper, whereas a thesis makes an assertion about the subject. Having a topic in mind helps you produce a thesis. Merely placing a title on top of your page to reflect your topic does not mean you have provided a thesis statement.

TIPS **FOR DEVELOPING A THESIS**

- **Answer a question.** Sometimes, especially in essay examinations, the thesis statement is suggested by the question. Often, all you have to do is think of a one-sentence answer to the question, and you have your thesis statement.

  Example question: What is job enrichment? Is job enrichment an attempt by management to exploit workers?

  Sample thesis statement: Job enrichment, an effort to increase productivity by making the job more attractive, is an attempt by management to exploit laborers by motivating them to work harder.

  In this thesis statement, the writer has both defined *job enrichment* and stated an opinion about the practice. The rest of the essay will give the reasons job enrichment, in this writer's opinion, is an attempt to exploit laborers.

- **Think about your subject.** Frequently, you have to work with a large-scale subject. As you know, it is up to you to limit the subject and decide what point you want to make about it. You may at first think you have no opinion about a subject, but you may have a question. You might have wondered why, for example, Japan seemed in years past to outdistance the United States in the production of everything from television sets to automobiles. Go to the library and the Web and read up on the subject. You may then decide that one reason Japan became a major industrial power is that the economy had not, since the end of World War II, had to support a military machine. Now you have a thesis.

- **Review your prewriting activities.** Look at your prewriting with an eye toward a central issue that may be brewing somewhere in your early, unedited thinking on a topic. Suppose that you're considering a paper on the subject of children's toys. It's near holiday time, you're a parent, and you've been giving lots of thought to toys lately. You've used free association to jot down anything that comes to mind on the topic. Your list might look like this:

Topic: Toys

1. Expense of toys
2. Shoddy construction: plastic parts don't fit together
3. Focus on violence: guns, destructive images
4. Too many batteries required
5. Sexist toys
6. Difficulty in putting together the parts of toys
7. Unclear, misleading assembly instructions

Considering your list, you note that three items (6, 7, and part of 2) relate to your frustrations with toy assembly. Putting together that kiddie gym really irritated you, didn't it? The more you think about that experience and others like it, the more you realize that item 7 on your list is the heart of the matter. The reason assembling toys is so difficult is that the instructions are unclear and misleading. There's your thesis statement: *Instructions accompanying disassembled toys are misleading.*

EXERCISE

Look at the following thesis sentences. What is the topic of each? What is the writer's main point—what does the writer want to say about the topic? How do you think each writer will go about supporting the thesis?

1. The costs of prescription drugs have skyrocketed, creating problems for consumers of all ages.
2. People use the label "terrorist" indiscriminately and therefore make unfair judgments based on race, color, or religion.
3. Some parents will do, say, or pay anything to get their children into the "right" nursery school.
4. Innovation by American automobile manufacturers has taken a back seat to advances by foreign competitors.
5. Through a variety of creative programs and police vigilance, it is possible to cut down dramatically on drunk driving among teens.

EXERCISE

Determine which of the following items are thesis statements and which are not. Also determine which thesis statements are too general or too lacking in unity to make a good paper. How does each statement meet the specifications for a thesis, as explained on pages 32–33? Revise the unacceptable thesis statements accordingly.

1. In a weak economy, employers do not hire quality workers.
2. Teenage drivers are a menace!
3. Americans are saving less and less money each year.
4. Curtailing drug use begins with education.
5. Readers now can download from their home computers many complete texts, including short stories, novels, and works of nonfiction.

EXERCISE

Return to the exercise on page 22. For any three topics you limited there, develop thesis statements that could be used successfully in a paper.

SUPPORTING YOUR THESIS: DETAILS

Once you've stated your thesis clearly, you need to consider how you will support it. The best way to convince a reader that your idea is worth considering is to offer details that back up your point and to present these details logically.

Chapter 20 presents the important topic of logic, and you no doubt will examine it fully later on. Here, it is important to know that logic involves the relation between the particulars and generalities as you present them in your paper. Logic is the process of reasoning inherent in your writing, and all readers expect a kind of clarity and intelligence that make the points and arguments understandable and easy to follow. Logical writing avoids what we call *fallacies*—that is, false notions, ideas founded on incorrect perceptions. We'll consider logic and logical fallacies in greater depth later in your course.

Using Sensory Details

In presenting details to support your point, you have many options. If you're drawing on your own personal experience, you can *provide examples* that illustrate your point. Examples drawn from experience rarely prove anything; however, they point out why you've made the generalization put forth in your thesis. When you use personal experiences to support a thesis, you should rely on **concrete sensory details**—colors, actions, sounds, smells, images of taste and touch. Details rooted in the senses make what you've experienced come alive for the reader. If you are narrating an event or describing a scene, concrete imagery will help your readers see things your way. Thus, if you're writing about the misleading instructions for assembling toys, you might show your frustration by describing your efforts to put together the offending kiddie gym—the hunt for an orange plastic tube, the pungent smell of epoxy glue, the rough silver hooks that don't fit the holes made for them, and the diagram labeled in Japanese characters and no English words.

George Orwell's "A Hanging" is a brilliant example of how concrete sensory details can support a thesis. In the paragraph below from Orwell's essay, note the rich imagery that the writer creates through sensory detail:

> One prisoner had been brought out of his cell. He was a Hindu, a puny wisp of a man, with a shaven head and vague liquid eyes. He had a thick, sprouting moustache, absurdly too big for his body, rather like the moustache of a comic man on the films. Six tall Indian warders were guarding him and getting him ready for the gallows. Two of them stood by with rifles with fixed bayonets, while the others handcuffed him, passed a chain through his handcuffs and fixed it to their belts, and lashed his arms tight to his sides. They crowded very close about him, with their hands always on him in a careful, caressing grip, as though all the while feeling him to make sure he was there. It was like men

handling a fish which is still alive and may jump back into the water. But he stood quite unresisting, yielding his arms limply to the ropes, as though he hardly noticed what was happening.

Using Data: Statistics, Cases, and Expert Testimony

Other kinds of supporting details draw on **data**—statistics and cases that demonstrate a point. For example, if your thesis is *Driver education courses have had a dramatic effect on improving the car safety record of young teenagers,* you'd need to cite comparative data of teens who took the course and those who didn't. You also would need to show the decrease, let us say, in speeding violations, drunk driving, and fatal accidents. Your analysis of the data would help readers see how you interpret the details. You might focus on a particularly illuminating case—the record of a young driver, say, before and after a driver's education course.

In supporting your thesis, you also might want to present expert testimony as supporting details. **Expert testimony** means the words and ideas of respected thinkers on your subject. Depending on your topic, you'll find an array of experts, thoughtful researchers, and other authorities who have considered the same issue and who have shared their observations in a variety of sources.

Without adequate support, your thesis is merely an assertion—an opinion. Unsupported assertions never win readers' respect.

Note how the writer uses particular cases, relevant data, and expert testimony in these paragraphs:

> Several studies have found that cruising for curb parking generates about 30 percent of the traffic in central business districts. In a recent survey conducted by Bruce Schaller in the SoHo district in Manhattan, 28 percent of drivers interviewed while they were stopped at traffic lights said they were searching for curb parking. A similar study conducted by Transportation Alternatives in the Park Slope neighborhood in Brooklyn found that 45 percent of drivers were cruising.
>
> When my students and I studied cruising for parking in a 15-block business district in Los Angeles, we found the average cruising time was 3.3 minutes, and the average cruising distance half a mile (about 2.5 times around the block). This may not sound like much, but with 470 parking meters in the district, and a turnover rate for curb parking of 17 cars per space per day, 8,000 cars park at the curb each weekday. Even a small amount of cruising time for each car adds up to a lot of traffic.
>
> —Donald Shoup

EXERCISE

For the three thesis statements that you developed for the exercise on page 35, indicate the kinds of details you might use to support them.

STRATEGY CHECKLIST: **Stating and Supporting Your Thesis**

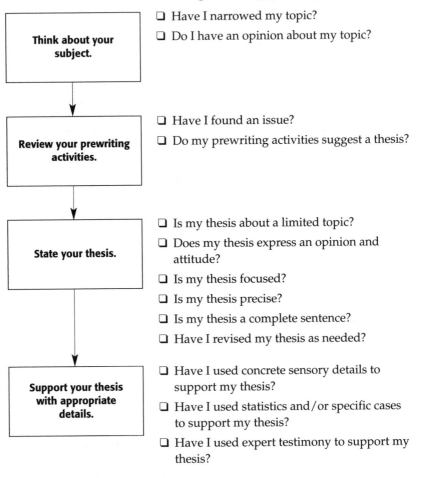

Think about your subject.

❑ Have I narrowed my topic?
❑ Do I have an opinion about my topic?

Review your prewriting activities.

❑ Have I found an issue?
❑ Do my prewriting activities suggest a thesis?

State your thesis.

❑ Is my thesis about a limited topic?
❑ Does my thesis express an opinion and attitude?
❑ Is my thesis focused?
❑ Is my thesis precise?
❑ Is my thesis a complete sentence?
❑ Have I revised my thesis as needed?

Support your thesis with appropriate details.

❑ Have I used concrete sensory details to support my thesis?
❑ Have I used statistics and/or specific cases to support my thesis?
❑ Have I used expert testimony to support my thesis?

5

Planning a Paper: Outlining

Proper planning is a key to writing a successful paper. As we saw in Chapter 3, John Fousek's two planning efforts—grouping related materials in lists and a rough outline—helped him to produce his drafts. This chapter examines a more rigorous kind of planning, **formal outlining**. A formal outline requires clearly defined headings and subheadings, which are arranged in a prescribed format of roman and arabic numerals and upper- and lowercase letters.

MAKING A FORMAL OUTLINE

A formal outline is a schematic presentation of your paper—a procedural diagram, if you will, in which you show the order of your topics and how they relate to each other. A formal outline gives a picture of the logical relations between the separate parts of the paper and the thesis or purpose.

When you produce a formal outline, follow the conventions of its format, as presented on pages 40–41. After your prewriting, you should have an idea of your thesis. Thus, always begin your outline by stating your thesis or purpose. As we have pointed out before, you may want to modify your thesis as your outline takes shape, so don't be concerned if you haven't stated your thesis exactly the way you want it.

Establishing Main Divisions

After you state your thesis, your next task is to determine the main divisions of the paper as suggested by the thesis. As you examine your prewriting, try to see how some of what you've written falls into large blocks of thought. If you've written preliminary thoughts by hand, circles and arrows or marks in different colored pens or pencils can help you make visual links among related ideas that may be spread out over the page. If you write by computer, you can experiment by grouping thoughts into blocks, saving your effort, and trying yet another plan. Some word processing programs have templates for outlining.

As the related thoughts come together, look at them as main points. If you can create a label for each thought block, you then can convert the label into a main heading. The main headings in your outline should match the number of blocks you have identified. If you see that your outline has more than five or so main points, reexamine it: You may be trying to do too much in your paper.

Adding Supporting Details

With thought blocks identified and labeled, you need then to think about the supporting details to place under each heading. The supporting points, of course, will pertain clearly to the main thought you stated in the heading. As you group these supporting points—some of which will appear in your prewriting, others to be invented as you produce the outline—they will become subheadings in your outline.

Formatting a Formal Outline

Begin by stating the thesis or purpose. Then indicate all major divisions of the paper with roman numerals. Mark the support for the major divisions with capital letters and additional support for those major divisions with arabic numerals. If you are planning a very long paper, you may want to make further subdivisions. To do so, next use small letters—*a, b, c*—and then arabic numerals in parentheses—*(1), (2)*—then lowercase letters in parentheses—*(a), (b)*.

A standard formal outline for a complex paper has the following format.

Complex Paper Formal Outline

Thesis or Purpose: [State the thesis or purpose of your paper here.]

I.   Major division

   A. First-level subdivision

      1. Second-level subdivision

      2. Second-level subdivision

         a. Third-level subdivision

         b. Third-level subdivision

            (1) Fourth-level subdivision

            (2) Fourth-level subdivision

   B. First-level subdivision

      1. Second-level subdivision

      2. Second-level subdivision

II. Major division

   A. First-level subdivision

      1. Second-level subdivision

      2. Second-level subdivision

   B. First-level subdivision

      1. Second-level subdivision

         a. Third-level subdivision

         b. Third-level subdivision

      2. Second-level subdivision

         a. Third-level subdivision

         b. Third-level subdivision

            (1) Fourth-level subdivision

            (2) Fourth-level subdivision

               (a) Fifth-level subdivision

               (b) Fifth-level subdivision

An outline for a short paper usually includes several major divisions and sometimes two or three subdivisions for each major topic. Remember that a word or a phrase in an outline can be expanded into a sentence—even a paragraph—in your essay.

Writing Topic and Sentence Outlines

Formal outlines are of two types, *topic outlines* and *sentence outlines*. A **topic outline** is one in which the writer uses just a few words or phrases to indicate the topics and subtopics that the paper covers. Topic outlines are sufficient for many short papers, especially those that classify or present a process. Longer papers and those that develop theses often profit from sentence outlines.

Here is a topic outline for a short paper on how to change automobile license plates.

Topic Outline

<u>Purpose</u>: To show how to change auto license plates.

I. Assemble materials

   A. Find screwdriver

   B. Find household oil

   C. Buy plastic screws

II. Remove old plates

   A. Oil screws to loosen rust

   B. Unscrew plates

   C. Discard metal screws

III. Mount new plates

   A. Position plate with screw holes

   B. Screw on plate using plastic screws

IV. Break and discard old plates

EXERCISE

1. What is the first major division of the license plate outline? The second? The third?
2. What supporting information does the outline indicate as subdivisions for the major division "Remove old plates"?
3. Why does the fourth major division not have any subdivisions?
4. What thesis could you propose for the essay that this outline suggests?
5. In what order has the writer chosen to arrange the thought blocks indicated as major divisions?

Longer papers and those that develop theses often benefit from sentence outlines. To write a **sentence outline**, you must sum up in one sentence what you want to say on each topic and subtopic. The sentence doesn't merely indicate the topic; it states what you intend to say about the topic. This kind of outline forces you to think through exactly what you want to say before you begin to write. By constructing a sentence outline, you will find out whether you really have support for your position. Look at the sentence outline below.

Sentence Outline

Thesis: My attitude toward the English language has changed from loathing to acceptance.

I. At first, I hated the English language.   *First major division*

    A. Knowing very little English, I felt isolated.   *First-level subdivision*

        1. I could not understand what people said to me. ⎤   *Second-level*
        2. I could not tell others what I thought or felt. ⎦   *subdivisions*

    B. The isolation I felt made me want to return to Greece.   *First-level subdivision*

II. Now, six months later, I like the English language very much.   *Second major division*

    A. The support of the Greek family I live with has ⎤   *First-level subdivision*
        helped me to accept English. ⎦

        1. They gave me courage to try to use the language.   *Second-level subdivision*

            a. They proved to me that they had learned ⎤
               the language. ⎟   *Third-level*
            b. They proved to me that they could talk with ⎟   *subdivisions*
               others in English. ⎦

        2. They held conversations with me in English.

    B. The teachers in my English classes have helped me to accept the language.

        1. They are approachable and helpful outside of class.

        2. They are good instructors in class.

      a. They explain material clearly.

      b. They discuss a variety of subjects.

         (1) The variety increases my vocabulary.

         (2) The discussions improve my comprehension and speech.

        } *Fourth-level subdivisions*

III. I go out of my way now to ensure my continuous contact with English.

    A. I study English regularly.

      1. I work with a tutor for one hour every day.

      2. I study grammar and vocabulary two hours every night.

    B. Since I meet few Greeks, I must speak English every day.

      1. I go to the supermarket to read and pronounce the names of consumer products.

        a. I love to say the weird names of candies and cereals.

          (1) Have you ever eaten Fiddle Faddle?

          (2) I have lots of fun with Captain Crunch, Sugar Frosted Flakes, and Count Chocula.

        b. I made friends with one of the stock boys who helps me when my English fails me.

      2. I always accept solicitation calls on the telephone just to practice my English.

EXERCISE

1. What are the major divisions of the outline? Put a checkmark beside each one. How do the major divisions relate to the thesis as stated as the first outline entry?
2. How do the items in I. A. 1. and 2. relate to the item in I. A.? To the item in I.? To the thesis?
3. Look at the various items connected to III. in the outline. Label each item appropriately as major division and first-, second-, third-, and fourth-level subdivisions. Be prepared to explain why you chose the labels you did.
4. Using any one of the thought blocks labeled as a major division as well as the various subdivisions beneath it, try your hand at writing the paragraph that the outline suggests.

PREPARING YOUR FORMAL OUTLINE

Whether your outline is a topic or a sentence outline, it should include a statement of the thesis or purpose of the paper (depending on your teacher's instructions) and an indication by means of roman numerals of the main points to be covered in the paper. Major and minor subdivisions, indicated by letters and arabic numerals, respectively, should show how the main points will be developed.

Here are other points to observe in preparing an outline:

TIPS FOR WRITING A FORMAL OUTLINE

- **Do not make single subdivisions.** If you decide to subdivide a point, you must have at least two subdivisions. If there is a I, there must be a II; if there is an A, there must be a B. If you cannot think of two divisions, rephrase the heading so no division is necessary.
- **Use parallel grammatical forms for headings of equal importance.** Parallel forms help show the relation of headings to one another. If heading I reads "Assembling the ingredients," heading II should read "Mixing the ingredients," not "Mix the ingredients."
- **Make sure the divisions of an outline do not overlap and that you stick to a single principle of division.** You should not, for example, discuss books in terms of fiction, nonfiction, and novels because novels are logically a subdivision of fiction. You should not discuss the branches of government in terms of legislative, judicial, executive, and crooked politicians because one might find crooked politicians in any of the branches.
- **Make sure headings and subheadings show a proper logical relation.** In discussing athletes, you should not establish Babe Ruth as one major division and baseball players as a second. You might, however, treat great home-run hitters as a major division and Babe Ruth and Hank Aaron as subdivisions.

One final note about outlines: They can be as helpful after you've written your paper as they are during the early stages of development. For example, if you choose to use only your prewriting activities or a rough outline as a guide to writing your first draft, a formal outline at this stage provides a visual scheme of how your ideas relate to each other logically.

As you develop your outline, ask yourself the questions in the "Strategy Checklist: Preparing a Formal Outline." Your answers to these questions can provide guidance as you write and revise your draft. You can determine if your major divisions relate logically to your thesis, and you can shift subdivisions or add new ones as necessary.

STRATEGY CHECKLIST: **Preparing a Formal Outline**

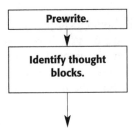

❑ Did I record my random thoughts on the topic?

❑ Did I identify and label related blocks of thought?

❑ Did I use the labeled thought blocks to develop the major divisions of my outline?

❑ Do the major divisions advance my thesis?

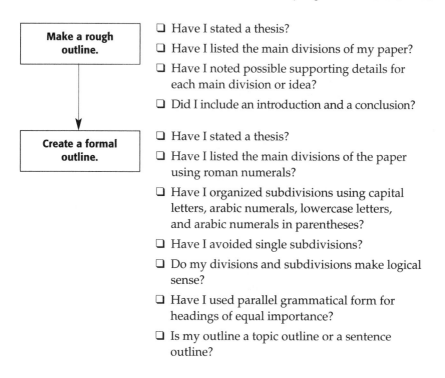

Make a rough outline.	❏ Have I stated a thesis?
	❏ Have I listed the main divisions of my paper?
	❏ Have I noted possible supporting details for each main division or idea?
	❏ Did I include an introduction and a conclusion?
Create a formal outline.	❏ Have I stated a thesis?
	❏ Have I listed the main divisions of the paper using roman numerals?
	❏ Have I organized subdivisions using capital letters, arabic numerals, lowercase letters, and arabic numerals in parentheses?
	❏ Have I avoided single subdivisions?
	❏ Do my divisions and subdivisions make logical sense?
	❏ Have I used parallel grammatical form for headings of equal importance?
	❏ Is my outline a topic outline or a sentence outline?

EXERCISE

Comment on the following topic outline.

Purpose: To classify the divisions of the federal government.

I.   The executive
   A. President

II. Legislative
   A. House of Representatives
   B. Senate
   C. Lawyers
   D. Committees

III. Judicial
   A. Supreme Court
   B. Judges
   C. Clerks

EXERCISE

What strengths and weaknesses do you see in the following sentence outline? Revise it so that it is more suitable to the writer's needs.

Thesis: Getting a broken appliance repaired by sending it to a service center requires careful packing and mailing.

I. Broken appliances can be repaired by service centers.
   A. It's generally easy to bring the appliance to a service unit if one exists in your city.
   B. Often, no such centers exist nearby.
      1. The manufacturer's center may be out of state.
      2. Local repair shops cannot do the work.
      3. Each company has its own designs and required parts.

II. Mailing the appliance requires attention to important details.
   A. You can find the mailing address easily.
      1. Check the literature that accompanied the object.
      2. Telephone the store where you purchased the object to find out the address.
   B. The biggest job is packing up the object and mailing it off.
      1. Find a strong cardboard box and pack the appliance well in order to prevent shifting and breakage.
      2. Close the carton with strong tape.
      3. Print mailing and home addresses carefully.
      4. Write a letter providing essential information.
         a. Tell what is wrong with the appliance and where you bought it.
         b. Address the envelope correctly and enclose the letter.
         c. Tape the envelope to the outside of the carton.
      5. The post office will weigh the package and tell you costs for mailing and insurance.

EXERCISE

Put the following information into a sentence outline that follows the suggested form.

- *First main heading:* Travel throughout America is increasing in popularity with people of all age groups.
- *Subheadings:* College and high school students find that travel adds to their education. People with young families feel that their children should experience people in different settings. Senior citizens find that travel gives life a sense of purpose.
- *Second main heading:* There are several popular methods of travel.
- *Subheading:* Hitchhiking is frequently used among teenagers.
- *Further divisions:* It allows inexpensive travel. It allows the traveler to meet many people. It is dangerous, however.
- *More subheadings:* Young families still choose small automobiles and camping equipment. Older people often take planes or trains.

6

Writing Your Paper

In this chapter we will review the characteristics common to almost all types of papers.

WRITING YOUR INTRODUCTION

To start, you need a beginning, or an **introduction**. The introduction consists of one or more paragraphs that set the stage for the essay. The simplest introduction identifies the subject and states the thesis. What matters in an introduction is to present the idea of the thesis in the most interesting manner possible. Sometimes, in addition to identifying the subject and stating the thesis, the introduction lists the divisions of the rest of the paper.

> Amid the growing pressure to study hard and make good grades, any student who admits to attending college to catch a mate risks alienation, hostility, and ridicule. I'm not sure that's fair. Although I firmly believe that students, while they are in college, should get the best education possible, I see no harm in their looking for a spouse at the same time. I believe college is an ideal place for an intelligent man or woman to look for a mate. For one thing, it's easy to meet eligible members of the opposite sex in college. Also, college provides a setting in which friendships can grow freely and naturally into love. Besides, an educated person surely wants a mate who shares his or her interests and tastes. What better place to find such a person than in college?

Here, the introduction identifies the subject—finding a mate while in college—and then states the thesis—*College is an ideal place for an intelligent man or woman to look for a mate.* The sentences following the thesis statement let you know how the writer will advance the argument in the body of the paper. You are prepared to expect the three reasons to be developed in such a way as to prove that college is an ideal place to find a mate.

Seeing Various Introduction Strategies

Although in short papers the one-paragraph introduction is most common, you are not limited to only one paragraph. Consider this four-paragraph introduction:

> "I don't like to do my Christmas shopping early. I enjoy the bustle of last-minute crowds."

> "Why should I start research for my term paper this early? I work best under pressure."

"I'll replace the washer on the bathroom sink Saturday when I have time to do it properly."

We recognize such statements for what they are—excuses for procrastination. But procrastination, far from being evil, can, in many cases, have positive effects.

The first three paragraphs give examples of the subject—procrastination. In the fourth paragraph the reader probably expects a humdrum list of ways to avoid putting off tasks, but instead the writer offers a surprising thesis: *Procrastination may be a good thing*.

Many other kinds of introductions can start an essay effectively. You might, for example, occasionally try dramatizing a situation:

Sheila felt light-headed: Her eyes would not focus and there was a slight hum in her ears. Her hands, wet and clammy, shook so that she could hardly write. She could not concentrate. She wanted only to run, to be away from that terrible scene.

Sheila had not just witnessed some horrible accident. She is a freshman composition student who has been told to write her first in-class composition. The following tips about writing under pressure may help alleviate the common pain of writing in class.

The scene described in the first paragraph attracts the reader's attention. The second paragraph explains the situation and anticipates the rest of the paper, which offers tips on writing under pressure.

Another option is to use an anecdote to illustrate the subject:

Mrs. Peters was busily talking to a neighbor over the telephone one afternoon when she experienced the sudden fear that her baby son had been hurt. She told her neighbor and ran to check the baby, supposedly napping in his crib upstairs. To her horror, she found the child unconscious on the floor. Evidently he had tried to climb out of the crib but, in the attempt, had fallen on his head. Mrs. Peters's "knowing" her baby was in danger is the kind of experience many of us have had at one time or another. This incident illustrates the kind of thought transference known as *telepathy*.

The anecdote in this introduction shows how telepathy, the subject of the paper, functions. The remainder of the paper explains how telepathy works.

As you can see, introductions take various forms. In many cases, as in the preceding paragraph, the thesis sentence appears at the end of the introduction. The examples here by no means exhaust the possibilities, but they do illustrate some ways of approaching a subject. Whatever form you choose, it's important to remember that the introduction must interest your readers—after all, you do want them to read the remainder of the paper—and it should in some way prepare readers for what follows.

TIPS FOR WRITING A STRONG INTRODUCTION

Consider these options as you plan to write an introduction for your paper.

- **Build to your thesis.** When you have a tentative thesis in place, you can build to it with a series of sentences. Your introduction should present the thesis in the most interesting manner possible. Spark your readers' interest and set a context for the thesis in your introduction.
- **Identify the paper's divisions.** Let the reader know how you will treat the subject in the body of your paper.
- **Seek variety with more than one paragraph.** Some topics benefit from a multiparagraph introduction that builds to the thesis.
- **Tell an anecdote.** A story relevant to your topic can appeal to readers and engage their interest.
- **Deal with the opposition.** If you're writing about why 16-year-olds should have the right to vote, build to your thesis by explaining why some people oppose such a plan.
- **Ask a challenging question.** You can stimulate your readers' interest with a thought-provoking question or series of questions that you will address in your essay.
- **Inject some humor.** Often a humorous statement can win readers over as you prepare to build to the serious topic at hand.
- **Quote a statement relevant to your topic.** Use a quote from books or current periodicals. *Bartlett's Familiar Quotations* or online quotation sites can be helpful resources.
- **Provide dramatic data or statistics.** You can give important background to your topic by citing data. Consider the introductory data in the first sentence of this brief introduction to a paper about presidential campaign contributions on college campuses:

> At three major universities, Harvard, Stanford, and Columbia, more than 80 percent of the dollars in 2008 presidential campaign donations went to Democratic candidates. But these figures mask a strong conservative Republican base on college campuses.

WRITING THE BODY PARAGRAPHS

The **body** of a paper provides support for the thesis presented in the introduction. Body paragraphs develop the writing plan or outline and should lead readers logically from one section to another without causing confusion.

Writing Topic Sentences

One method of leading your reader is to write clear topic sentences for each paragraph. A **topic sentence** is to a paragraph what a thesis is to a paper: It expresses the central idea of the paragraph. The remainder of the paragraph gives support for the topic sentence.

Stated Topic Sentences

Topic sentences generally appear at the beginning of a paragraph, but they can appear anywhere in a paragraph.

Topic Sentence at the Begining

Mrs. Jackson, my landlady's mother, is very nosy. Living on the first floor of the building affords her easy knowledge of the comings and goings of everyone living there. No matter how many times I descend the stairs in one day, I always find Mrs. Jackson peeking out of her front door. Usually she makes some statement or asks some question: "You really get around a lot. I guess you're going to the grocery now, huh?" I must give an explanation, denial, or confirmation of her guess—rather loudly, I might add, because of her hearing problem. Whenever company calls, they too are detained and cross-examined on the first floor. "Who are you going to see?" "Are you a relative?" "I guess you've known her a long time." Never does a visitor get up the stairs without first conversing with Mrs. Jackson.

Topic Sentence at the End

He drank noisily and chewed with his mouth open. He stuffed food into his mouth with his fingers and wiped his chin with the sleeve of his coat. He made loud, vulgar comments to the waitress, who had difficulty hiding her anger as other customers turned to stare. His idea of conversation was to regale his date with statistics about the World Series or facts about his expensive new car—especially its expense. *An hour with Bruce in the city's most costly restaurant made Jane wish she had dined at home alone on a tuna fish sandwich.*

Topic Sentence in the Middle

A fire-warning detector will "smell" smoke and sound an alarm; a guided missile will "see" and pursue a radar echo or the hot engines of a bomber; a speed governor will "feel" when a shaft is spinning too fast and act to restrain it. *But... quotation marks are appropriate in all such cases, because these machines do not have minds and they do not perceive the world as human beings do.* Information from our eyes, ears, and other senses goes to our brains, and of some of it (by no means all) we are aware as a vivid part of our conscious experience, showing us the world we inhabit.

—Nigel Calder, *The Mind of Man*

On rare occasions, writers do not state the topic sentence directly at all; instead, they imply it:

Implied Topic Sentence

Often when I find some passage in a book especially impressive—especially bright, say, or especially moving—I find myself turning to the dust jacket, if the author's picture is there, to communicate, to say a kind of "Well done." Coretta Scott King's photograph, soft, shadowed, and lovely, is on the jacket of her book *My Life with Martin Luther King, Jr.* I must have turned to it a dozen times in the reading of this book.

Here, the paragraph's central idea—that Coretta Scott King's book *My Life with Martin Luther King, Jr.* is especially impressive—is so clear that a statement of it is unnecessary; indeed, to state it directly would mar the grace of the paragraph. Implied topic sentences are tricky, though; use them cautiously. An idea that seems quite clear to you may not be as clear to your reader.

In summary, a topic sentence states the central idea of the paragraph. Wherever you decide to put your topic sentence, keep your readers in mind. They should not experience any confusion in following your thoughts. The central idea of every paragraph must be clear enough to lead readers easily from one point of your paper to another.

Using Transitions

Another way to help readers follow your thoughts is to use **transitions**, words or phrases that show the logical connections between ideas. Transitional words like *and, but, however, therefore, next*, and *finally* act as signals. They say to a reader, "Here's an additional point," or "A contrast is coming up," or "Now, I'm drawing a conclusion." Transitions make connections between ideas clear and therefore easy to follow.

COMMON TRANSITIONAL EXPRESSIONS

To show space relations

above, adjacent to, against, alongside, around, at a distance from, at the, below, beside, beyond, encircling, far off, forward, from the, in front of, in the rear, inside, near the back, near the end, nearby, next to, on, over, surrounding, there, through the, to the left, to the right, up front

To show time relations

afterward, at last, before, earlier, first, former, formerly, further, furthermore, immediately, in the first place, in the interval, in the meantime, in the next place, in the last, later on, latter, meanwhile, next, now, often, once, previously, second, simultaneously, sometime later, subsequently, suddenly, then, therefore, third, today, tomorrow, until now, when, years ago, yesterday

To indicate something added to what has come before

again, also, and, and then, besides, further, furthermore, in addition, last, likewise, moreover, next, nor, too

(Continued on next page)

To give examples or to intensify points

after all, as an example, certainly, for example, for instance, indeed, in fact, in truth, it is true, of course, specifically, that is

To show similarities

alike, in the same way, like, likewise, resembling, similarly

To show contrasts

after all, although, but, conversely, differ(s) from, difference, different, dissimilar, even though, granted, however, in contrast, in spite of, nevertheless, notwithstanding, on the contrary, on the other hand, otherwise, still, though, unlike, while this may be true, yet

To indicate cause and effect

accordingly, as a result, because, consequently, hence, since, then, therefore, thus

To conclude or summarize

finally, in brief, in conclusion, in other words, in short, in summary, that is, to summarize

Here are some examples of transitions in sentences:

I do not need to tell you how important the election is. *Nor* do I need to remind you to vote tomorrow.

Laura is always on one kind of diet or another. *Yet* she never seems to lose any weight.

Medicare can be a blessing to elderly people. The difficulty of filling out all the required forms, *however*, sometimes makes them wonder how blessed they are.

I have been a thrifty stay-at-home dad most of my life. It was a surprise to my children, *therefore*, when I went off to Europe first class last summer.

Avoiding Too Many Transitions

Used sensibly, transitions contribute to the smoothness of your paper. However, too many transitions can be as distressing to a reader as too few. This example overuses transitional words:

The children wanted to see the animals in my woods. *However*, they made too much noise. *In the first place*, all twenty of them shouted. *Moreover*, they screamed. *Furthermore*, they threw rocks into the streams. *Therefore*, birds, frogs, even bugs went rushing to the hills. *As a result*, the children saw no animals. *Nor* should they have expected to see animals after making so much noise. *Nevertheless*, I was sorry that they thought they might see what only hours of silence and days of watching ever bring to sight.

Now look at how the paragraph actually appears in *The Inland Island* by Josephine Johnson:

> "Where are all your animals?" the little children cried, running . . . through the woods—twenty little children, panting, shouting, screaming, throwing rocks into the streams. Birds, frogs, even bugs went rushing to the hills. How sad that the children thought they might see what only hours of silence, days of watching ever bring to sight.

Use transitions, but use them only to signal a logical connection that would not otherwise be obvious.

Using Sentences and Paragraphs as Transitions

In making connections between ideas, you are not limited to single words and short phrases. Often the topic sentence serves both as a transition and as an indicator of the central idea of a paragraph.

> *Besides making life difficult for his parents,* Charles sent his first-grade teacher home with a nightly headache.

> *Although the Puritans observed a strict code of behavior,* their lives were often filled with great joy.

In sentences of this kind, the introductory adverbial phrase or clause (shown here in italics) points back to the preceding paragraph to provide a transition. At the same time, the rest of the sentence points forward to the subject matter of the paragraph for which it is the topic sentence.

Occasionally, an entire paragraph may serve as a transition. The good **transitional paragraph**, like the transitional topic sentence, points back to what has gone before and points forward to what is yet to come. Note the successful use of these transitional paragraphs:

> So much for the preparation of the surface. Now we are ready to paint.

> Thus, Jackie Robinson had to confront a long tradition of bigotry in the major leagues. How did he meet this challenge?

> With all these arguments in favor of state-run lotteries, opponents of such lotteries can still raise some valid points.

EXERCISE

See the excerpt from John Fousek's paper on pages 87–88. How would you revise the over-coordinated sentence?

Developing Paragraphs: Unity and Coherence

In addition to leading your reader from one paragraph to another, you need to be certain that the paragraphs themselves are logically and adequately developed.

A **paragraph**—a group of related sentences developing a single topic—must be unified, coherent, and complete.

Paragraph Unity

A paragraph must be **unified**—that is, all the sentences in the paragraph must develop one idea, the one contained in the topic sentence. Anything that doesn't contribute to the idea should be omitted from the paragraph. One of the following two paragraphs appears exactly as it was written by Lewis Thomas, a skilled essayist whose paragraphs are beautifully unified.

Paragraph 1

[1]Viewed from the distance of the moon, the astonishing thing about the earth... is that it is alive. [2]The photographs show the dry, pounded surface of the moon in the foreground, dead as an old bone. [3]Aloft, floating free beneath the moist, gleaming membrane of bright blue sky, is the rising earth, the only exuberant thing in this part of the cosmos. [4]If you could look long enough, you would see the swirling of the great drifts of white cloud, covering and uncovering the half-hidden masses of land. [5]If you had been looking for a very long, geologic time, you could have seen the continents themselves in motion, drifting apart on their crustal plates, held afloat by the fire beneath. [6]It has the organized, self-contained look of a live creature, full of information, marvelously skilled in handling the sun.

Paragraph 2

[1]Viewed from the distance of the moon, the astonishing thing about the earth... is that it is alive. [2]The great technological advances that made it possible for man to walk on the moon also made it possible to send photographs back to earth. [3]Such are the miracles of modern science that you sat in your living room and watched the astronauts romp, enjoying their gravity-less freedom. [4]Soon, however, you saw something much more important, the photographs of the moon. [5]The photographs show the dry, pounded surface of the moon in the foreground, dead as an old bone. [6]It is so dead you marvel that poets for centuries have hymned its praises. [7]On the other hand, aloft, floating free beneath the moist, gleaming membrane of bright blue sky, is the rising earth, the only exuberant thing in this part of the cosmos. [8]If you could look long enough, you would see the swirling of the great drifts of white cloud, covering and uncovering the half-hidden masses of land. [9]If you had been looking for a very long, geologic time, you could have seen the continents themselves in motion, drifting apart on their crustal plates, held afloat by the fire beneath. [10]It has the organized, self-contained look of a live creature, full of information, marvelously skilled in handling the sun.

The first paragraph is the paragraph taken from Lewis Thomas. In the second—and longer—one, sentences 2, 3, 4, and 6 obviously do not advance Thomas's idea that the earth is alive. Instead, they distract the reader, and the paragraph loses its central idea in the confusion.

TIPS FOR ACHIEVING PARAGRAPH UNITY

- Give each paragraph a controlling idea by means of a topic sentence.
- Check each sentence in a paragraph to see that it supports the main idea.
- Revise or eliminate any sentence that distracts from the main idea.

Paragraph Coherence

A paragraph must have **coherence**. This means that the sentences must be smoothly integrated. You can't expect your readers to follow your thought if the sentences do not follow some intelligible order. Is the following paragraph orderly? Can you follow the writer's thoughts?

> Yesterday was one big disaster. When I found my right rear tire flat as a board, I laid my head on the steering wheel and wept. The burned bacon didn't help, either; especially after that cold shower, I needed a hot meal. I had worked so hard on my paper I didn't think it was fair that the professor gave me a "D" on it. Sleeping through the alarm always starts my day off wrong. And now I've got to write a 20-page term paper for history. I should have stayed in bed.

Using a simple **chronological order** can make this paragraph coherent:

> Yesterday was one big disaster. I slept through the alarm. Late, I rushed to the bathroom. No more hot water. Teeth chattering from a cold shower, I decided to cook a hot breakfast—and burned the bacon. I gulped down some cold shredded wheat and dashed to my car. By running two traffic lights, I made it to my English class on time and eagerly waited for the professor to return our papers. I had worked hard and was sure I had made at least a "B," if not an "A." Then I saw a big red "D" at the top of my paper. It didn't seem fair. I went on to my history class, and the professor assigned a 20-page term paper. I decided to cut my remaining classes and go home. When I got to my car and found the right rear tire flat as a board, I laid my head on the steering wheel and wept. I should have stayed in bed.

You can achieve order in a number of other ways as well. One of these lies in the use of **space order**—from left to right, from top to bottom, or, as in the following example, from near to far.

> It was a rimy morning, and very damp. I had seen the damp lying on the outside of my little window, as if some goblin had been crying there all night, and using the window for a pocket-handkerchief. Now I saw the damp lying on the bare hedges and spare grass, like a coarser sort of spiders' webs; hanging itself from twig to twig and blade to blade. On every rail and gate, wet lay clammy, and the marsh-mist was so thick, that the wooden finger on the post directing people to

our village—a direction which they never accepted, for they never came there—was invisible to me until I was quite close under it.... The mist was heavier yet when I got out upon the marshes, so that instead of my running at everything, everything seemed to run at me....

—Charles Dickens, *Great Expectations*

You can sometimes **enumerate reasons** by listing them (italics added):

I have sought love, *first*, because it brings ecstasy—ecstasy so great that I could often have sacrificed all the rest of life for a few hours of this joy. I have sought it, *next*, because it relieves loneliness—that terrible loneliness in which one shivering consciousness looks over the rim of the world into the cold unfathomable lifeless abyss. I have sought it, *finally*, because in the union of love I have seen, in a mystic miniature, the prefiguring vision of the heaven that saints and poets have imagined. That is what I sought, and though it might seem too good for human life, that is what—at last—I have found.

—Bertrand Russell, "What I Have Lived For"

Perhaps one of the most useful logical relations, comparing one thing to another, helps you achieve coherence:

In science fiction, which is the literature of extrapolation, there is to be found the recurrent theme of the omniscient computer which ultimately takes over the ordering of human life and affairs. Is this possible? I believe it is not; but I also believe that the arguments commonly advanced to refute this possibility are the wrong ones.... It is said, for example, that computers [unlike humans] "only do what they are told," that they have to be programmed for every computation they undertake. But I do not believe that I was born with an innate ability to solve quadratic equations or to identify common members of the British flora; I, too, had to be programmed for these activities, but I happened to call my programmers by different names, such as "schoolteacher," "lecturer," or "professor."

—W. T. Williams, "Computers as Botanists"

Another strategy for achieving coherence is **repetition**.

I know how a prize watermelon looks when it is sunning its fat rotundity among pumpkin vines and "simblins"; I know how to tell when it is ripe without "plugging" it; I know how inviting it looks when it is cooling itself in a tub of water under the bed, waiting; I know how it looks when it lies on the table in the sheltered great floor space between house and kitchen, and the children gathered for the sacrifice and their mouths watering; I know the crackling sound it makes when the carving knife enters its end, and I can see the split fly along in front of the blade as the knife cleaves its way to the other end; I can see its halves fall apart and display the rich red meat and the black seeds, and the heart standing up, a luxury fit for the elect; I know how a boy looks behind a yard-long slice of that melon, and I know how he feels; for I have been there. I know the taste of the watermelon which has been honestly come by, and I know the taste of the watermelon which has been acquired by art.

—Mark Twain, *Autobiography*

Pronouns help achieve coherence. They refer readers to a previously identified noun (the antecedent) and help the writer connect the ideas without having to name the nouns again and again.

> The Deadbeat Dad has emerged as our principal cultural model for ex-fathers, for obviously failed fathers. As a cultural category, the Deadbeat Dad has become our primary symbol of the growing failure of fatherhood in our society. We demonize him in part because he reminds us of our fatherlessness. He represents loss. He forces us to reduce our expectations. Consequently, we vilify him, we threaten him—we demand that he pay—largely because he so clearly embodies the contemporary collapse of good-enough fatherhood.
>
> —David Blankenhorn, *The Deadbeat Dad*

Use any of these methods—or any others that work—to achieve coherence. The important thing is to achieve it—to make the relation between and among sentences clear to the reader.

TIPS FOR ACHIEVING PARAGRAPH COHERENCE

- Be sure that your sentences follow each other logically.
- Use appropriate—but not excessive—transitions.
- Order details appropriately through chronological or spatial order or through a list.
- Compare one thing to another.
- Use repetition.
- Link ideas with pronouns.

WRITING A STRONG CONCLUSION

The easiest way to conclude a paper is to mention again its major ideas. The following example concludes a paper in which the writer explains membership in a book club:

> Interesting reading, the exchange of ideas, and new friends—these were my reasons for joining a book club. I have not been disappointed.

Some conclusions merely restate the thesis, although in different words to avoid monotony.

> There's an explanation for everything, it's true, but some explanations are more readily acceptable than others. That's the way it is.
>
> —George E. Condon

Some conclusions interpret the significance of the material presented in the body of the paper.

> Since these personality characteristics depend on the growth of the layers of the little egg from which the person developed, they are very difficult to change.

Nevertheless, it is important for the individual to know about these types, so that he can have at least an inkling of what to expect from those around him, and can make allowances for the different kinds of human nature, and so that he can become aware of and learn to control his own natural tendencies, which may sometimes guide him into making the same mistakes over and over again in handling his difficulties.

—Eric Berne

An anecdote sometimes effectively concludes a paper. Following is the conclusion to a paper about the rewards given Dr. Jonas Salk for his polio vaccine:

Probably the greatest tribute Dr. Salk received was unwittingly paid by a small boy whose father, having shown his son the research center, told him that Dr. Salk invented the polio vaccine. The boy, looking puzzled, said, "Daddy, what's polio?"

Quotations and questions can serve to conclude papers.

Samuel Johnson defined a patron as "one who looks with unconcern on a man struggling for life in the water, and when he has reached ground encumbers him with help." Shall we be merely patrons of the needy?

Some of the most effective conclusions attempt to set a broader, more general context for the topic. Such a conclusion helps the reader see that the limited topic you have advanced has relevance beyond your immediate concerns in the paper. By developing a larger application for the topic, you provide a new significance for it.

A student writer produced this thesis sentence in an effort to show the different shades of meaning for the word "excitement":

Excitement means one thing to a seven-year-old and something quite different to a girl in her teens.

In the first body paragraph the writer tells of the excitement she felt on a day her whole third-grade class visited her house to see the backyard cherry tree in bloom. In the next paragraphs she tells of a political demonstration she participated in and the excitement and fear of being jostled in a crowd and then knocked to the ground by people fleeing the police. Here is the conclusion to the essay:

In both instances I experienced excitement; one moment simple and innocent, and the other complex and explosive. Since such different situations aroused the same kind of emotion, I wonder if our emotions are reliable at all until we have a full chance to test them with time and experience. I have to laugh when I hear my thirteen-year-old neighbor say she loves her high school boyfriend. Love is an emotion, and to rely on an early or untested experience for the definition for me is ridiculous. Still, many young people marry at seventeen or eighteen, claiming deep love for their partners. Then, of course, in too many cases, the divorce courts spring into action. Decisions based on emotions must be very carefully made so that we understand the full range of meaning we attach to any special feeling.

—Sarah Fogel

The conclusion establishes a new, general context. The essay itself is about excitement; the conclusion deals with an altogether different emotion, love; yet the example in the conclusion works very well to help the writer make her larger point.

TIPS FOR WRITING A STRONG CONCLUSION

- Refer to the major ideas in the paper.
- Restate the thesis in different words.
- Interpret the significance of the ideas presented.
- Use a lively anecdote.
- Present a quotation.
- Raise a question.
- Establish a new context for the topic.

EXERCISE

For the draft of your own paper, examine the introduction, body, and conclusion in light of the guidelines explored in this chapter. What changes, additions, or deletions should you make in the draft? Revise your paper and submit it to your instructor and classmates for their comments and suggestions.

7

Revising for Thought, Content, and Structure

Like all papers, John Fousek's first draft (see Chapter 3, page 29) needs revising and editing. These two interrelated terms identify critical stages in the development of a successful paper.

When you **revise**, you rethink the ideas and concepts in your paper and change them to reflect your new thoughts. Revision means literally *looking again*. In revising your paper, you want to present and explore any fresh insights you've developed, make necessary changes in focus and direction for your topic, and add essential details. You may have to scrap whole sentences and paragraphs or shift them around for better organization. You may have to change your thesis or alter your supporting details dramatically. And sometimes you have to start all over. When you revise, you also make changes in language and expression. You reshape sentences for clarity and emphasis, you improve the style, you attend to appropriate word choice, diction, and sentence structure.

The information that we have provided in previous chapters should guide you in developing your first and subsequent drafts. But you do have to make a conscious effort to apply the guidelines in Chapters 1–5 not only when you produce a rough draft, but also when you begin the all-important process of revision. In your first effort to produce another draft, focus on the content of your essay.

Try to make your paper as clear as possible. Check on organization and development of ideas. Examine your introduction and conclusion. Consider the unity, coherence, and completeness of your paragraphs. Where should you add information? What unexplored feature of your topic could you open for your readers' advantage? How could you connect related thoughts in different parts of your paper?

REVISING TO IMPROVE YOUR THESIS

As you develop your paper, your thoughts may take you on a track that you never anticipated. In such a case you have three options:

- Revise your thesis so that it addresses the issues you have raised.
- Eliminate any ideas that do not adhere to the thesis you intended.
- Start all over with a new thesis.

You can see how John Fousek's thesis evolved through the various drafts of his paper.

First draft thesis	Intermediate draft thesis	Final draft thesis
But he has a lot of shortcomings that really burn me up. He can be a real pain.	I like Jim very much but he has one habit that I see as an annoying shortcoming. Jim doesn't close things.	But Jim has one shortcoming that irritates me: He doesn't close things.

John moved from the broad thesis in his first draft—his roommate Jim's shortcomings in general—to the more specific notion of Jim's forgetting to close things.

PROGRESS REMINDERS: Revising Your Thesis

❏ Have I stated my topic and my attitude toward it clearly enough?

❏ Am I sure that my topic, and thus my thesis, is limited enough? If not, what can I do to limit the topic and thesis further?

❏ If I chose not to write a thesis sentence, can I at least state it in a complete sentence?

❏ Is my thesis appropriately focused? How can I improve its focus, if necessary?

❏ Is the language of my thesis precise enough? If not, what words could I change to improve its specificity?

❏ Does my thesis cover the evidence and details I intend to use to support my ideas?

REVISING FOR APPROPRIATE SUPPORTING DETAILS

In the paper "My Roommate," John Fousek added a number of sensory details to help the reader see exactly what items his roommate Jim did not close. (See pages 87–88.) For example, the sentence "Spoons and knives clink together as he pokes through the nearest open drawer looking for things in the mess" adds an intense visual image to paragraph 3. But John also saw that he had extraneous detail. He had to eliminate the whole of paragraph two, beginning with "Jim must be allergic to dishes...." This paragraph no longer suited John's new focus in his paper, which is to present Jim's failure to close things.

PROGRESS REMINDERS: Revising for Supporting Details

❏ Have I included details that clearly support my thesis?

❏ If I'm presenting data or using quotations, do they enhance my position effectively?

❑ Have I included extraneous details that I should prune?

❑ Do my details add specificity to generalizations so that the reader can see my point clearly?

❑ If I'm drawing on personal experience, have I used concrete sensory detail—color, action, sound, smell—to bring the reader into the scene?

❑ Do the details fit the paragraphs in which they appear? Does the topic of each paragraph allow the details I have presented, or do I need to move some details to other paragraphs where the details will fit better logically?

❑ Have I attributed the source of my details when I have drawn on someone else's exact words or ideas?

REVISING FOR BETTER ORGANIZATION

When you write a draft of your paper, you must be sure that the sentences and paragraphs make sense in their current order. Would moving a section of the paper strengthen its presentation? Would a few sentences in one paragraph sound better in another? Would moving sentences around make your ideas more logical? In John Fouseks's intermediate draft (pages 87–88), you'll see that paragraph 4 now incorporates paragraph 6 from the first draft (pages 29–30). John's complaint about Jim's not closing the bathroom door works better as part of a more general observation about the failure to close items in the bathroom.

PROGRESS REMINDERS: Revising for Better Organization

❑ Have I followed my outline? If not, can I revise my outline and see that I still have presented the ideas sensibly?

❑ Do my points follow each other logically? Does each idea come after the one before it in a rational way?

❑ Have I used a conscious organization plan for presenting my points? Have I built from the least to the most important point or used some other plan that better suits my thesis?

❑ Are the main divisions of my paper discrete?

❑ Should I shift some sentences or paragraphs so that the ideas in my paper unfold more logically than they do now?

REVISING FOR PURPOSE AND AUDIENCE

After you have a first draft, you want to look very carefully at your writing to see whether or not you have made your purpose and audience clear. In regard to purpose, you must be sure that the way you wanted to treat your topic is obvious. If someone were to ask you, "What exactly are you trying to accomplish in your paper?" would you be able to answer the question simply and directly? If so, what parts of your paper most effectively make your purpose clear? In regard to audience, have you used technical language that only an expert would understand? Have you defined terms if you are using highly technical language? What assumptions have you made about your audience that your writing reflects?

PROGRESS REMINDERS: Revising for Purpose and Audience

- ❏ Is my intent clear—that is, can I state simply and clearly what the purpose of my essay is?

- ❏ How does my thesis inform the purpose of my essay? Can I revise my thesis to help make my purpose even clearer than it is?

- ❏ Have I stayed consistently focused on my purpose, or have any sentences moved off track and need revision?

- ❏ Do the quality and quantity of supporting details contribute successfully to my purpose?

- ❏ Is it clear to me whom I expect to read the essay? If not, what adjustments can I make in language, structure, detail, or organization to ensure that I'm reaching my intended audience?

- ❏ Have I successfully anticipated any questions or objections that readers may have about my topic or supporting information?

- ❏ Does my vocabulary suit the audience I have in mind for my essay? Do I have to replace or define key terms for readers to understand my ideas better?

- ❏ Is my tone—my attitude toward my readers—consistent? Am I trying to sound funny, desperate, angry, hopeful, impatient—and does my expression reflect this or some other intended attitude fruitfully?

REVISING FOR SUITABLE STRUCTURE: INTRODUCTION, BODY PARAGRAPHS, CONCLUSION

As you revise, be sure that you have considered the key structural elements—introduction, body paragraphs, and conclusion—and the way they contribute to the success of your paper.

In John Fousek's essay, note the strong introduction in his final draft.

Introduction: Final Draft

My roommate, Jim, and I have shared a small apartment for the past two years. On the whole, we get along very well. We are both students, and we both work, so we don't spend much time together; but when we do, we cooperate. Jim, who is good at it, does most of the cooking;

> I do most of the cleaning. We find the arrangement satisfactory. And I like Jim. He is generous, witty, honest. Our two-year association has, for the most part, been a good one. But Jim has one shortcoming that irritates me: He doesn't close things.

Although from the first draft John's **introduction** achieved its goal of building to the thesis and setting the stage for the main point of the paper, his revisions tweaked the introduction; he tightened some of the sentences, removed some unnecessary language, and improved significantly on his thesis statement.

But sometimes an introduction will require a complete overhaul, and you shouldn't shrink from the job of a thorough revision.

The **body paragraphs** in any essay must contribute to the thesis by providing information that supports the topic. The topic in each paragraph must relate clearly to your thesis. As you revise, be sure to check carefully on how the sentences in your paragraphs relate to the topic sentence (unity) and how the sentences stick together in an intelligible order (coherence). See pages 53–57. Your use of transitions here is important, and you want to be sure that you have used linking words wisely but sparingly

John made a number of revisions in his body paragraphs, as you can see from the drafts on pages 87–88 and 94–96. We have already noted how he eliminated completely the second body paragraph of the first draft. Now look at the evolution of paragraph 3.

Paragraph 3 in the first draft has become paragraph 2 in the intermediate draft. John realized the unnecessary repetition in his first draft of paragraph 2 and reduced it sharply—by half, from 70 words to 35, five sentences to three. The new paragraph in the intermediate draft has little more than a topic sentence indicating that Jim doesn't close things and provides little useful supporting information for the assertion. From a bloated paragraph, John produced an excessively deflated one. Wisely, he rejected this paragraph in his next try.

In the final draft, observe how John once again has expanded his ideas into a substantial body paragraph, rich in details but empty of needless repetition. The details support the topic sentence and reinforce the thesis with specific references to Jim's sloppiness and his habit of never closing drawers.

Body Paragraph: Final Draft

> Jim, for example, almost never closes a drawer or a closet door, and his failure to do so is often a source of embarrassment to me. The problem is that I am compulsively neat, and Jim, I'm sorry to say, is a slob. It seems never to have occurred to him that the contents of a drawer could be organized. When he does his laundry, he just empties his bag of clean clothes into a drawer—white socks, underwear, a rainbow of T-shirts with college crests, pajamas, graying handkerchiefs. When the drawer is full, he begins filling the next one. Then when he needs clean socks or a shirt, he

rolls the contents of the drawer around until he finds what he wants, often leaving rejected items hanging over the edge of the drawer. His clothes closet is just as messy as the drawers. He does the same kinds of things in the kitchen. Spatulas, flatware, eggbeaters, knives clink together as he pokes through the nearest open drawer to find his favorite tool for beating eggs or mincing onions. If he'd organized the drawer in the first place, the rattle of kitchenware wouldn't disturb my study time before every meal. Since Jim doesn't close drawers or closets, our apartment usually looks like the site of a rummage sale at closing time. The appearance offends my neat soul and embarrasses me when friends visit us.

The **conclusion** of your essay is an essential component of the whole paper: It creates for your reader the final impression of your writing. Don't always settle just for a restatement of the main ideas or for a paraphrase of your thesis.

John Fousek changed his conclusion significantly from draft to draft. In his first attempt, John's conclusion merely restates his thesis with another example as support. The intermediate draft's conclusion adds words but little else of import. But the conclusion in the final draft brings the main point of the essay to a close, and then applies his experience with Jim in a new context: how John is better able now "to handle the frustrations of some of my friends' strange habits in general." And the final sentence provides a neat closing to both the conclusion and the essay itself.

Conclusion: Final Draft

When that frigid air blasts my wet body, my irritation with Jim reaches its peak. Nevertheless, because he is such a great guy and because I know his failure to close things is, in the scheme of human problems, just a minor bad habit, I try to overlook it. I shut my mouth and take a deep breath. In fact, by learning to deal with this annoyance I think I've learned a little about how to handle the frustrations of some of my friends' strange habits in general. I keep a good sense of humor and I hold my temper. After all, I'd rather have opened closets and drawers than a door closed on friendship.

PROGRESS REMINDERS: Revising for Suitable Structure

❏ Does my introduction build appropriately to my thesis? Is my thesis itself clear?

❏ Have I considered a variety of strategies for improving my introduction, such as identifying my paper's divisions, telling an anecdote, asking a challenging question, quoting a statement relevant to my topic, or providing dramatic data or statistics (see pages 36–37)?

❏ Do my body paragraphs have a stated topic sentence or at the very least an implied topic sentence that readers can understand?

❑ Does each paragraph's topic relate clearly to my thesis?

❑ Are the sentences in each paragraph unified, that is, clearly supporting the main idea? Should I revise or eliminate any distracting sentences?

❑ Do the sentences cohere; that is, do they follow each other in some logical way, such as chronologically, spatially, by means of cause and effect or comparison and contrast, through repetition or parallel structure?

❑ Have I checked for transitions to be sure that I have used them appropriately (and not excessively) to link sentences and paragraphs?

❑ Have I developed a strong conclusion that at the very least recaps briefly the main ideas of my paper? Have I drawn on other useful strategies for conclusions: using an anecdote or a quotation from an expert, interpreting the significance of the ideas I've presented, or establishing a new context for my topic?

8

Revising to Improve Language

Jonathan Swift, the author of *Gulliver's Travels*, once defined good style as "proper words in proper places." Gustave Flaubert, the great French novelist, felt that the writer's craft was embodied in the quest for *le seul mot juste*, "the single right word." Nearly all writers can learn to hit the right word simply by becoming more alert to the possibilities of language.

REVISING YOUR LANGUAGE

Denotation and Connotation

Traditionally, the most logical way to begin thinking about right and wrong words when you revise your paper is through the distinction between denotation and connotation:

- The **denotation** of a word is its explicit, surface meaning, its bare "dictionary meaning."
- The **connotation** of a word is its implicit meaning, the meaning derived from the emotions associated with the word in people's minds.

Words like *Las Vegas* or *Ireland*, for example, simply denote a particular city or country—a mere geographical location—but for many people, they also have an emotional significance that has nothing to do with geography. The connotative meanings of a word do not always appear in a dictionary, but they are as vital a part of the word's full meaning as are denotations.

The Importance of Connotation

Developing a sensitivity to the connotations of words is an invaluable asset for all writers. The right word will be the one with the right connotations—the connotations that most precisely reflect the writer's intended meaning and produce the desired reaction from the writer's audience. Was the person who had too much to drink *inebriated, intoxicated, drunk, looped, smashed, tipsy, high, crocked, pickled, loaded,* or *blotto*? Was the overweight person *plump, fat, pudgy, obese, chubby, portly, chunky, corpulent, stout,* or *stocky*? Writers always think about the fine distinctions in connotation that separate words with similar denotations and never automatically assume that the first word that springs to mind is the right one.

EXERCISE

Rearrange each group of words by connotation, from the least favorable term to the most favorable. In many cases, opinions will differ; there are few purely right and purely wrong answers.

1. unromantic, realistic, pragmatic, hardheaded
2. thin, skinny, slender, bony, emaciated
3. weep, cry, blubber, bawl
4. squabble, disagreement, quarrel, brawl
5. knowledgeable, bright, shrewd, smart, brainy

Abstract Writing and Concrete Writing

Although the distinction between denotation and connotation is valuable to writers, it is sometimes easier to see the immediate, practical consequences to a writer's quest for the right word in the distinction between abstract writing and concrete writing:

- **Abstract writing** is writing that lacks specific details and is filled with vague, indefinite words and broad, general statements.
- **Concrete writing** is characterized by specific details and specific language.

Consider the following examples of abstract and concrete writing.

Abstract ⟶	Concrete
Too much poverty exists in this country.	I see one-third of a nation ill-housed, ill-clad, ill-nourished.
Mr. Jones is a tough grader.	Mr. Jones flunked 75 percent of his class and gave no higher than a C to the students who passed.
Computers now execute many of the tasks that only humans could do many years ago.	Today's technology allows computers to perform tasks like processing banking transactions, obtaining research from thousands of sources, and sending information overseas.

Nothing is technically wrong with these examples of abstract writing, but we need only compare them to the rewritten concrete versions to see their basic inadequacy. They convey less information. They are less interesting. They have less impact. There is nothing wrong with them except that they could be much better.

Using Specific Details

The use of specific details is the most direct way to avoid abstract writing. Here's a useful rule:

> *Never* make an unsupported general statement that you do not back up with specific details.

This rule sounds easy enough, but it means what it says. It means a writer should never try to get by with sentences such as, "The day was too hot"; "The hero of the story was very ambitious"; "The administration is corrupt"; "The Industrial Revolution brought about many changes." Without specific details the sentences are worthless. "The day was too hot" is uninteresting and unpersuasive. *Back it up*. The reader should know that the temperature was 93 degrees, that Bill's sweaty glasses kept slipping off his nose, that a cocker spaniel who had managed to find a spot of shade was too exhausted and miserable to bother brushing away the flies. Specific details give the writing life and conviction that abstractions alone can never achieve.

One more point about specific details: Within reason, *the more specific the better*. As long as the detail is relevant—as long, that is, as it supports the generalization and is not instantly obvious as too trivial for consideration—the writer is unlikely to go wrong by being too specific.

To summarize: Support all your generalizations with relevant, specific details. Remember that, within reason, the more specific the details, the better the writing.

Abstract (weak)

The telephone is a great scientific achievement, but it can also be a great inconvenience. Who could begin to count the number of times that phone calls have come from unwelcome people or on unwelcome occasions? Telephones make me nervous.

Specific (strong)

The telephone is a great scientific achievement, but it can also be a great big headache. More often than not, that cheery ringing in my ears brings messages from the Ace Bill Collecting Agency, my mother (who is feeling snubbed for the fourth time that week), salespersons of encyclopedias and magazines, solicitors for the Police Officers' Ball and Disease of the Month Foundation, and neighbors complaining about my dog. That's not to mention frequent wrong numbers— usually for someone named "Arnie." The calls always seem to come at the worst times, too. They've interrupted steak dinners, hot tubs, Friday night parties, and Saturday morning sleep-ins. There's no escape. Sometimes I wonder if there are any telephones in padded cells.

EXERCISE

Invent two or three specific details to back up each of the following generalizations. Use your imagination. Remember, the more specific the better. Don't settle for a detail like "He reads many books" to support the statement "My teacher is very intellectual."

1. Some television commercials are extremely entertaining.
2. Some television commercials are extremely irritating.
3. Most people are foolish about their own health.
4. After enough time goes by, anything can become a bore.
5. Thunder showers are dangerous.

Using Comparisons

Another way of avoiding abstract writing and increasing the liveliness of concrete writing is to use effective figures of speech, particularly **comparisons**. Good comparisons are attention-getters. They can add a helpful spark to otherwise pedestrian writing.

Two cautions are in order. First, use comparisons in moderation. The more comparisons a piece of writing contains, the less impact each one is likely to have. Second, and more important, avoid the routine, trite comparisons that fill our language. Don't write "It was as easy as pie" or "It was as easy as taking candy from a baby." Try to be fresh and different. Rather than be trite, avoid comparisons altogether.

Make sure, too, that you phrase your comparisons correctly, whether you are using them for lively specific detail or as a simple means of making a point—"Alice is smarter than Sally," for example. Beware of illogical sentences (see pages 141–146).

EXERCISE

Make up *two* logical phrases to complete each of the following comparisons. Be prepared to tell which of your phrases is better and why.

1. I have no more chance of passing this course than...
2. My brother is more dependable than...
3. The congressman's explanation was as plausible as...
4. If you'd buy an insurance policy from him, you're the kind of person who...
5. I haven't had a more hectic day since...

9

Revising and Editing to Improve Style

WORDINESS AND ECONOMY

Wordiness is a major writing problem. It is hard to avoid because it can turn up for any number of reasons, and writers usually don't realize that they are being wordy. Nobody wants to be a windbag, yet unneeded words sneak into nearly everyone's writing.

Before discussing the different kinds of wordiness, we should clear up one point: Wordiness results from using words that don't do anything—it has no direct connection to the number of words. A poor writer can produce a wordy paragraph on the meaning of freedom; a good writer can produce a whole book on the same subject that is not wordy. If the words contribute to the effect the writer wants, if eliminating any of them would sacrifice something valuable, then the writer is *not* being wordy. Only when words can be eliminated without any harm being done do we find real wordiness.

There are four major sources of wordiness: deadwood, pointless repetition of meaning, inadequate clause cutting, and delay of subject.

Cutting Deadwood

Some words are like deadwood on a tree or bush—unless you remove them, they sap the strength of the healthy words around them. Moreover, an attentive writer can remove **deadwood** with little or no tampering with the rest of the sentence, as in the examples that follow.

Deadwood	Improved
His hair was red in color.	His hair was red.
Pollution conditions that exist in our cities are disgraceful.	Pollution in our cities is disgraceful.
The building has a height of 934 feet.	The building rises 934 feet.
She was in a depressed state of mind.	She was depressed.
Disneyland struck us as a fascinating kind of place.	Disneyland struck us as fascinating.

In this day and age we live in, people seem totally apathetic about everything.

People today seem totally apathetic.

The hero of the story was an individual in the high-income bracket.

The hero of the story was rich.

Avoiding Pointless Repetition of Meaning

Pointless repetition of meaning is a special kind of deadwood. Aside from adding useless words, such repetition reflects writers' lack of confidence in themselves—their fear that their point will not be clear unless they make it twice. Unfortunately, this overemphasis usually suggests sloppy thinking to the reader, rather than a desire for accuracy.

Pointless repetition ⟶	Improved
The film was very interesting and fascinating.	The film was fascinating.
Our streams are filthy and dirty.	Our streams are filthy.
The author gives examples of different and varied criticisms of the novel.	The author gives examples of different criticisms of the novel.
To begin with, in the first place, the story has terrific suspense.	In the first place, the story has terrific suspense.

EXERCISE

Point out any instances of deadwood and pointless repetition in the following sentences.

1. At this point in time, we have no travel plans.
2. In my opinion, I think depression is a terrible kind of illness.
3. We have ignored and neglected the basic fundamental essentials for too long a period of time.
4. Men and women of both sexes must join the combat to fight for a better world.
5. Rebecca Lobo is an individual who excels in the area of basketball.

Cutting Wordy Clauses

Cut a cumbersome clause into a shorter phrase or, if possible, a single word. This **clause cutting** can result in a tighter, more economical structure, with the phrase or word more firmly incorporated into the sentence than the original clause ever was.

Wordy clause ⟶	Improved
The woman who had red hair was afraid.	The red-haired woman was afraid.
Some of the students who were more enthusiastic wrote an extra paper.	Some of the more enthusiastic students wrote an extra paper.
The story was very exciting. It was all about ghosts.	The ghost story was very exciting.

Avoiding Delay of Subject

The phrases *there is, there has, it is,* and *it has*—in all tenses—are frequent causes of wordiness. Nothing is wrong with these phrases in themselves. Too often, however, they are used carelessly and delay a sentence or clause from getting down to business.

Wordy delay ———————————————————➤	Improved
There are too many people who care only for themselves.	Too many people care only for themselves.
It has often been commented on by great philosophers that philosophy solves nothing.	Great philosophers have often commented that philosophy solves nothing.
There have been a number of conflicting studies made of urban problems.	A number of conflicting studies have been made of urban problems.

EXERCISE

Rewrite these sentences to make them more economical, cutting clauses and eliminating wordy delay of subject wherever possible.

1. The man who lives next door to me walks his two poodles every morning that it is cool and sunny.
2. There have been many complicated plans that have been proposed to reduce the number of nuclear weapons that are stationed in Europe.
3. Many people who frequently travel by plane may experience some delays, which are caused by new airport security measures recently put in place.
4. The idea of a guaranteed annual wage is a notion that conflicts with many traditional middle-class values.
5. Another time, when he was shown the list of the names of the officers who had been appointed to serve under him at the Battle of Waterloo, the Duke commented, "I don't know if they will frighten the French, but, by Gad, they terrify me!"

PASSIVE AND ACTIVE VERBS

In most English sentences, the subject performs an action.

John likes this poem.
The critic saw the movie.
The senator is going to vote for the bill.

The verb in such sentences is said to be in the **active voice**. The active voice is direct, clear, and concise; in most sentences, it is what we expect.

Too often, however, instead of using the active voice, writers substitute the more stilted **passive voice**. A verb in the passive voice combines a form of *to be* with the past participle of the verb: *is given, has been delivered, was mailed.* Thus, instead of *acting*, the subject of the sentence is *acted upon*.

This poem is liked by John.
The movie was seen by the critic.
The bill is going to be voted for by the senator.

Compared to the active voice, the passive is generally awkward, exceedingly formal, and wordy.

On occasion, the passive voice doesn't sound bad, of course. Such occasions may arise when the actor is unknown, insignificant, or nonexistent, or when a deliberately impersonal tone is required. Don't be afraid of the passive when it seems normal and unforced—as in the last part of the preceding sentence—but always be alert to its dangers. When you use the passive voice, you should always have a reason for choosing it over the active voice.

Here are a few examples of perfectly acceptable passives:

The game was delayed because of rain.
The eighteenth century has been called the Age of Enlightenment.
Your prompt attention to this request for payment will be appreciated.

EXERCISE

Change the passive voice to the active voice wherever appropriate in the following sentences.

1. Fewer novels are being read by teenagers these days.
2. At the corner restaurant, all of the tacos are freshly made each day.
3. The director was convicted of embezzling funds and using the money for herself.
4. The doctor was advised to get malpractice insurance.
5. The doctor was advised to get malpractice insurance by his lawyer.

CORRECTING FAULTY PARALLELISM

What Is Parallelism?

Essentially, **parallelism** means expressing ideas and facts of equal (or coordinate or "parallel") importance in the same grammatical form. Parallel grammatical structure reinforces a writer's thoughts by stressing the parallel importance of the various sentence elements, and so makes life easier for the reader. Many of the most famous phrases in our language draw strength in part from effective use of parallelism:

...*life, liberty,* and the *pursuit* of happiness.	(group of three nouns)
...*of the people, by the people,* and *for the people.*	(three prepositional phrases)
Love me or *leave me.*	(two imperatives)
Early *to bed* and early *to rise* / Makes a man *healthy,* and *wealthy,* and *wise.*	(two infinitives/three adjectives)
I come *to bury Caesar,* not *to praise him.*	(two infinitives with objects)

I came, I saw, I conquered.   (three independent clauses)

Better be *safe* than *sorry*.   (two adjectives)

Avoiding Faulty Parallelism

Now notice how faulty parallelism or lack of parallelism can sabotage a sentence.

Incorrect	Correct
You can get there by *car, bus*, or *fly*. (noun, noun, verb)	You can get there by *car, bus*, or *plane*. (noun, noun, noun)
I thought the climactic episode in the story was *shocking, offbeat*, and *I found it very amusing*. (adjective, adjective, independent clause)	I thought the climactic episode in the story was *shocking, offbeat*, and very *amusing*. (adjective, adjective, adjective)
She *liked* people and *was liked* by people. (active voice, passive voice)	She *liked* people and people *liked* her. (active voice, active voice)

Descriptive words added to some of the parallel elements do not break the basic parallelism and can be valuable in avoiding monotony.

Judith had *brains, talent*, and an extremely charming *personality*.	(still parallel: a group of three nouns, even though one is modified by an adjective, and the adjective is modified by an adverb)
The man owned a *mansion* and a fine *collection* of modern etchings.	(still parallel: two nouns, even though one of them is modified by an adjective and followed by a prepositional phrase)

EXERCISE

Which of the following sentences use faulty parallelism? Which use parallelism correctly? Which use inappropriate parallelism? Make corrections in the sentences that need them.

1. She enjoys running, mountain climbing, and the movies.
2. Some day I will go bungee jumping, parasailing, and buy a boat.
3. The principal said the main issues were discipline, academic achievement, and good attendance at the pep rally.
4. Percy Bysshe Shelley wrote some of the greatest poems in the English language, lived a spectacularly scandalous private life, and had a weird middle name.
5. Steven Yip's résumé shows that he is hardworking, responsible, and an experienced manager.

FAULTY SUBORDINATION

Which of the following observations on that great new epic movie, *The Return of the Hideous Vampire*, is likely to be most significant?

It was produced by Paramount.
It is one of the best horror movies of the last ten years.
It was filmed in Technicolor.

Which of these facts about Earnest N. Dogood deserves the most emphasis?

He is a Republican.
He has announced his candidacy for president of the United States.
He is a senator.

You should have chosen the second item in both cases.

Yet a skillful writer will **subordinate** some of those facts, arranging the sentence or paragraph so that some parts are clearly secondary to others. This process is sometimes called **sentence combining**.

Above, we have three pieces of information about a movie. Below, with proper subordination the writer collects the three related observations, reserves the independent clause for the most important one, and tucks away the rest in a less conspicuous place.

The Return of the Hideous Vampire, a Technicolor film produced by Paramount, is one of the best horror movies of the last ten years.

Here are a few examples of how subordination can improve writing:

Unsubordinated ──────────▶	Subordinated
Jane is a wonderful person. She is very shy. She is extremely kind to everybody.	Although very shy, Jane is a wonderful person who is extremely kind to everybody.
	or
	Although she is a wonderful person who is extremely kind to everybody, Jane is very shy.
This play explores the fate of love in a mechanized society. It is highly symbolic, and it has two acts.	This highly symbolic play of two acts explores the fate of love in a mechanized society.

EXERCISE

Rewrite the following sentences, making effective use of subordination.

1. Some scientists are skeptical about life on other planets. Astronomers calculate that there are many Earth-like planets. Some evidence exists that microbes once survived on Mars.

2. He is an ignorant young man. He is boorish. He is ugly. He is cheap. Why did I say "yes" when he asked me to go to the party?
3. Cape Cod is crowded. It's overcommercialized. It's expensive. I love it.
4. The nuclear age is in its seventh decade. We should reevaluate atomic energy. People are very emotional about it.
5. Jill was going up the hill to fetch a pail of water, and Jack was helping her. Then Jack fell down.

REVISING FOR SENTENCE VARIETY

Varying Sentence Length

Sentences come short, medium, and long—and the simple principle for effective writing is to try for variety. Don't take this principle more rigidly than it's intended. Don't assume, for instance, that every single short sentence must be followed by a long one, and vice versa. A string of short or long sentences can sometimes be effective, providing that it is eventually followed by a sentence that varies the pattern. Common sense and alertness will tell you when variety is needed. Just remember that too many sentences of the same length bunched together can create a monotonous style and a restless reader.

Monotonous ⟶	Improved
I thought the course was going to be easy, but I was wrong, because after a two-week sickness early in the term I could never find the time to catch up with the assignments, and I kept getting poor grades. I wish I had had the foresight to see what was coming and had taken the initiative either to drop the course or to ask the teacher for an incomplete, but pride or vanity kept me plugging away, and nothing did any good.	I thought the course was going to be easy, but I was wrong. After a two-week sickness early in the term, I could never find the time to catch up with the assignments, and I kept getting poor grades. Why didn't I drop? Why didn't I ask for an incomplete? If I'd known for sure what was coming, I probably would have done one or the other. Pride or vanity kept me plugging away, however, and nothing did any good.

Varying Sentence Structure

Regardless of sentence length, a group of sentences can become monotonous if each sentence uses the same basic structure. Remember only that there are many different ways of structuring a sentence, and wise writers never limit themselves to one method. Variety is again the key.

Monotonous ————————————➤	Improved
Entering the personnel manager's office, Bill wanted to make a good impression. Smiling, he shook hands. Sitting down, he tried not to fidget. Answering the questions politely, he kept his voice low and forced himself not to say "uh." Being desperate for a job, he had to be at his best. Wondering if his desperation showed, he decided to risk a little joke.	Entering the personnel manager's office, Bill wanted to make a good impression. He smiled, shook hands, and tried not to fidget when he sat down. He answered questions politely, keeping his voice low and forcing himself not to say "uh." Bill was desperate for a job. He had to be at his best. Wondering if his desperation showed, he decided to risk a little joke.

EXERCISE

The following groups of sentences are monotonous. Rewrite them to add greater variety in sentence length and structure.

1. Tired and bored, I gazed vacantly out the window. Energetic and powerful, a robin dug for worms. Cheerful and bright, a cardinal chirped melodiously in a treetop. Ashamed and humbled, I watched their total involvement in life.

2. Certificates of deposit from local banks are insured by a federal agency, so they are extremely safe investments, but your money is tied up in them for long periods of time unless you are willing to accept stiff penalties for early withdrawal, and they also do not always pay particularly high rates of interest. You may find it more beneficial to invest in a conservative mutual fund specializing in government bonds, which will give you great safety, too, but it also offers excellent returns on your money and permits you to withdraw money by check any time you wish.

3. Eager to begin their vacation, the family loaded the minivan. Filled with enthusiasm, they drove for twenty-five minutes. Shocked by the sudden failure of the engine, they pulled the car to the side of Interstate 90. Horrified at their poor planning, they realized they had forgotten to fill the tank with gas.

10

Revising and Editing for Additional Style Problems

TRITENESS

A **trite expression**, or **cliché**, is a word or phrase that has become worn out through overuse. Many trite expressions may once have been original and even brilliant, but through constant repetition they have lost whatever impact they once had. If a writer uses many trite expressions, a reader may be tempted to assume that the thoughts are as secondhand as the language.

The best way to deal with triteness is to eliminate it. Apologetic little quotation marks do not help. If the writer has been trite, quotation marks call even more attention to the fault and let the reader know that the triteness was no accident.

The following list contains a number of trite expressions. Avoid them. Choose ten from the list and try to think of original and effective ways to express the same ideas.

Trite Expressions

more fun than a barrel of monkeys	peer pressure
worth its weight in gold	do unto others
stop on a dime	tender loving care
fresh as a daisy	meaningful dialog
happy as a lark	turned on
hard as nails	a good time was had by all
make a long story short	white as snow
no use crying over spilled milk	Mother Nature
a penny saved is a penny earned	Father Time
cool as a cucumber	spread like wildfire
pretty as a picture	the crack of dawn
in the pink	dog-eat-dog
hale and hearty	every cloud has a silver lining
under the weather	sick as a dog
go at it tooth and nail	work like a dog
generation gap	easy as pie
broaden one's horizons	sweet as sugar

a matter of life and death

sly as a fox

stubborn as a mule

rat race

Old Glory

trial and error

the bigger they are, the harder they fall

sad but true

south of the border

armed to the teeth

flattery will get you nowhere

male chauvinist pig

a bolt from the blue

open-and-shut case

slow as molasses

do your own thing

last but not least

In addition to these phrases, we express some familiar—and important—ideas in the same language so often that the ideas themselves seem trite unless we word them differently. Here is a partial list of such potentially trite ideas:

Trite Ideas

Getting to know people of different backgrounds is a good thing.

College is more difficult than high school.

Pollution is a major problem in the United States.

Education is necessary for many jobs.

We live in a technological society.

We need to think more about people who are less fortunate.

Nature is beautiful.

Adults have more responsibilities than children.

This issue is very complicated.

EUPHEMISMS

A **euphemism** is a word or phrase used as a polite substitute for a more natural but less refined word or phrase. Euphemisms can be handy to have around, especially in social situations. As a rule, though, you should avoid euphemisms, especially in your writing. They generally seem pretentious, fussy, and old-fashioned. The natural, honest word is usually the best one, so long as honesty is not confused with exhibitionistic crudeness or vulgarity.

Euphemisms ⟶	Direct language
low-income individual	poor person
urban poverty area	slum
sanitation worker	trash collector
custodian *or* superintendent	janitor
mortician *or* funeral director	undertaker
conflict	war

EXERCISE

Locate the trite expressions and euphemisms in the following sentences and suggest alternatives.

1. He had once established a meaningful relation with a member of the fair sex, but time flies, and she moved on to greener pastures.
2. When the senior citizen stepped into the street and began walking as slow as molasses, I had to stop my car on a dime to avoid an unfortunate incident.
3. Excessive ingestion can significantly increase adipose tissue.
4. The army executed a strategic withdrawal.
5. It made my blood boil to hear that officers of the law were accused of assaulting an unarmed gentleman who was as helpless as a kitten.

REPETITION, GOOD AND BAD

Repetition can help or hurt your writing depending on how you use it. When used to add clarity or dramatic impact, repetition is a major stylistic resource. At other times, however, repetition can interfere with good style, and writers need to be aware of its dangers.

Repetition for Clarity

Repetition can help to clarify meaning and get the writer and reader from one sentence or clause to another. One of the simplest and most valuable transitional devices for a writer is the repetition of a key word or phrase, sometimes in slightly altered form, from a preceding sentence or clause:

> Critics tend to make too much of a fuss about *symbols*. *Symbols* are not obscure artistic tricks. Our own daily lives are filled with *symbols*.

Repetition for Impact

Repetition can often add effective dramatic impact, as in the following example.

> We've shrugged at scandals. We've shrugged at violence. We've shrugged at overpopulation and pollution and discrimination. Now it's time to stop shrugging.

If not handled skillfully and tastefully, repetition for impact can also lead to foolish emotionalism or unnecessary stress on the obvious:

> Must cruel developers have their way forever? What of the flowers? What of the trees? What of the grass? What of the homeless birds and squirrels and bunnies?

Undesirable Repetition of Meaning

Avoid restating a point that is already sufficiently clear. For example:

The American flag is red, white, and blue *in color*.

She was remarkably beautiful. *She was, in fact, quite exceptionally good-looking.*

(See the discussion of wordiness in pages 71–73.)

Undesirable Repetition of the Same Word

Although repetition of a word or word form can help to clarify a point or serve as a transitional device, if used too often it can become monotonous and irritating.

I am *very* pleased to be here on this *very* distinguished occasion. Your *very* kind remarks and your *very* generous gift have left me *very* much at a loss for words, but *very* deeply appreciative.

Beware of using different forms of the same word through carelessness. The result can be an awkward and confusing sentence.

We had a *wonderful* time seeing the *wonders* of Florida.

People must be made more *aware* of the need for increased *awareness* of our environment.

Undesirable Repetition of Sounds

Save rhymes for poetry. Avoid a horror like this:

The church is reexamining its position on the condition of the mission.

Go easy on **alliteration**, the repetition of sounds at the beginning of words. Every once in a while, alliteration can be effective, but when a writer is obviously pouring it on, the results are silly at best.

The orchestra's bold blowing of the brasses thrilled me to the bottom of my being.

EXERCISE

Point out any undesirable repetition in the following sentences and make the necessary corrections.

1. Endless streams of tourists threaten to ruin our state's rivers, brooks, and streams.
2. Let's not bring up that argument anymore. Let's never discuss it again.
3. Despite efforts to forget, I find that the mind will remind us of our errors.
4. I am sure that avarice adds fuel to his already active aspirations for advancement.
5. I asked her to marry me, and she said yes. She said yes!

SLANG

By and large, slang is inappropriate for the comparatively formal, analytical writing that college courses most often demand. But when you feel sure that a slang expression can genuinely communicate something you could not otherwise convey as well, don't be afraid to use it. When you do use it, avoid the coy quotation marks that some writers put around slang to show that they are really sophisticated people who could use more formal language if they wanted to. Good slang should seem natural, and if it is natural, it doesn't need quotes.

> Once thought of as the intellectual leader of a generation, Thompson turned out to be just another jerk with the gift of gab.
>
> Billed as a luxury resort, the hotel was a high-priced dump.

Be careful about using slang, however. Don't use it to show how up-to-date you are; slang changes so fast that what seemed current yesterday is often embarrassingly old-fashioned tomorrow. Don't use slang to show your reader what a folksy person you are; that technique almost always fails. Avoid crude sentences like these:

> In *Hamlet*, Hamlet's girlfriend, Ophelia, goes nuts.
>
> This profound political allegory really turned me on.
>
> Albert Einstein was one of the big brains of the twentieth century.

EXERCISE

Correct any inappropriate use of slang or fancy writing in the following sentences.

1. The cacophony emanating from the foyer indicated to us an altercation among our offspring.
2. Good writers eschew prolixity.
3. Through all the vicissitudes of life, Benjamin Franklin kept his cool.
4. Little Billy became lachrymose when his mother turned off the boob tube.
5. Many liberal policy makers concur with welfare recipients who express sentiments indicating their desire to obtain employment as long as it isn't flipping burgers at some burger joint.

SEXIST LANGUAGE

Sexist language is language that displays prejudice and stereotyped thinking about the roles, character, and worth of both sexes, though women have most frequently been its victims.

To prevent or eliminate sexist language, pay particular attention to the following suggestions.

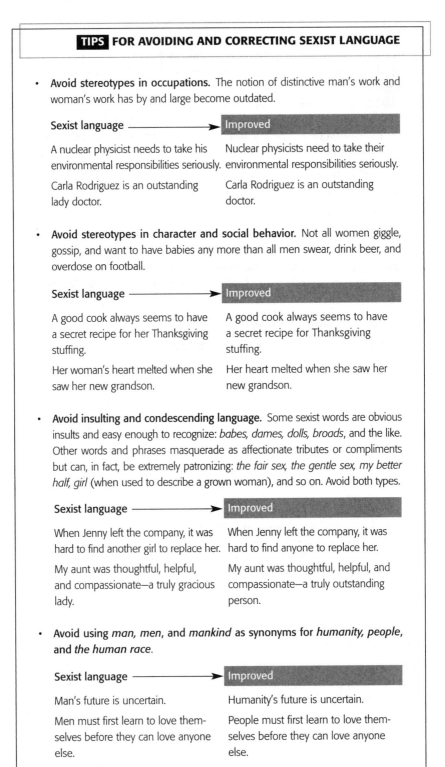

TIPS FOR AVOIDING AND CORRECTING SEXIST LANGUAGE

- **Avoid stereotypes in occupations.** The notion of distinctive man's work and woman's work has by and large become outdated.

  Sexist language ⟶ Improved

Sexist language	Improved
A nuclear physicist needs to take his environmental responsibilities seriously.	Nuclear physicists need to take their environmental responsibilities seriously.
Carla Rodriguez is an outstanding lady doctor.	Carla Rodriguez is an outstanding doctor.

- **Avoid stereotypes in character and social behavior.** Not all women giggle, gossip, and want to have babies any more than all men swear, drink beer, and overdose on football.

  Sexist language ⟶ Improved

Sexist language	Improved
A good cook always seems to have a secret recipe for her Thanksgiving stuffing.	A good cook always seems to have a secret recipe for Thanksgiving stuffing.
Her woman's heart melted when she saw her new grandson.	Her heart melted when she saw her new grandson.

- **Avoid insulting and condescending language.** Some sexist words are obvious insults and easy enough to recognize: *babes, dames, dolls, broads*, and the like. Other words and phrases masquerade as affectionate tributes or compliments but can, in fact, be extremely patronizing: *the fair sex, the gentle sex, my better half, girl* (when used to describe a grown woman), and so on. Avoid both types.

  Sexist language ⟶ Improved

Sexist language	Improved
When Jenny left the company, it was hard to find another girl to replace her.	When Jenny left the company, it was hard to find anyone to replace her.
My aunt was thoughtful, helpful, and compassionate—a truly gracious lady.	My aunt was thoughtful, helpful, and compassionate—a truly outstanding person.

- **Avoid using *man, men*, and *mankind* as synonyms for *humanity, people*, and *the human race*.**

  Sexist language ⟶ Improved

Sexist language	Improved
Man's future is uncertain.	Humanity's future is uncertain.
Men must first learn to love themselves before they can love anyone else.	People must first learn to love themselves before they can love anyone else.

- Avoid using the pronoun *he* when sex is unknown or irrelevant.

Sexist language ─────────────────▶ Improved

Sexist language	Improved
We need a person who can offer a few hours of his time each week.	We need a person who can offer a few hours of time each week.
A liar needs to make sure that he has a good memory.	Liars need to make sure that they have good memories.

EXERCISE

Rewrite the following sentences to eliminate sexist language.

1. After moving from her neighborhood of the past twenty-five years, Julie most missed the girls' nights out every Tuesday.
2. A collegiate athlete must be able to manage his time well.
3. Marjorie Small is a fully ordained lady minister.
4. Forget about elections and wars. The fate of man is determined more by climate than by anything else.
5. She shouldn't let these disappointments bother her pretty little head. All she really needs is a good cry.

EXERCISE

Comment on the stylistic problems in each of the following sentences, and rewrite the sentences where necessary.

1. Your ugly buck teeth can now be corrected more quickly and economically than was once the case.
2. This paper will demonstrate that Beyoncé is more than just a pretty face.
3. In my opinion, I believe that George W. Bush will go down in history as an extremely controversial president.
4. Recent government funding cuts mean that you may no longer be able to feed your hungry children.
5. Thus the poem clearly shows, in my humble opinion, that Dickinson was a shrewd observer.

11

One Student Writing: Revising and Editing in Action

Strongly linked to the revision process is **editing,** a critical step in refining your paper. When you edit, you look at your paper for errors in grammar, usage, spelling, and punctuation. You also refine any word choices that seem off for the intent of your paper.

When you **proofread,** you take a final look at your paper for any errors that you may have missed in your editing process. You look for spelling mistakes, omitted commas, and transposed letters that your word processing program may have missed. Proofreading usually does not require the production of yet another draft: You can make corrections in ink directly on your final draft.

In an effort to anticipate the range of problems and errors that appear in student writing, we have appended a minibook, an alphabetical list of characteristic grammar, spelling, punctuation, and mechanics problems that you may encounter as you produce your drafts. (See pages 197–235.) Check the entries often; make the minibook an essential tool when you edit and proofread your drafts.

PEER REVIEW: LEARNING FROM OTHER STUDENTS

John Fousek shaped his draft by working first with another student in a peer-critiquing session in class.

Some instructors build peer review sessions into regular writing activities. In peer review, you and your classmates comment on each other's drafts. Sometimes you work in small groups and offer comments and suggestions orally. Or, you can write comments directed at specific questions posed by fellow writers or by your teacher on a peer-response checklist.

Following the instructor's guidelines for using a peer-response guide or checklist, the person who read John's paper gave him this written evaluation.

Peer Evaluation Guide and Student Response

> 1. What is the main point of the paper?
> *You are trying to show what annoys you about your roommate, that he doesn't close things.*

2. What is the best part of the paper?
The bathroom examples—funny! I've had toe shampoos, too! I also like the open drawers part.

3. What recommendations for improvement can you make?
   a. *Add more details. Show some of the stuff in the drawers—how they're dumped in. Maybe describe the bathroom, too?*
   b. *I agree with your question—watch trite and slang words. "Like a bomb hit it" must go!*

These comments from one of John's classmates will be very helpful as John attends to the next draft.

REVISING AND EDITING: ONE STUDENT WRITING

Back at the computer, John developed his next draft, shown following. The handwritten comments are his own.

INTERMEDIATE DRAFT

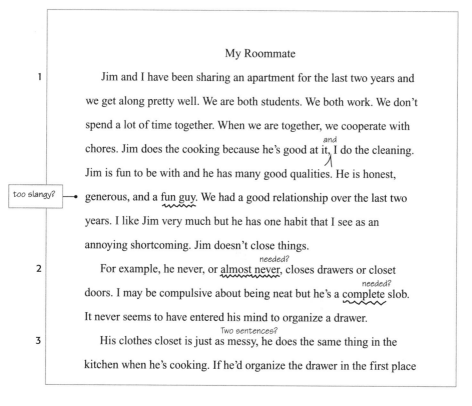

My Roommate

1   Jim and I have been sharing an apartment for the last two years and we get along pretty well. We are both students. We both work. We don't spend a lot of time together. When we are together, we cooperate with chores. Jim does the cooking because he's good at it, ~and~ I do the cleaning. Jim is fun to be with and he has many good qualities. He is honest,

too slangy? → generous, and a *fun guy*. We had a good relationship over the last two years. I like Jim very much but he has one habit that I see as an annoying shortcoming. Jim doesn't close things.

2   For example, he never, or *almost never*, closes drawers or closet [needed?] doors. I may be compulsive about being neat but he's a *complete slob*. [needed?] It never seems to have entered his mind to organize a drawer.

3   *Two sentences?* His clothes closet is just as messy, he does the same thing in the kitchen when he's cooking. If he'd organize the drawer in the first place

the noisy silverware wouldn't bother me. Spoons and knives clink together as he pokes through the nearest open drawer looking for things in the mess. Our apartment usually looks like a messy rummage sale.

Too general?

| Need more detail? |

I really get embarrassed when any of my friends visit and they see the place looking so messy.

4

| New sentence? |

I'm bothered even more by Jim's failure to close bathroom objects, for example, he never closes the shampoo cap. This makes me lose my ~~cool~~ composure more than anything. When I'm showering, I always grab the shampoo bottle by the cap. A̷ loose cap always results in shampoo on my toes and not in my hair, which at this point is soaking wet. Because I am economically minded, ~~moneywise~~ watching a green puddle of shampoo going down the drain wasted every day really upsets me. Jim forgets to close the bathroom door after using the facilities while I shower. The bathroom has grown warm and steamy during the cou͎r͏se

| Two sentences? |

of my shower, the cold morning air chills me. Jim's thoughtlessness is very annoying.

5

| Repeats too much. Revise conclusion? |

Jim is such a great guy, and I know his failure to close things is a minor bad ha̷bit, and I try to overlook it. However, it does tend to irritate me, especially when cold air hits me right after I'm out of the shower.

EXERCISE

1. How does the revised first paragraph compare and contrast with the first paragraph in the earlier draft on page 29? What improvements has John made? What further suggestions would you make for revision and editing?
2. Where else in the essay has John made significant changes from first draft to intermediate draft? What other recommendations would you make?

No doubt you noted the advances in John's paper. He tightened the introduction and sharpened the thesis sentence. (See Chapter 7, pages 63–64.) He eliminated some colloquial expressions. He provided some concrete language; "a green puddle of shampoo" is a good image.

Improvements aside, you probably saw as well several areas for John to explore in further revision and editing. John's paper would benefit significantly from even more sensory language (see page 36–37). In paragraph 1, better coordination and subordination would link related thoughts and eliminate the bumpy ride from sentence to sentence. In addition, some of John's sentences still ramble a bit and ideas are repeated, as in the last few sentences of the third paragraph. Note how many times John refers to messy conditions; the repetitive language needs revision and editing here. Some of the ideas throughout the essay should be reordered or more smoothly connected (or both), and some of the paragraphs should be joined. John's first and last paragraphs, vital elements in any paper, could be strengthened (see Chapter 6).

Although John made handwritten changes to correct some mistakes, his sentences contain many structural errors—particularly run-ons and fragments. In the revision process, some of these errors may disappear simply because new or reorganized sentences will replace some of those with mistakes. Nevertheless, a pattern of errors emerges here, and John must address them as he revises, edits, and proofreads in successive drafts. The "Strategy Checklist: Revising, Editing, and Proofreading Your Drafts" on pages 92–94 will help you consider revising and editing strategies as you develop your paper. The mini-book at the end of *Writing Papers in College: A Brief Guide* identifies characteristic grammar and usage problems and how to solve them.

Learning from Your Instructor's Comments

Your instructor may read an early draft of your writing and (or) your final copy. In either case, she no doubt will use a system of marking symbols (like those at the end of this book), as well as marginal comments and final summary remarks to suggest changes and corrections for you to consider. Pay careful attention to any comments you receive. When you revise your work again, think through your instructor's suggestions as you make the changes and corrections your instructor indicates. If you are responding to comments on a final draft, you should answer any questions and rewrite any segments you've been asked to.

Reproduced on page 90 are the last two paragraphs of John Fousek's intermediate draft, together with his teacher's marginal comments and symbols. Note especially his instructor's summary comments at the end of the paper.

LAST TWO PARAGRAPHS OF INTERMEDIATE DRAFT
WITH INSTRUCTOR'S COMMENTS

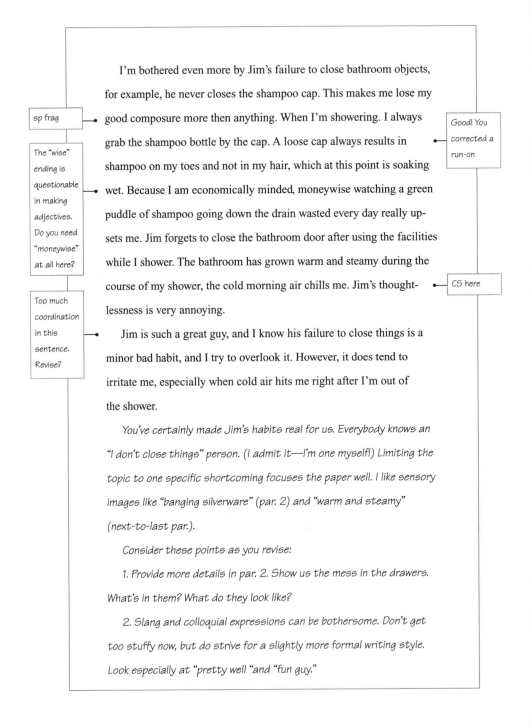

sp frag

The "wise" ending is questionable in making adjectives. Do you need "moneywise" at all here?

Too much coordination in this sentence. Revise?

Good! You corrected a run-on

CS here

I'm bothered even more by Jim's failure to close bathroom objects, for example, he never closes the shampoo cap. This makes me lose my good composure more then anything. When I'm showering. I always grab the shampoo bottle by the cap. A loose cap always results in shampoo on my toes and not in my hair, which at this point is soaking wet. Because I am economically minded, moneywise watching a green puddle of shampoo going down the drain wasted every day really upsets me. Jim forgets to close the bathroom door after using the facilities while I shower. The bathroom has grown warm and steamy during the course of my shower, the cold morning air chills me. Jim's thoughtlessness is very annoying.

Jim is such a great guy, and I know his failure to close things is a minor bad habit, and I try to overlook it. However, it does tend to irritate me, especially when cold air hits me right after I'm out of the shower.

You've certainly made Jim's habits real for us. Everybody knows an "I don't close things" person. (I admit it—I'm one myself!) Limiting the topic to one specific shortcoming focuses the paper well. I like sensory images like "banging silverware" (par. 2) and "warm and steamy" (next-to-last par.).

Consider these points as you revise:

1. Provide more details in par. 2. Show us the mess in the drawers. What's in them? What do they look like?

2. Slang and colloquial expressions can be bothersome. Don't get too stuffy now, but do strive for a slightly more formal writing style. Look especially at "pretty well "and "fun guy."

3. *Smooth out transitions and logic as I've indicated in the margin.*

4. *Proofread carefully for those run-ons, comma splices, and*

fragments—these can be major problems on a final draft. See relevant

sections in the minibook (at the end of Writing Papers in College*) for*

review and practice.

5. *The conclusion lacks impact. Can you interpret the significance*

of your experience with Jim? Go beyond the immediate experiences you

share with the readers here.

Good try for an intermediate draft, John. Revise! Revise! Revise!

EXERCISE

Read the excerpt from John Fousek's paper on page 90 and make the grammatical and spelling changes that respond to the marginal comments written by John's teacher.

PROOFREADING

Proofreading is the part of the editing process in which you reread your paper particularly for errors. This step in the writing process is best accomplished at two stages.

First, proofread your draft after you make revisions and edit before you produce the final copy for submission. At this point, check for problems in grammar, syntax, spelling, and usage. Proofread the paper a second time just before you turn it in to catch mistakes you may have overlooked. At this stage, you can make minor revisions neatly on the final copy. However, if you discover major problems that require extensive reworking, you should produce another copy. Do not submit for evaluation a paper containing numerous changes and corrections.

You'll find the following pointers useful as you proofread.

TIPS FOR CAREFUL PROOFREADING

- **When you proofread, read slowly.** Your purpose is to check for errors, and quick readings make errors hard to find.
- **Proofread after you have made revisions and editing changes.** Do not try to revise and proofread at the same time. If you attend to errors when you revise, you won't be focusing on issues related to the content and clarity of your paper. Thus, treat proofreading as a separate activity, after you're satisfied with your writing and revising.
- **Be familiar with the types of errors that you tend to make and keep them in mind as you proofread.** If you tend to write run-on sentences or fragments, proofread your paper for those mistakes especially. Keep a record of your own errors and consult it before proofreading.
- **If you must make minor revisions on a final copy, use blue or black ink, not pencil.** Cross out errors neatly with one line and insert changes directly above the mistake or in the margin, if you need more room. Remember, extensive changes on a draft mean that you must do another draft before submitting it. Use a caret (^) for insertions.

$$\text{She admonished} \overset{her}{\underset{\wedge}{}} \text{brother for being late.}$$

PUTTING IT ALL TOGETHER

In Part One, you've examined many key features in developing a paper for your writing course and have done numerous exercises designed to help you produce and revise a draft. Since your revised copy will be the draft you submit for evaluation, take time to review the following checklist as you rework your drafts. The tips are stated as general questions to ask yourself as you revise, edit, and proofread.

We've devised similar checklists, more specific for the focused writing task at hand, for each chapter in Part Two, "Methods of Development."

STRATEGY CHECKLIST: Revising, Editing, and Proofreading Your Drafts

Revise for thought and content.

- ❑ Does my thesis state the topic clearly and give my opinion about the topic?
- ❑ Is my thesis sufficiently limited?
- ❑ Have I provided sufficient details to support my assertions?
- ❑ Have I used precise and appropriate language?

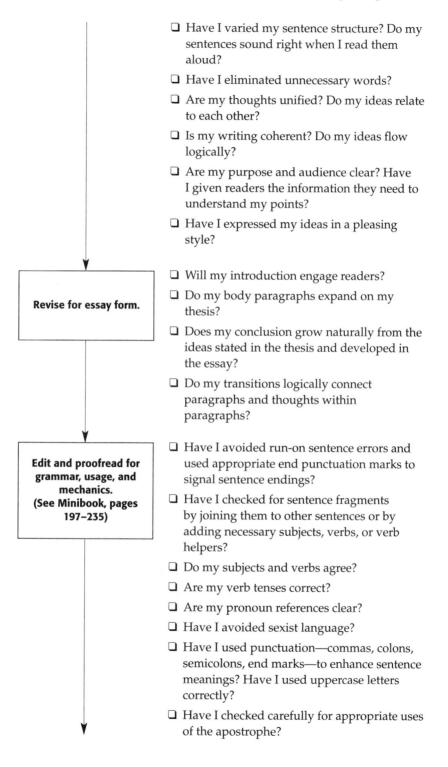

❏ Have I varied my sentence structure? Do my sentences sound right when I read them aloud?

❏ Have I eliminated unnecessary words?

❏ Are my thoughts unified? Do my ideas relate to each other?

❏ Is my writing coherent? Do my ideas flow logically?

❏ Are my purpose and audience clear? Have I given readers the information they need to understand my points?

❏ Have I expressed my ideas in a pleasing style?

Revise for essay form.

❏ Will my introduction engage readers?

❏ Do my body paragraphs expand on my thesis?

❏ Does my conclusion grow naturally from the ideas stated in the thesis and developed in the essay?

❏ Do my transitions logically connect paragraphs and thoughts within paragraphs?

**Edit and proofread for grammar, usage, and mechanics.
(See Minibook, pages 197–235)**

❏ Have I avoided run-on sentence errors and used appropriate end punctuation marks to signal sentence endings?

❏ Have I checked for sentence fragments by joining them to other sentences or by adding necessary subjects, verbs, or verb helpers?

❏ Do my subjects and verbs agree?

❏ Are my verb tenses correct?

❏ Are my pronoun references clear?

❏ Have I avoided sexist language?

❏ Have I used punctuation—commas, colons, semicolons, end marks—to enhance sentence meanings? Have I used uppercase letters correctly?

❏ Have I checked carefully for appropriate uses of the apostrophe?

❑ Have I used quotation marks correctly and consistently to indicate someone else's words?

❑ Have I checked the spelling of difficult words in a dictionary? If I used a computer spell check, did I look especially for homonyms and misused (but correctly spelled) words that the computer may have missed?

❑ Did I check appropriate sections in this book for more detailed explanations of grammar, usage, and mechanics problems in my writing?

FINAL DRAFT: ONE STUDENT WRITING

After reading his paper over several times, discussing it with friends and his writing teacher, making revisions, and producing new drafts, John finally submitted the following paper to his instructor.

FINAL DRAFT

My Roommate, Jim

1   My roommate, Jim, and I have shared a small apartment for the past two years. On the whole, we get along very well. We are both students, and we both work, so we don't spend much time together; but when we do, we cooperate. Jim, who is good at it, does most of the cooking; I do most of the cleaning. We find the arrangement satisfactory. And I like Jim. He is generous, witty, honest. Our two-year association has, for the most part, been a good one. But Jim has one shortcoming that irritates me: He doesn't close things.

2   Jim, for example, almost never closes a drawer or a closet door, and his failure to do so is often a source of embarrassment to me. The problem is that I am compulsively neat, and Jim, I'm sorry to say, is a slob. It seems never to have occurred to him that the contents of a drawer

could be organized. When he does his laundry, he just empties his bag of clean clothes into a drawer—white socks, underwear, a rainbow of T-shirts with college crests, pajamas, graying handkerchiefs. When the drawer is full, he begins filling the next one. Then when he needs clean socks or a shirt, he rolls the contents of the drawer around until he finds what he wants, often leaving rejected items hanging over the edge of the drawer. His clothes closet is just as messy as the drawers.

He does the same kinds of things in the kitchen. Spatulas, flatware, eggbeaters, knives clink together as he pokes through the nearest open drawer to find his favorite tool for beating eggs or mincing onions. If he'd organized the drawer in the first place, the rattle of kitchenware wouldn't disturb my study time before every meal. Since Jim doesn't close drawers or closets, our apartment usually looks like the site of a rummage sale at closing time. The appearance offends my neat soul and embarrasses me when friends visit us.

3   The irritation I experience because of open drawers and closets, however, is nothing compared with the irritation that Jim's failure to close things in the bathroom produces. Jim's failure to tighten the cap on the shampoo bottle, for example, causes me to completely lose my composure when I am showering. Because I am in the habit of grasping the shampoo bottle by its cap, a loose cap results in the annoyance of shampoo on my toes instead of in my hair. And because I am a frugal sort, I hate seeing a green puddle of unused shampoo oozing down the drain each day. Jim also often fails to close the bathroom door after using the facilities while I shower. Since the bathroom has become warm and steamy during the course of my shower, the cold draft of morning air chills and distresses me, and the idea that he has been so thoughtless bothers me.

4   When that frigid air blasts my wet body, my irritation with Jim reaches its peak. Nevertheless, because he is such a great guy and because I know his failure to close things is, in the scheme of human problems, just a minor bad habit, I try to overlook it. I shut my mouth and take a deep breath. In fact, by learning to deal with this annoyance I think I've learned a little about how to handle the frustrations of some of my friends' strange habits in general. I keep a good sense of humor and I hold my temper. After all, I'd rather have opened closets and drawers than a door closed on friendship.

EXERCISE

How does John's intermediate draft compare and contrast with the first draft? What advice did he take from the peer critique? What other changes did he make?

EXERCISE

How does John's final draft compare and contrast with his intermediate draft? What additions has he made? How has he improved the level of detail in the intermediate draft? How has he improved the structure of his paragraphs? Where has he eliminated unnecessary words and sentences? How has he corrected grammatical errors?

12

Description

When most students receive an assignment like "Write a **description** of a person, place, or thing" (a car, a wedding, a painting, or a temper tantrum), their first impulse is often to describe what the person, place, or thing looks like. Although many excellent descriptions do just that, in deciding on your subject and how to treat it, you don't need to limit your choices so severely. Most good descriptive writing appeals to the reader's senses, and sight is only one of our five senses. For example, an essay titled "Good Old Franks and Beans" would describe taste; "Nighttime Noises" would describe sound; "Real Men Don't Use Cologne" would describe smell; and "Kids Need Cuddling (and So Do I)" would stress how good it feels to be cuddled—the sense of touch. A piece of descriptive writing generally will explore more than one of the senses: The glories of franks and beans could involve sight and smell as well as taste, for example. Strong specific writing (see pages 36–37) is filled with life, and sensory appeal is likely to be built right in.

WRITING YOUR DESCRIPTIVE PAPER

The following guidelines for descriptive writing should be helpful.

TIPS FOR WRITING A DESCRIPTIVE ESSAY

- **Don't take inventory. You must have a thesis.** Periodically, shopkeepers need to take inventory. The procedure is vital to business survival, but if you try to include every piece of information you have on your subject in a descriptive essay, you are inviting disaster.

  The writer who takes inventory may begin this way:

  > My friend Judy is twenty years old. She is a solid C student. She has black hair, has brown eyes, and weighs 115 pounds. Her family is comfortably middle class. Judy is very nearsighted but is vain about her appearance and often does not wear her glasses. She's been my friend for many years, and I like her.

  (Continued on next page)

This paragraph is simply a random collection of stray descriptive facts. No logic, no principle, seems to be at work here except the desire to get everything in—to take inventory. If the writer is only taking inventory, all facts are of equal importance, which means, in effect, that no facts are of any importance.

A descriptive essay needs a thesis. Notice how a thesis and a few additional phrases can transform the mess about Judy into a coherent start for a potentially effective paper.

> There is nothing at all special about my friend Judy. Judy is such a completely ordinary twenty-year-old woman that I often wonder how our friendship has lasted so long and stayed so warm.
>
> Just for starters, consider these totally ordinary facts about her. Physically, she has absolutely undistinguished black hair and brown eyes, stands an average 5 feet 4 inches, and weighs an average 115 pounds. Scholastically, she is a solid C student. By solid I *mean* solid. In two years at college, I can't recall her once getting a daring C– or an exciting C+. Her family—you guessed it—is comfortably middle class, not too rich and not too poor. Even in her little flaws, Judy is just what you'd expect. Like so many people of her age, she tends to be vain about personal appearance and all too frequently tries to get by without her glasses, even though she's very nearsighted.

The important thing to remember here, then, is don't describe simply to describe. Description always serves the broader purpose identified in your thesis.

- **Use lively, specific details.** The most effective way of communicating an immediate sense of your subject is to use specific details rooted in sensory language—color, action, sound, smell, touch, taste. Don't tell your reader that a room is old and neglected: Indicate the squeaky floorboard next to the door, the lint collected in the coils of the radiator, the window propped up with a sooty stick of wood. If you do the job with details, the sense of age and neglect will come through. The more precise the detail, the greater its potential for arousing the attention of your reader.

- **Choose a principle of organization that presents the descriptive details in a logical sequence.** The organizing principle you select should help create a coherent paper. In describing a snowstorm, for instance, you might organize by **time,** presenting the storm from the first hesitant flakes through the massive downfall to the Christmas-card quietness at the end of the storm. In describing a landscape, you might organize by **space,** beginning with the objects farthest from the observer and working your way closer. A physical description of a person could go from top to bottom or bottom to top.

Fortunately, not all principles of organization have to be this rigid. You could build a landscape description by progressing from the most ordinary details to the least ordinary details. If the top-to-bottom approach to a description of a person strikes you as dull or inappropriate, you might organize the paper by unattractive features and attractive features or first impressions and second impressions. The important consideration is that you provide some clear principle to give structure to the paper.

STRATEGY CHECKLIST: Writing and Revising Your Descriptive Paper

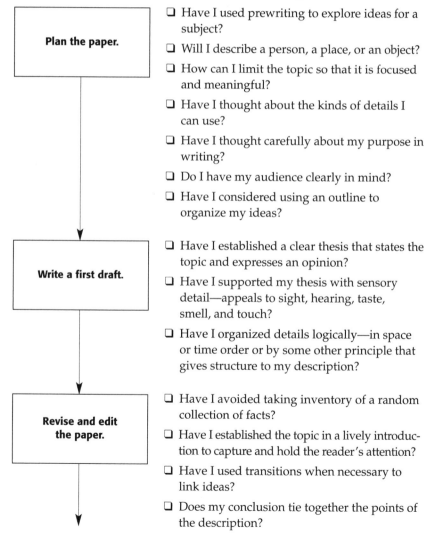

Plan the paper.

❑ Have I used prewriting to explore ideas for a subject?

❑ Will I describe a person, a place, or an object?

❑ How can I limit the topic so that it is focused and meaningful?

❑ Have I thought about the kinds of details I can use?

❑ Have I thought carefully about my purpose in writing?

❑ Do I have my audience clearly in mind?

❑ Have I considered using an outline to organize my ideas?

Write a first draft.

❑ Have I established a clear thesis that states the topic and expresses an opinion?

❑ Have I supported my thesis with sensory detail—appeals to sight, hearing, taste, smell, and touch?

❑ Have I organized details logically—in space or time order or by some other principle that gives structure to my description?

Revise and edit the paper.

❑ Have I avoided taking inventory of a random collection of facts?

❑ Have I established the topic in a lively introduction to capture and hold the reader's attention?

❑ Have I used transitions when necessary to link ideas?

❑ Does my conclusion tie together the points of the description?

Proofread the paper.

❏ Have I proofread for grammar, spelling, and mechanics?

Writing Topics

If you cannot easily decide on a topic for your description paper, you might want to try one or more of these suggestions.

1. An office party
2. A religious leader
3. A loyal pet
4. A street corner
5. An afternoon schoolyard
6. People waiting in a line
7. Sloppy eaters
8. Doctor's waiting room
9. Restaurant waiters
10. Bad drivers
11. A school cafeteria
12. An amusement park
13. A hospital room
14. The contents of a wallet or pocketbook
15. Summer nights
16. A natural disaster
17. A morning at the beach
18. My best friend
19. The biology lab
20. A favorite food

13

Narration

"Last night, as I was driving home from work, I stopped for the light at Fifty-fifth and Main. I was just sitting there minding my own business when, all of a sudden...."

"You'll never guess what the kids did today."

"That reminds me of the time...."

Think of how often during a conversation you say something like "That reminds me of the time..." and then tell a story.

We all tell stories, and for many reasons. Usually we tell stories just to share our daily experience with others. Frequently, however, we tell stories to make a point. Sometimes the point is simply, "Yes, I've had an experience like that, too. I know how you feel." That kind of story helps establish a bond between people. At other times, we tell stories that illustrate ideas. A pastor, for example, does not merely say that repentance will bring forgiveness; he reads the story of the prodigal son from the Bible. Or we tell stories to make people laugh: "Once there was a person named Mike who had a friend named Pat, and...." Whatever the case, we enjoy telling and hearing stories, and you have been telling and hearing them all your life. So the assignment to write a narrative paper should be one you will enjoy.

A **narrative** is a story. To *narrate* means "to tell, to give an account of." Narratives take many forms. A novel is a narrative. So is a short story. A biography is a narrative because it tells the story of a person's life. Historical narrative traces events over time. Often a narrative is a brief story included in a longer work to illustrate an idea. (An argument calling for the enforcement of safety standards in steel mills, for example, might include a story about a worker who lost two fingers because a hot steel bar fell on her.) A **narrative paper** tells a story, usually of a personal experience, that makes a point or supports a thesis. The purpose of a narrative paper is to recreate an experience in such a way that your readers can imaginatively participate in it and share it with you.

WRITING YOUR NARRATIVE PAPER

As you plan and write your paper, keep the following principles in mind.

TIPS FOR WRITING A NARRATIVE ESSAY

- **Limit the subject.** Almost any experience you have had can serve as subject matter for a narrative paper. But you must limit the subject, and, in a narrative paper, time usually determines the limits of your subject. Your goal is to tell a story so dramatically and so completely that your readers can share the experience. A subject such as your summer as a camp counselor, therefore, is too broad—unless you want to write a book. But you could tell about the time a skunk got into your RV. Even one day in the city provides too much material for a complete and dramatic story. But some part of that day—the hour you spent watching a pair of cardinals in the park teach their baby how to fly—can make a good story. It's probably no exaggeration to say that the subject cannot be too limited.

- **Have a thesis.** The experience you narrate is not as important as its significance to you. Why did the experience matter to you? Why do you want to tell about it? Did it change you in some way? Did it embarrass you? Did it make you happy? Sad? Was it thrilling? Frustrating? Did it lead to a decision? Did you learn something about yourself or about others or about the world around you? Were you disappointed? Any little event in your life—even taking out the garbage—can make good subject matter for a narrative paper if you determine the significance of the experience and tell the story well.

    The thesis is important because it controls the content of the paper. It helps you decide what to put in the paper and what to leave out. We tolerate rambling spoken narratives, when we must, out of consideration for a speaker's feelings. Even so, we wish the person would get to the point. But we won't tolerate written narratives that ramble because we don't have to. We can always put the book or paper down. So have a thesis; it helps keep the narrative under control.

- **Use specific details.** Remember, a narrative recreates an experience for your readers. In most cases, you can make your readers feel what you felt if you use specific details. What you learned in the last chapter about descriptive writing will help you considerably here and elsewhere when you need to marshal concrete sensory language.

    A word of caution, however. The details you use, like everything else in your paper, should support your thesis. Extraneous details, no matter how vivid, always feel like padding and frustrate readers.

- **Use language that sounds natural.** Your readers should feel that an intelligent, articulate friend is telling them a story. The language of a narrative, therefore, should sound conversational, which means you should avoid two extremes—the pompous and the inarticulate.

    As, for the first time, I entered the portals of the edifice that housed my new employer and donned the attire specified for my position, I felt apprehensive.

> Like, man, that first day, ya know, was like...well, when I put that waiter's jacket on, ya know, I was scared.

Try, instead, something like this:

> I was nervous that first day on the job. When I put on my white waiter's jacket, my hands trembled.

These sentences sound natural, and they give a conversational tone to the narrative.

Another way to give a natural sound to your narrative is to use direct quotations when appropriate (see "Quotation Marks," pages 221–223).

> "Are you having a good time?" she asked.

> "Not really," I replied, "but I don't want to spoil the party for you and the kids."

Direct quotations are also good for revealing the personality and feelings of the characters in your narrative:

> "Get lost," he growled.

> "I'm not your doormat!" she screamed.

Direct quotations, then, are useful in developing a narrative. Don't feel, however, that you must fill your paper with them.

- **Give order to the narrative.** Like the descriptive paper discussed in Chapter 12, most papers contain, first, an introduction, which includes the thesis statement; next, a body, which supports the thesis and is organized according to the principle of time, space, or logic; and, finally, a conclusion, which restates the thesis and gives a sense of finality to the paper. A narrative paper also should contain these three parts, but the development of each part is somewhat different from that of other papers.

- **Introduce your narrative.** The introduction does not necessarily include a thesis statement. Instead, it may set the scene for the narrative:

> It was in Burma, a sodden morning of the rains. A sickly light, like yellow tinfoil, was slanting over the high walls into the jail yard. We were waiting outside the condemned cells, a row of sheds fronted with double bars, like small animal cages. Each cell measured about ten feet by ten and was quite bare within except for a plank bed and a pot of drinking water. In some of them brown silent men were squatting at the inner bars, with their blankets draped round them. These were the condemned men, due to be hanged within the next week or two.
>
> —George Orwell, "A Hanging"

Sometimes the introduction gives the background—the facts that led to the experience being narrated:

> In 1969, I was a senior on the Luther Burbank High School basketball team. The school is on the south side of San Antonio, in one of the city's many barrios. After practice one day our coach announced that we were going to spend the following Saturday scrimmaging with the ball club from Winston Churchill High, located in the city's rich, white north side.
>
> —Rogelio R. Gomez, "Foul Shots"

(Continued on next page)

Indeed, sometimes a narrative paper doesn't even have an introduction. In this case, the writer simply begins with the first event of the story:

> "There's a gun at your back. Raise your hands and don't make a sound," a harsh voice snarled at me. I raised my hands.

- **Sequence your body paragraphs.** Written narrative depends on chronological organization. It is possible to begin with the present and then portray an earlier episode:

> As I sit in my soft leather easy chair that I keep in front of the fireplace this time of year and gaze at brightly burning pine logs, I remember a Christmas ten years ago when I was not so comfortable.

But the heart of the narrative—what happened ten years ago—should proceed chronologically. You must present the events in the order that they occurred: First this, then that, and later something else. And you should let your readers know, by means of transitions, what the chronology is. Transitions are, of course, important to any piece of writing, but the kinds of transitions that indicate the passage of time are essential to a narrative paper:

> then, next, soon, later
> at four o'clock, a few minutes later, on the way back, the next morning
> After I removed the bullets…
> I must have been asleep a couple of hours when a shout awakened me.

- **Conclude your narrative.** Finally, the narrative's conclusion as well is different from other conclusions. In some narratives, the thesis of the paper appears for the first time in the conclusion. The writer tells a good story in the introduction and body and then states the significance of the story at the end of the paper:

> At last I admitted to myself that the raccoons had won. I was tired of getting up in the middle of the night to gather the garbage they scattered about the backyard. I was tired of trying to find a garbage can that they could not open. I was, in fact, tired of the country. As I crept wearily back to my bedroom, I knew *the raccoons had taught me a valuable lesson: I did not belong in the country; I belonged in a high-rise apartment in the heart of the city.* And that's just where I moved two weeks later.

At other times, when the main point of the narrative is sufficiently clear within the piece, the conclusion may imply the thesis without restating it, or it may take up other ideas stated or hinted at in the narrative.

In any event, the conclusion for a narrative paper should do what all good conclusions do: give the paper a sense of completeness.

STRATEGY CHECKLIST: Writing and Revising Your Narrative Paper

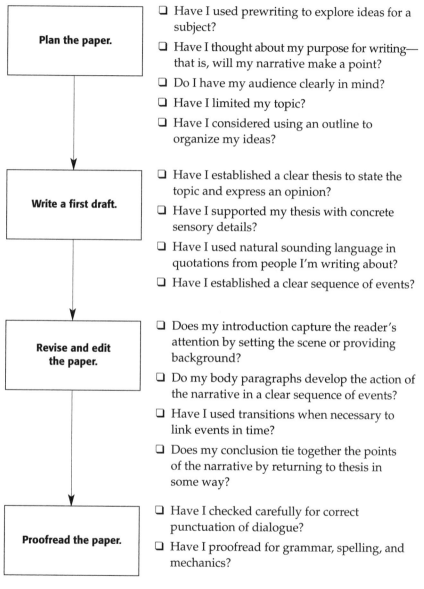

Plan the paper.

- ❏ Have I used prewriting to explore ideas for a subject?
- ❏ Have I thought about my purpose for writing—that is, will my narrative make a point?
- ❏ Do I have my audience clearly in mind?
- ❏ Have I limited my topic?
- ❏ Have I considered using an outline to organize my ideas?

Write a first draft.

- ❏ Have I established a clear thesis to state the topic and express an opinion?
- ❏ Have I supported my thesis with concrete sensory details?
- ❏ Have I used natural sounding language in quotations from people I'm writing about?
- ❏ Have I established a clear sequence of events?

Revise and edit the paper.

- ❏ Does my introduction capture the reader's attention by setting the scene or providing background?
- ❏ Do my body paragraphs develop the action of the narrative in a clear sequence of events?
- ❏ Have I used transitions when necessary to link events in time?
- ❏ Does my conclusion tie together the points of the narrative by returning to thesis in some way?

Proofread the paper.

- ❏ Have I checked carefully for correct punctuation of dialogue?
- ❏ Have I proofread for grammar, spelling, and mechanics?

Writing Topics

If you are having trouble deciding on a topic for your narrative paper, you might find it helpful simply to choose one of the following proverbs, quotations, or commonsense statements and then write a narration supporting or attacking it.

1. Money can't buy happiness.
2. Money is the root of all evil.
3. I never met a man I didn't like.
4. If you can't take the heat, get out of the kitchen.
5. When the going gets tough, the tough get going.
6. You can't tell a book by its cover.
7. If at first you don't succeed, try, try again.
8. There's no such thing as a bad boy.
9. Nobody knows the trouble I've seen.
10. A penny saved is a penny earned.
11. Small children, small problems; big children, big problems.
12. Spare the rod and spoil the child.
13. Hell hath no fury like a woman scorned.
14. Good fences make good neighbors.
15. A stitch in time saves nine.

14

Example

An **example**—or **illustration**—represents, or sometimes shows, the primary nature of the larger group to which it belongs: A rattlesnake is an example of a reptile; kidnapping is an example of crime; a Cadillac is an example of General Motors products. An **example paper** relies almost solely on examples to support the thesis, and learning to manage this kind of paper well will help prepare you for all the varieties of papers you will have to write.

Nearly all good writing depends heavily on examples or illustrations as an important means of supporting ideas—and for sound reasons. Examples give concreteness and, therefore, clarity to ideas. A writer may say, for instance, that going to school can be frustrating, and, as a student, you nod your head in agreement. But how can you be sure that you and the writer have the same understanding of frustration? When the writer goes on to tell stories about the causes of her frustration—when she writes about her inability to stand on her head in her physical education class, or her ineptness at dissecting a cat in her anatomy class, or her habitual failure to recharge the batteries of her calculator before going to her math class—you understand what the writer means by frustration. The examples give to the abstract idea *frustration* not only clarity but also concreteness, and the concreteness does much to make the idea interesting.

Because concreteness and clarity are essential to good writing, example often shapes even the smallest sentence sequence:

> To convince a reader, good writers usually offer support for their generalizations. In the Declaration of Independence, for example, Thomas Jefferson cited twenty-eight violations of basic human rights to support his assertion that George III was a tyrant.

Similarly, examples can develop an entire paragraph:

> History and legend tell us that some of the greatest scientific discoveries are the result of inspirations caused by chance occurrences. Three brief examples can demonstrate this point. First, Archimedes' noticing the rise of the water level as he submerged himself in a tub led to the formulation of the laws of liquid displacement, the foundation of many of the laws of modern physics. Second, Sir Isaac Newton discovered the law of gravity because an apple fell on his head while he was sitting under a tree. Third, after being caught in a strong current of hot rising air while flying his gas balloon, George Alexander Whitehead thought about the occurrence and developed the fundamental principles of meteorology. These and other incidents show that many of the greatest scientific developments spring from lucky accidents that stimulate work in a specific direction.

WRITING YOUR EXAMPLE PAPER

Writers can shape sentences and paragraphs by means of example, but our concern in this chapter is to look at an entire paper developed by example. In such a paper, the writer offers well-developed examples to support a thesis. The success of the paper will depend largely on the quality of these illustrations and on their arrangement. We have some suggestions.

TIPS FOR WRITING AN EXAMPLE ESSAY

- **Be specific.** Remember, the purpose of an example is to give concreteness and clarity to an idea, and you won't get either with vague language (see pages 68–70). Notice the concrete language and the specific details in the following passage:

  > I spent a good part of my life close to nature as a migratory worker, lumberjack, and placer miner. Mother Nature was breathing down my neck, so to speak, and I had the feeling that she did not want me around. I was bitten by every sort of insect, and scratched by burrs, foxtails and thorns. My clothes were torn by buck-brush and tangled manzanita. Hard clods pushed against my ribs when I lay down to rest, and grime ate its way into every pore of my body. Everything around me was telling me all the time to roll up and be gone. I was an unwanted intruder. I could never be at home in nature the way trees, flowers and birds are at home…in the city. I did not feel at ease until my feet touched the paved road.
  >
  > —Eric Hoffer, "Cities and Nature"

  Obviously, good examples use specific details expressed in concrete language.

- **Make certain that your examples are examples, and that your generalization, or thesis, is one that examples can support.** If Maria is the only woman in your school who has dyed her hair green, you cannot generalize that green hair is a fad in your school and then cite the one case as an example, no matter how vividly you describe Maria's new hair color. You can, however, use Maria's green hair as an example of her eccentricity if she really is eccentric—if she exhibits several other odd characteristics. An example is one of many, and a generalization is that which is usually or frequently or generally true of its subject.

- **Play fair.** Try to select examples that represent an honest cross-section of your subject. If you want to show, for instance, that most of the teachers in a particular school are boring lecturers, try to find examples of some who are young, some who are middle-aged, and some who are nearing retirement. Again, some of your examples should be women and some men, some perhaps single and some married. Your examples should also indicate a fair distribution among departments. You don't want your examples to suggest that all boring lecturers are middle-aged, married men who wear glasses and teach English. Rather, you want to show that boring teachers pop up everywhere and too often in this particular school, reflecting many backgrounds and subject areas—and even ways of being boring.

Of course, you don't always have to use several examples to make your point. Often, a good way to develop a thesis is to use one **extended example.** Even so, you should select the example according to the same rules of fairness that apply to the selection of numerous examples. It must truly represent an honest cross-section of the subject.

The following passage from Sasha Abramsky's essay "When They Get Out" for *The Atlantic* does just that. In it, the writer illustrates the painful effects of incarceration on the lives of exprisoners.

> The most extraordinary of the people I met was a thirty-nine-year-old named Edmond Taylor, who had served a total of eighteen years in a variety of New York's toughest prisons for crimes ranging from drug dealing to violent assault. Out of prison for the past couple of years, Taylor has dedicated himself to change; he works full time as a counselor, helping other prisoners to adjust to life on the outside....
>
> A highly articulate man, more capable than most of understanding what led him into violence and helped to destroy half his life, Taylor explained that he had spent nearly four years in "the box"—some of that time in Clinton Dannemora prison, near the Canadian border, for being what he described as "a vocal critic" of conditions within the prison. Describing his reaction to being released from isolation back into the general prison population, he said, "First there's fear, then there's anger, and the anger takes over. It's violent anger. Very quick. No thought of the magnitude of the consequence of the violence. An individual bumped me, rushing to get to the gym. And I rushed up behind him and hit him with a pipe. He went into a coma." Taylor went straight back into the box. I asked how long it had taken him to recover from isolation. He looked surprised by the question, and said, "Honestly, I've still not recovered. I've been out of isolation five and a half years. Ms. Page is my boss. If she was to confront me when I had a lot on my mind, anger would come up before rational thought. Anger. Strike back. Now it's not so much physical as verbal. In another situation it would cause me to lose my job." Then Taylor told me a shameful secret. Shortly after he got out of prison, he was living with his brother. His brother criticized him for some of the attitudes he'd brought out of prison with him. "I felt fed up, and I attacked him." Taylor said. "I grabbed him, choked him, lifted him off his feet, threw him to the ground. I pummeled him causing him to get several stitches above the eye. I grabbed a kitchen knife—I don't remember any of this; he told me afterward—and put it to his neck and said. 'I should kill you. I hate you.' The realization that I put my hands on my baby brother—the only person at that time who'd ever been in my corner..."
>
> —Sasha Abramsky, "When They Get Out"

(Continued on next page)

On reading this passage, we accept Abramsky's generalization not only because he tells the story of Edmond Taylor so vividly but also because it illustrates the uncontrollable anger of prisoners kept in isolation and then released into the general prison population. The writer uses one extended example to make his point: He focuses on the violent reactions of a single prisoner and his efforts to keep his own anger in check as he attempts to help others.

One extended example, then, can serve to support a thesis if the example is fully and convincingly developed. More often than not, however, you can build a stronger argument with several short examples. In this case, you need to give order to your examples, and this brings us to our last tip on writing an example paper.

• **Think about the arrangement of your examples.** Sometimes the best arrangement is chronological. The examples in the paragraph on page 107 about scientific discoveries, for instance, are presented in chronological order—from the ancient to the modern world. At other times, a spatial order works best. In supporting a thesis about the restaurants in your town, you might offer examples from several sections of the town, and those examples could be arranged geographically from north to south, east to west.

Or consider this: Many writers like to save their best example for last in order to achieve a dramatic conclusion. Others like to use their best example first to awaken interest. Certainly, the first and last are likely to get the most attention from a reader. Since some examples are more dramatic and convincing than others, you would do well to bury the weaker ones in the middle of the paper. Of course, if all your examples are equally excellent, you have nothing to worry about.

STRATEGY CHECKLIST: Writing and Revising Your Example Paper

Plan the paper.

❑ Have I used prewriting to explore ideas for a subject?

❑ Have I limited my topic so that my examples will support it effectively?

❑ Have I concentrated on using specific examples to support my thesis?

❑ Have I thought carefully about my purpose in writing?

❑ Do I have my audience clearly in mind?

❑ Have I considered using an outline to organize my ideas?

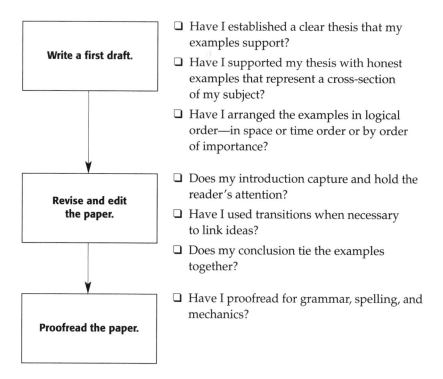

Write a first draft.	❑ Have I established a clear thesis that my examples support? ❑ Have I supported my thesis with honest examples that represent a cross-section of my subject? ❑ Have I arranged the examples in logical order—in space or time order or by order of importance?
Revise and edit the paper.	❑ Does my introduction capture and hold the reader's attention? ❑ Have I used transitions when necessary to link ideas? ❑ Does my conclusion tie the examples together?
Proofread the paper.	❑ Have I proofread for grammar, spelling, and mechanics?

Writing Topics

If you are having difficulty deciding on a topic for your example paper, you might find some help among our suggestions. Use examples to support or attack one of the following statements.

1. Watching the news does not guarantee that you get the whole story.
2. Students on college campuses are turning more and more conservative in their politics.
3. Some television commercials are more entertaining than most of the scheduled programs.
4. The senior year in high school is more fun than hard work.
5. Many dangers await the desert hiker.
6. Teenagers do not know how to manage money.
7. Student government teaches important values.
8. Religion leaves many serious problems unsolved.
9. The United States has become the world's police force.
10. Computer dating is more popular now than ever.
11. Hazing rituals are unfortunate features of high school sports.
12. The chores on a farm are endless!
13. Not all problems can be solved— we just have to live with them.
14. Some modern conveniences have turned out to be very inconvenient.
15. Affirmative action has (has not) benefited America.

15

Process

The **process** paper indicates a series of actions, changes, or functions that bring about an end or a result. The most familiar kind of process paper is the "how-to" paper, a step-by-step set of instructions on how to do or make something—how to change a tire, how to bake a cake, how to do aerobic exercise, how to assemble a bicycle. Some process papers explain how something is done, not necessarily a procedure the reader or even the writer can perform—how viruses attack cells, how a cellular phone works, how companies design video games, for example.

WRITING YOUR PROCESS PAPER

Follow these guidelines for writing process papers:

TIPS FOR WRITING A PROCESS ESSAY

- Choose carefully the kind of process you will write about—showing how to carry out a process or explaining a process that you don't expect a reader to carry out. If you're an expert at some task like baking a rhubarb pie or setting up a tank for saltwater tropical fish or making the best coffee your side of the Mississippi, you can draw on your personal experiences to explain the process. But don't be fooled into a complacent attitude about it: Because you're an expert doesn't mean that your reader will easily understand the materials you need, the language of the activity, or even the appropriate sequence of events. In most cases you have to state the obvious. The point here is that if you're writing for an audience who may not know how to carry out the process you're explaining and is looking to you for careful guidance, you have to make sure that you omit no important steps.

  On the other hand, you might choose to explain a process that you don't expect someone to carry out, and that explanation requires additional strategies. If you know from experience how to take apart a clock, for example, and want to explain how it's done without expecting someone to perform the intricate task, you'll need to follow the suggestions in the previous paragraph, of course. Leave nothing out. Assume that your readers have little knowledge of the task at hand. But you may be interested in a process whose steps you yourself do not know—how plants carry out photosynthesis, how double-entry bookkeeping works, what steps we can take to reduce greenhouse gases, for instance. In these cases, you'll need to do research in the library or on the Web so that you understand the process fully enough to explain it to someone else. And here, too, you must make a thorough go of it so readers don't come away puzzled about any steps.

- **Make certain that the explanation is complete and accurate.** If, for example, you want to describe the process for baking a cake, you would mislead your reader if you omitted the instruction to grease and flour the pan. It's surprisingly easy to leave out important steps. You will be writing about a process you know extremely well, and you probably perform some steps—such as greasing a pan—without consciously thinking about them.

- **Maintain strict chronological order.** Tell your reader what to do first, what to do second, and so on. Once the cake is in the oven, it is too late to remind the baker to stir walnuts into the batter.

- **If a particular kind of performance is called for in any part of the process, indicate its nature.** Should the batter be stirred vigorously or gently? Should an applicant for a job approach the interviewer humbly, aggressively, nonchalantly? Besides indicating the nature of the action, you should also tell the reader why such action is called for. Readers are more likely to follow instructions if they understand the reasons for them.

- **Group the steps in the process.** A process may include many steps, but you usually can group them in their chronological order, under logical headings.

  Suppose you want to explain how to make a favorite dish—stir-fried shrimp, for example. You could develop paragraphs around two headings as part of a rough outline as shown following. Because they often require such precise steps in strict order, process papers lend themselves to outlining. You should develop an outline (see Chapter 5) as a check on the accuracy of your presentation.

  A. Assembling ingredients
    1. Raw shrimp
    2. Oil
    3. Red and green peppers
    4. Almonds
    5. Hot chiles
    6. Orange rind
    7. Orange juice
    8. Cornstarch
  B. Assembling utensils
    1. Wok
    2. Sharp kitchen knife with small blade
    3. Cooking fork
    4. Wooden spoon
    5. Measuring cup and measuring spoons

(Continued on next page)

Other headings to organize steps logically for this topic might include "C. Mixing ingredients" and "D. Cooking ingredients." A number of steps may be involved in each of the divisions A, B, C, and D, but reading the steps in paragraphs that address the groups separately is far less overwhelming and confusing to readers than beginning with step 1 and ending with step 19. What steps would you include under the "C" and "D" headings for a process paper on making stir-fried shrimp?

- **Pay careful attention to your audience.** Who will read your process paper? Who do you anticipate as your main audience? For example, a paper explaining a quick way to change the oil in a car would use one approach to address a group of experienced auto mechanics but quite another one to address car owners eager to save on repair costs but unfamiliar with the parts of an automobile.

- **Define terms that might be unfamiliar to the reader or that have more than one meaning.** To most of us, *conceit* means extreme self-love, but to a literary scholar, it means an elaborate and extended metaphor. The scholar, when writing instructions for first-year students on analyzing a poem, would have to define the term for readers.

- **Have a thesis.** It's possible just to present a clear set of instructions and stop. But the most interesting process papers do have theses. You can easily state your topic and your attitude toward it if you choose a process that you're passionate about.

- **Anticipate difficulties.** One way to prevent difficulties for your readers is to warn them in advance when to expect problems:

  This step requires your constant attention.
  Now you will need all the strength you can muster.
  You'd better have a friend handy to help with this step.

  Another way to anticipate difficulties is to give readers advice on how to make the process easier or more pleasant. Wearing old clothes isn't essential to the process of shampooing a carpet, of course, but you've learned from experience that dirty suds can fly and soil clothing, and you want to pass that information on. Similarly, it's possible to apply organic garden insecticides without using a face mask, but you've learned that the unpleasant odors can cause severe coughing and sneezing even if the products are considered harmless. Naturally, you want to warn your readers about how to avoid possible side effects.

- **Tell the reader what to do if something goes wrong.** In many processes, one can follow the instructions faithfully and still encounter problems. Prepare your reader for such cases.

  If, at this point, the pecan pie is not firm when you test the center, reduce the heat to 250 degrees and cook it 15 minutes longer.
  If, even after careful proofreading, you find a misspelled word at the last minute, carefully cross out the word and neatly print the correction by hand.

- **Use other rhetorical strategies as needed.** It's hard to write a process paper without drawing on some of the other writing strategies explored in this book. Narrative, for example, will help you frame the chronological sequence of steps to take in the process you're explaining. You may need to use descriptive details to identify some object. If you look ahead to the chapters on cause and effect (18) and definition (19), you might find explanations there that will help you develop your topic. The point is that you should mix rhetorical approaches as needed to write the best process paper that you can.

- **Weigh your options for an introduction and a conclusion.** An introduction to a how-to paper, in addition to presenting the thesis, might state when and by whom the process would be performed. It could also list any equipment needed for performing the process, and it might briefly list the major headings or divisions of the process. Don't forget about the need for a conclusion. You want the last thought in your reader's mind to be about the process as a whole, not about the comparatively trivial final step.

STRATEGY CHECKLIST: Writing and Revising Your Process Paper

Plan the paper.	❏ Have I chosen a process that I understand thoroughly?
	❏ Will I explain a process that I expect readers to perform, or will I explain how something is done or made without expecting readers to perform the action?
	❏ Have I thought carefully about my purpose in writing?
	❏ Do I have my audience clearly in mind?
	❏ Have I used an outline to organize my ideas?
	❏ Have I addressed any issues raised by readers about my outline?
Write a first draft.	❏ Have I done any necessary research if I'm explaining a complex process?
	❏ Have I made the process interesting with an introduction that engages readers?
	❏ Have I developed a thesis?
	❏ Have I explained the process completely and accurately in chronological order?
	❏ Have I provided reasons for performing some steps, where necessary?
	❏ Have I identified all the steps in the process and grouped them logically?

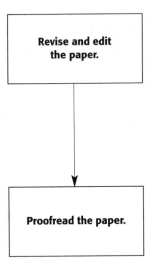

❑ Have I identified all necessary materials and equipment?

❑ Have I defined unfamiliar terms for the reader?

❑ Have I anticipated any problems people performing the process might face?

❑ Have I adapted my language and instructions for the person who is performing the action or someone just trying to understand it?

❑ Have I proofread for grammar, spelling, and mechanics?

Writing Topics

If you cannot easily decide on a topic for your process paper, you might want to use one of these suggestions as a topic idea:

1. How to be a working mother
2. How to use the Internet
3. How to achieve peace in the Middle East
4. How to teach math concepts to preschoolers
5. How to adopt a child in your city or state
6. How a steam engine works
7. How to get an A in English
8. How to make your favorite sandwich
9. How to prevent juvenile crime
10. How to manage stress
11. How to read a book
12. How a light bulb works
13. How to enjoy a concert
14. How to waste time
15. How to listen to music

16

Comparison and Contrast

A *comparison* shows the similarities between two or more things; a *contrast* shows the differences between two or more things. Used interchangeably, if imprecisely, each term often includes the other. Asked to compare, you'll probably contrast automatically as well. Asked to contrast, you can't escape comparing too. Many teachers use the unambiguous term **comparison–contrast** to signal the task of showing likenesses and differences. No matter what the term, the most common kind of essay question on examinations calls for comparison and contrast. It is important, then, to master the techniques of this method of development.

WRITING YOUR COMPARISON–CONTRAST PAPER

Everyone uses comparisons, sometimes to explain the unfamiliar, and sometimes just to establish a superficial similarity: "He is as slow as a snail," for example. But to produce a good comparison–contrast paper, the writer must apply logical principles to the consideration of similarities and differences.

TIPS FOR WRITING A COMPARISON–CONTRAST ESSAY

- **Compare and contrast according to a single principle.** You might compare automobiles and airplanes as means of transportation, or you might compare them as causes of air pollution. The principle in the first instance might be ease of travel; in the second, pollution. In each case, the principle determines the similarities and differences discussed in the paper. If you're concerned with ease of travel, you won't mention the variety of colors that both airplanes and automobiles can be painted. If you're concerned with pollution, you won't mention the comfort of adjustable seats.

  In a sense, this means developing a thesis. However, you usually must establish a principle for comparison–contrast before you can arrive at a thesis: the meaning of the similarities and differences. Having examined the similarities and differences according to the principle of ease of travel, you might establish as a thesis that travel by air is more convenient than travel by automobile.

  (Continued on next page)

- **Compare and contrast according to a single purpose.** One useful purpose is to clarify. For an audience that knows little about soccer, for example, you could make the game understandable by comparing it to football, a game with which more American audiences are familiar. A foreign student might explain the courtship and wedding customs of his or her country by contrasting them to their American equivalents.

    A second purpose of comparison–contrast is to show the superiority of one thing over another: Spiffy Peanut Butter is a better buy than Spunky Peanut Butter, say; or living in a high-rise apartment is easier than living in a house; or travel by air is more convenient than travel by automobile.

    A third purpose of comparison–contrast is to use the two items as examples of a generalization. Toni Cade Bambara and Toni Morrison show in their writings that African Americans want to be thought of as individuals rather than as stereotyped representatives of causes or groups.
- **Be fair with your comparison–contrasts.** If you see an exception to the comparison you have made, mention it. This is known as *qualification*, and often it can win the reader's respect and confidence.
- **Follow an established pattern of organization.** A comparison–contrast paper can be organized in one of three ways: subject by subject, point by point, or a combination of the two.

COMPARISON–CONTRAST PATTERNS

Subject-by-Subject Pattern

For short papers, one of the clearest patterns of organization—for comparison *or* contrast—is the **subject-by-subject pattern** or **block method**. If you select this pattern, you first discuss one side of the subject completely, and then you discuss the other side. You must, of course, stress the same points in discussing each side of the subject; otherwise there will be no comparison. The diagram on the right will help you visualize the block method.

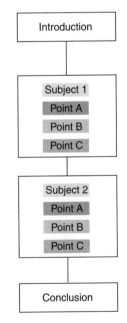

Point-by-Point Pattern

A second pattern of development is the **point-by-point** or **alternating pattern.** Although this pattern is most frequently used in writing long papers, it is by no means restricted to them. In this pattern, the writer establishes one or more points of comparison or contrast and then applies those points to each side of a subject. We can represent this pattern in a diagram like the one on the right.

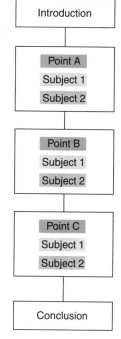

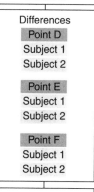

Combined Pattern

The point-by-point pattern and the subject-by-subject pattern are most useful for stressing only the similarities between two items or only the differences between two items. Sometimes, however, you may want to give weight to similarities *and* differences. To do so, you can combine the two patterns, as in the following student examples.

The diagram on the left represents the combined pattern visually.

STRATEGY CHECKLIST: Writing and Revising Your Comparison–Contrast Paper

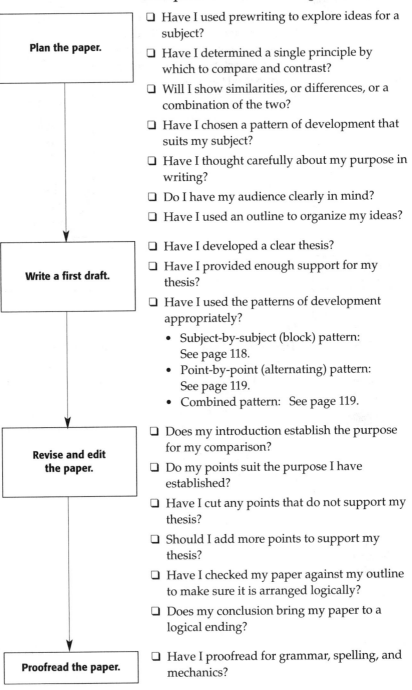

Plan the paper.

❑ Have I used prewriting to explore ideas for a subject?

❑ Have I determined a single principle by which to compare and contrast?

❑ Will I show similarities, or differences, or a combination of the two?

❑ Have I chosen a pattern of development that suits my subject?

❑ Have I thought carefully about my purpose in writing?

❑ Do I have my audience clearly in mind?

❑ Have I used an outline to organize my ideas?

Write a first draft.

❑ Have I developed a clear thesis?

❑ Have I provided enough support for my thesis?

❑ Have I used the patterns of development appropriately?

- Subject-by-subject (block) pattern: See page 118.
- Point-by-point (alternating) pattern: See page 119.
- Combined pattern: See page 119.

Revise and edit the paper.

❑ Does my introduction establish the purpose for my comparison?

❑ Do my points suit the purpose I have established?

❑ Have I cut any points that do not support my thesis?

❑ Should I add more points to support my thesis?

❑ Have I checked my paper against my outline to make sure it is arranged logically?

❑ Does my conclusion bring my paper to a logical ending?

Proofread the paper.

❑ Have I proofread for grammar, spelling, and mechanics?

Writing Topics

If you are having difficulty deciding on a topic for your comparison–contrast paper, the following suggestions might be helpful. Bear in mind that the number of comparison–contrast topics is almost infinite, and ours just begin to scratch the surface. Our suggestions are intended more to start your own thoughts flowing than to be specific, final topics.

1. Any past-versus-present topic: cars, sports teams or athletes, places you've lived, girlfriends or boyfriends, movie stars, musical styles, clothes, ways of celebrating a holiday, a change in your attitude toward someone or something, attitudes before and after 9/11.
2. A which-is-better topic: two competing products, cultures, newscasters, restaurants, television sitcoms, business establishments, seasons of the year, cats versus dogs, breeds of dog, methods of disciplining children.
3. Two contrasting types of people: teachers, police officers, drivers, salespeople, political leaders, "dates," hairstylists, servers at restaurants.
4. Two contrasting (but sometimes confused) emotions or character traits: love and infatuation, courage and recklessness, pride and arrogance, snobbery and good taste, fear and terror.
5. Two contrasting views on a controversial issue: dealing with terrorists, compulsory drug testing for high school athletes, abortion, SUV drivers, censorship, pornography, to name a few possibilities.

17

Classification and Division

Classification and division are among humanity's most advanced, yet most basic, modes of thought. These thinking skills allow us to see relations among parts and so make the world around us more comprehensible.

CLASSIFICATION AND DIVISION IN ACTION

Saturday night is just around the corner, and you've decided to spend a quiet evening at home—cook some pasta, make a salad, rent a movie from the video rental shop, and pick up the latest Stephen King book for a little nighttime terror before bed. If you're walking, biking, driving, or taking a bus, you're already plotting the most efficient route. Maybe it's Blockbuster video rental first, Pathmark Supermarket second, and the local library last.

At Blockbuster, signs direct you to different groups of films—new releases, comedies, adventure classics, romances, and others. You decide on *Knocked Up*—you've seen it at least twice before—but its antics seem to be the perfect antidote to Stephen King. So you head over to the comedies section and take what you want from the shelf. There's a two-for-one special tonight—well, maybe you'll be bored the third time around with Seth Rogan, Katherine Heigl, and Paul Rudd and company—so you head over to the adventure classics section; your friend Consuelo has been raving about *The Thin Red Line*, a World War II film set in the Pacific that she calls beautiful poetry, and you find your way to the right shelf for that film too.

At Pathmark, your first stop is at the produce area for the makings of a small salad, then to the boxes of macaroni and spaghetti piled high in the pasta section (it's linguine tonight, you've decided), and then over to the shelves marked "Sauces" for a jar of Ronzoni's meat sauce. Finally, you go to the frozen food section, check out the ice-cream bin, and pick Ben and Jerry's Cherry Garcia.

Off to the library then; this branch has a section called New Releases near the checkout desk. You look for the King book and note that one copy is in the group of books to rent with a daily fee and another copy is in the group of free books—from which you grab your copy and head home.

USING DIVISION (OR ANALYSIS)

When you established your route for picking up the various items you needed for Saturday night at home, you used *division*, maybe even unconsciously. You considered the whole map of your town or neighborhood and divided it into separate units to make your trip easier. The video shop, the supermarket, the library—these are the sections of your larger surrounding geography. When you divide, you break down something (here, your town or neighborhood) into parts or sections. Your purpose in dividing was for ease of transport and so you divided the entity into units that served your purpose. Clearly, many other possibilities exist for dividing the neighborhood you live in, all depending on the purpose for the division. You could separate the neighborhood by the way people vote in elections; by the ethnic makeup of various sections; by the architectural varieties of buildings; by the lawns and flower gardens and what they look like; and by the school districts and the businesses—the options are numerous.

In the process of division—which, incidentally, many people call *analysis*—you break down an entity into its discrete parts, all based on some organizing principle. Division moves from the general to the specific; you look at a large category and try to understand it better by seeing what makes it up. When you analyze a Big Mac, a rock song, a television program, a magazine ad, or a poem, you divide it into distinct elements in order to understand the parts and how they contribute to the whole.

Division

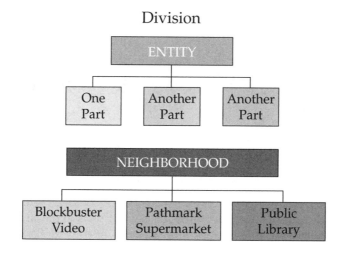

USING CLASSIFICATION

As you scooted around town to the video shop, the supermarket, and the library, you used a different, but related, thinking skill. When you searched for movies, pasta, vegetables, ice cream, and a King thriller, you relied on *classification*. To locate specific items, you had to identify the large group into which someone had placed them. Classification creates large entities from discrete components.

Classification

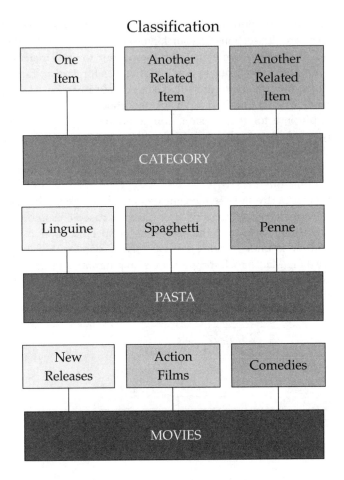

HOW ARE CLASSIFICATION AND DIVISION DIFFERENT?

Do you see the differences? *Division* moves from the larger group to the smaller parts. *Classification* moves from the smaller parts to the larger group. Division and classification as rhetorical strategies often work hand in hand and overlap considerably.

If you wanted to write about preparing for your Saturday night at home, as we've revealed it here, you might explain how you *divided* your neighborhood into entities that let you move easily from one stop to the other. Then you'd explain how *classification* at your various stops helped you set up an evening of leisure according to your own design.

To take another example, if you wanted to write about violence on television, you might *divide* the topic into news shows, daytime soap operas, and children's programs. Selecting one or more of these, you might then *classify* the soaps, for example. You might identify categories of violence that you saw on the soap operas, such as violence against children; violence among husbands, wives, and lovers; and violence at the workplace. Each category would require supporting details to make your classification stick—but we'll have more to say later about how to write your classification essay.

REVIEWING DIVISION STRATEGIES

As you've seen, another name for division is *analysis*. When you analyze—a poem or short story, a process or procedure, or the reasons for some behavior or action—you divide the issue into components. In analysis by *division*, you break down a subject usually thought of as a single unit into each one of its parts. An analysis of a stereo system, for example, requires naming and describing each of its components. An analysis of a breakfast cereal requires a listing of the number of calories and the grams of protein, carbohydrates, fat, and sodium in a single serving. An analysis of a process—how to change a light bulb or how to make iron ore into steel—requires discussing the separate steps of the process. So, in fact, if you have written a process paper, you have already used one major form of division.

If you wrote a literary analysis using comparison–contrast strategies (see pages 117–121), you used division to break the piece of literature into the components that concerned you before you showed similarities and differences.

When you write a cause and effect paper, often called *causal analysis* (see Chapter 18), division will help you separate an entity—an event, an action, or a consequence—into components.

We deal, therefore, with analysis (division) in other sections of this book. This chapter focuses on *classification*.

WRITING YOUR CLASSIFICATION PAPER

As you have seen, **classification** is the process by which we categorize members of a large group—ideas, people, plants, animals, books, pasta, films, and so on—on the basis of a single principle. Classification enables us to cope with a large body of material by organizing it into smaller, more workable categories. Besides, we all like to classify. We do it naturally. Students classify their professors as boring or stimulating. Homemakers classify their cooking utensils, perhaps as those used often and those used occasionally, and place them in drawers and cupboards accordingly. But whether used for fun or for profit, classification has certain requirements, many of which you have already used in developing outlines.

TIPS FOR WRITING A CLASSIFICATION ESSAY

- **Determine the basis for classification and then apply it consistently.** To classify automobiles, you would not want to establish as the categories "foreign cars," "expensive cars," and "sedans" because these classes do not have the same basis of classification. The first class is based on country of origin, the second on price, and the third on body style. A member of one class would be likely to overlap into others. A Rolls-Royce or a Mercedes, for example, could fit into any of the three classes. Logic would require selection of a single basis of classification such as price and then sticking to the issue of price with subclasses like "expensive," "medium-priced," and "low-priced."

- **Define terms that might be unfamiliar to your audience or that are used in a special way.** A writer using technical terms like *mesomorph, ectomorph*, and *endomorph* to describe human body types would need to define those terms. Even familiar terms like *mature* and *immature* or *realistic* and *unrealistic* may often require definitions because their interpretations can vary. Similarly, suppose you invent names for your categories. You might, for instance, classify joggers as red-faced wobblers, short-legged two-steppers, and long-legged striders. You must share with your reader your understanding of these made-up terms.

- **Decide whether you need only describe each category fully or whether you need to add clarifying examples.** A classification of people as overweight, underweight, and normal, for example, would require merely a complete description of each type. Readers could, on the basis of the description, decide which category the various people they meet belong to. On the other hand, a classification of the present Supreme Court justices as liberals or conservatives, besides giving the characteristics of liberal and conservative justices, should also give the names of the justices who belong to each category and some explanation of why they appear in each group.

- **Have a thesis.** In one sense, of course, the classification itself provides the basis for a thesis. If you assert that there are three classes of teachers or four classes of pet owners or five classes of social drinkers and can support your assertion, you have a thesis. But, as usual, your thesis should express your opinion about or attitude toward your subject. You could show, for example, that one of the categories is preferable to the others, or that all the categories are silly or despicable or admirable. Having a thesis gives force and interest to your categories.

- **Establish some kind of order.** In some cases, you can order your categories according to time, from earliest to latest. Or, depending on your thesis, several other possibilities for ordering the categories present themselves. You might order the categories from worst to best, best to worst, least enjoyable to most enjoyable, or weakest to strongest, for example. In most listings, you may have more interesting comments to make about some classes than about others. Arrange your classes so that the less interesting ones are in the middle of your paper. Hook your readers with a strong first category and leave them satisfied with an even stronger last category. The practice of ordering categories will make an important contribution to your classification papers.

STRATEGY CHECKLIST: Writing and Revising Your Classification Paper

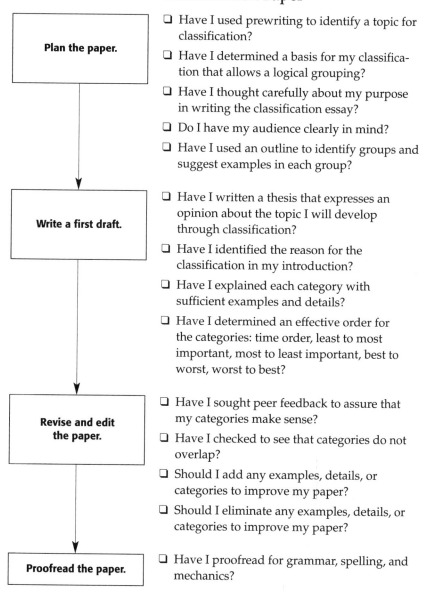

Plan the paper.

❑ Have I used prewriting to identify a topic for classification?

❑ Have I determined a basis for my classification that allows a logical grouping?

❑ Have I thought carefully about my purpose in writing the classification essay?

❑ Do I have my audience clearly in mind?

❑ Have I used an outline to identify groups and suggest examples in each group?

Write a first draft.

❑ Have I written a thesis that expresses an opinion about the topic I will develop through classification?

❑ Have I identified the reason for the classification in my introduction?

❑ Have I explained each category with sufficient examples and details?

❑ Have I determined an effective order for the categories: time order, least to most important, most to least important, best to worst, worst to best?

Revise and edit the paper.

❑ Have I sought peer feedback to assure that my categories make sense?

❑ Have I checked to see that categories do not overlap?

❑ Should I add any examples, details, or categories to improve my paper?

❑ Should I eliminate any examples, details, or categories to improve my paper?

Proofread the paper.

❑ Have I proofread for grammar, spelling, and mechanics?

Writing Topics

The following list of subjects may offer you some ideas for a topic for your classification paper. Notice how some subjects can easily be limited further than they are: "Summer jobs" could be limited to summer jobs at resorts, "outstanding teachers" to outstanding physical education teachers, and so on.

1. Tyrants
2. Attitudes toward Christmas
3. Campus parties
4. Outstanding teachers
5. Summer jobs
6. Major classes of love
7. Automobiles
8. Male or female chauvinists
9. Types of chili (or pizza or burgers)
10. Natural disasters
11. People at a sporting event
12. TV preachers
13. Good drugs
14. Concert goers
15. Voters
16. Holiday gifts
17. Terrorism
18. Shoppers
19. The contents of my handbag (or bookbag or briefcase)
20. Great leaders

18

Cause and Effect

Many of the papers you write in college will require analysis of causes or circumstances that lead to a given result: Why does the cost of living continue to rise? Why do people with symptoms of cancer or heart disease put off consulting a doctor? In questions of this type, the **effect** or result is given, at least briefly. Your job is to analyze the causes that produce the effect.

Other assignments will require that you discuss the results of a particular case: What are the positive and negative effects of legalizing lotteries? What are the effects of giving direct legislative power to the people? What is the effect of noise pollution on our bodies? In questions of this type, the **cause** is given, and you must determine the effects that might result or have resulted from the cause.

WRITING YOUR CAUSE AND EFFECT PAPER

Cause and effect papers do not call for the rigid structure demanded of classification and process papers. Nevertheless, writers must meet some logical demands.

TIPS FOR WRITING A CAUSE AND EFFECT ESSAY

- **Do not confuse cause with process.** A process paper tells *how* an event or product came about; a cause and effect paper tells *why* something happened.
- **Avoid the *post hoc* fallacy.** That a man lost his billfold shortly after walking under a ladder does not mean that walking under the ladder caused his loss. Similarly, that a woman lost her hearing shortly after attending a loud rock concert does not prove that her deafness is a direct result of the band's decibel level. (See the discussion of *post hoc* fallacies in Chapter 20 on pages 141–142.)
- **Do not oversimplify causes.** Getting a good night's sleep before an exam doesn't cause a student to receive the highest grade in the class. The rest certainly won't do any harm, but familiarity with the material covered on the exam, intelligence, and an ability to write also have something to do with the grade. Almost all effects worth writing about have more than one cause.

(Continued on next page)

- **Do not oversimplify effects.** Even though it may be true that many people lose money by gambling on lotteries, that does not mean legalizing lotteries will result in nationwide bankruptcy.
- **Follow an established pattern of organization.** Once you have determined the causes or effects that you wish to discuss, you can organize your paper in several ways. In a paper devoted primarily to cause, the simplest way to open is to identify the effect in the introduction, then to develop the reasons for that effect in the body of the paper. If, for example, you want to explain a recent rise in the cost of living, you might begin with an indication of the rise (effect)—the cost of living has risen dramatically during the past three years and promises to go even higher in the coming year—before dealing with the causes. Similarly, a paper devoted primarily to effect usually begins with a description of the cause. If your subject is the probable effects of a proposed tax increase, you might begin with a description of the proposal itself (cause) before discussing effects.

STRATEGY CHECKLIST: Writing and Revising Your Cause and Effect Paper

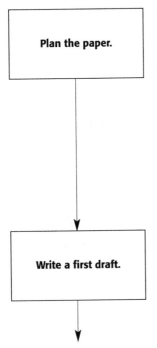

Plan the paper.

❏ Have I used prewriting to explore topics?
❏ Have I identified a topic that I can explore through causal analysis?
❏ Am I prepared to explain *why* something happened instead of *how* it happened?
❏ Will my topic lend itself to either causes or effects, or a combination of both?
❏ Have I thought carefully about my purpose in writing?
❏ Do I have my audience clearly in mind?
❏ Have I used an outline to organize my ideas?

Write a first draft.

❏ Have I developed a clear thesis that expresses an opinion about the topic I will develop through cause and effect analysis?
❏ Have I written an introduction that presents the topic and makes my focus clear?
❏ Have I avoided oversimplifying causes and effects?

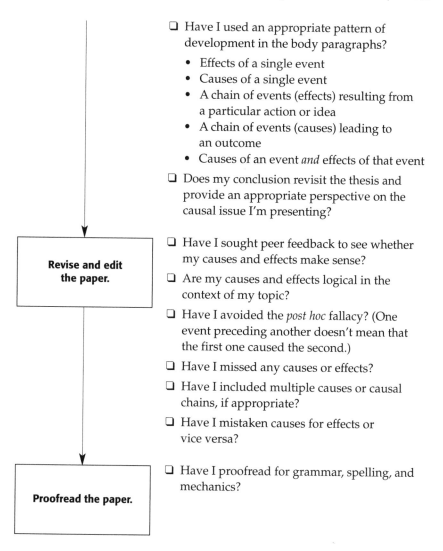

❑ Have I used an appropriate pattern of development in the body paragraphs?
- Effects of a single event
- Causes of a single event
- A chain of events (effects) resulting from a particular action or idea
- A chain of events (causes) leading to an outcome
- Causes of an event *and* effects of that event

❑ Does my conclusion revisit the thesis and provide an appropriate perspective on the causal issue I'm presenting?

Revise and edit the paper.

❑ Have I sought peer feedback to see whether my causes and effects make sense?

❑ Are my causes and effects logical in the context of my topic?

❑ Have I avoided the *post hoc* fallacy? (One event preceding another doesn't mean that the first one caused the second.)

❑ Have I missed any causes or effects?

❑ Have I included multiple causes or causal chains, if appropriate?

❑ Have I mistaken causes for effects or vice versa?

Proofread the paper.

❑ Have I proofread for grammar, spelling, and mechanics?

Writing Topics

If you cannot easily decide on a topic for your cause and effect paper, you might want to try one or more of the following suggestions. You can treat most of the subjects as material for a cause-only, effect-only, or cause and effect paper.

1. One of your personality quirks
2. Effects of going to college
3. Why people smoke cigarettes despite their proven dangers
4. A change of mind about something or someone
5. The popularity of Christian bands in mainstream music
6. Results of the 2010 Gulf oil spill
7. Growth or decrease in the popularity of a style of music
8. Growth or decrease in the popularity of a hairstyle
9. Growth or decrease in the popularity of a clothing style

10. Street gangs
11. Why sexism remains a problem
12. Global warming
13. Teaching preschoolers to read
14. Emphasis on computers in American schools
15. Why teenagers drink alcohol
16. Blind dates
17. Excessively strict or lenient parents
18. Internet spam
19. Election fraud
20. World hunger

19
Definition

From time to time, you may have found yourself in a shouting match with friends over a question such as, which is the all-time great concert group—the Beatles, the Rolling Stones, Queen, or Pink Floyd. Eventually, some wise soul says, "Hey, wait a minute. What's your idea of a great concert group?" The speaker has demanded a **definition** of the term that has sparked the debate. You may find that one person's standard for "great" is how many albums the group sold. Another may appreciate how the group subtly improvises on a theme. And another may insist that "great" means having long-lasting effect on music worldwide. Then you realize, perhaps, either that your respective ideas of a great group are so different that you can't have a discussion or that, once you understand each other's terms, you have no real disagreement.

When writing, you won't have the advantage of another person asking what you mean. If you want to appear reasonable when you present an idea, you sometimes have to define terms.

Often, a dictionary won't be much help. It may be a good place to start, but at times a dictionary definition won't explain a term fully. Take the word *great*, for example. A dictionary tells you that it means "remarkable or outstanding in magnitude, degree, or extent," and so it does; but how does such a definition help you distinguish between one rock group and another? To do so, you could begin with a dictionary definition, to be sure, but you must let your reader know what you believe the positive or desirable qualities of a rock group are. You must provide an **extended definition**.

As you have no doubt learned on your own, much of your course work—in psychology, history, sociology, biology, and so on—depends on extended definitions. So you know that certain terms, then, require a more elaborate definition than a dictionary gives. The burden is on the writer to explain the meaning of the term. Sometimes in a long paper you have to write an extended definition that may take up one or two paragraphs. Occasionally, a definition can become the paper itself.

The following kinds of terms often need defining:

WORDS AND TERMS FOR DEFINITION

- *Judgmental words*—words that reflect opinions—need definition. Whether subjects being discussed are *good, better, best; bad, worse, worst; beautiful, ugly; friendly, unfriendly; wise, foolish; fair, unfair*; and so on, is a matter of opinion.
- *Specialized terms*—terms with a special meaning to a given group—need definition. Almost every professional or occupational group uses terms that the members of the group understand but that require explanation for those outside the group—for example, *psychosis*, a psychological term; *neoclassicism*, a literary term; *writ*, a legal term; and *gig*, a show-business term.
- *Abstractions*—general words like *love, democracy, justice, freedom*, and *quality*—need definition.
- *Controversial terms* like *male chauvinist, nuclear buildup*, and *affirmative action* need definition.
- *Slang terms* like *bro, phat, cool, the 'hood, bling*, and *hot* may need definition for many audiences.

WRITING YOUR DEFINITION PAPER

You can present your extended definition in one of two ways—formally or informally.

Beginning a Formal Definition

A **formal definition** contains the three parts of a dictionary definition: (1) the term itself—the word or phrase to be defined; (2) the class—the large group to which the object or concept belongs; and (3) the differentiation—those characteristics that distinguish it from all others in its class.

Term ⟶	Class	⟶ Differentiation
A garden	is a small plot of land	used for the cultivation of flowers, vegetables, or fruits.
Beer	is a fermented alcoholic beverage	brewed from malt and flavored with hops.
Lunch	is a meal	eaten at midday.

To write an extended formal definition, you first need to develop a one-sentence definition of the term. Keep the following cautions in mind:

TIPS FOR WRITING ONE-SENTENCE DEFINITIONS

- **Make sure to include the class.** Don't write, "Baseball is when nine players...." Write instead, "Baseball is a *sport* in which nine players...."
- **Restrict the class.** Speak of a sonnet not as a kind of literature but as a kind of poem.
- **Include no important part of the term itself or its derivatives in the class or differentiation.** Don't say that "a definition is that which defines."
- **Make certain that the sentence defines and does not simply make a statement about the term.** "Happiness is a Madonna concert" doesn't have the essential parts of a definition of happiness.
- **Provide adequate differentiation to clarify the meaning.** Don't define a traitor as "one who opposes the best interests of his or her country." That definition doesn't exclude the well-meaning person who misunderstands the country's best interests and opposes from ignorance. Try instead, "A traitor is one who opposes the best interests of his or her country with malicious intent."
- **Don't make the definition too restrictive.** Don't define a matinee as "a drama presented during the day." That definition doesn't include other forms of entertainment, such as ballets or concerts, which also could be held in daytime.

EXERCISE

Using a dictionary whenever necessary, write one-sentence formal definitions for the following terms.

1. Politics
2. Joy
3. Intelligent design
4. Philosophy
5. Democracy
6. Terrorist
7. Cold fusion
8. Chauvinism
9. Hanukkah
10. Inflation

Writing Your Formal Definition Paper

Once you have composed a one-sentence formal definition, its three parts can become the major divisions of your paper. The introduction to your paper might contain the term and its one-sentence definition. That sentence could become the thesis for your paper. Or, in addition to providing a one-sentence definition, you could express an attitude toward the term.

The next division of your paper could discuss the class, and the final division, the differentiation. In these discussions, you can make your idea clear by using specific details, by making comparisons and using analogies, by giving examples or telling anecdotes, and sometimes by tracing the history of the term. Often you will be able to quote or refer to the definitions others have given the term. This technique is particularly useful if experts disagree over the meaning of the term. An especially effective tool is *exclusion*, showing what the term is *not*:

> *Gourmet* cooking does not mean to me the preparation of food in expensive wines; it does not mean the preparation of exotic dishes like octopus or rattlesnake; it does not mean the smothering of meat with highly caloric sauces. *Gourmet* cooking to me means the preparation of any food—whether black-eyed peas or hollandaise sauce—in such a way that the dish will be as tasty and attractive as it can be made.

In advancing your discussion of class and differentiation, you can use any rhetorical method or combination of methods of development you have studied. In fact, what makes definition such an interesting rhetorical challenge is that you can draw on most of the familiar patterns of essay development. For example, suppose you wanted to define the term *happiness*. You could use a variety of approaches, as indicated here.

APPROACHES TO YOUR ESSAY TOPIC
DEFINING THE TERM *HAPPINESS*

Possible approach	Mode of development
Provide accurate sensory details to describe the face and actions of a happy person you know.	Description (Chapter 12)
Tell a story about a moment when you were truly happy.	Narration (Chapter 13)
Provide several illustrations (examples) of happiness.	Example (Chapter 14)
Explain how to be happy or unhappy.	Process (Chapter 15)
Compare one state of happiness with another; contrast happiness with sadness.	Comparison–Contrast (Chapter 16)
Divide happy people into groups or categories.	Classification (Chapter 17)
Explain the conditions necessary for true happiness or the outcomes of happiness in a person's life.	Cause and Effect (Chapter 18)
Argue that happiness is not achievable in America today.	Argumentation (Chapter 20)

Writing Your Informal Definition Paper

Although many terms lend themselves to the three-part formal definition, some are better explained by **informal definition**. What is a good teacher, for example? or a bad marriage? or an ideal home? Clearly, one can define such topics only in a subjective or personal way; your purpose is to show what the term means to you. In such instances, it is probably wise to avoid a rigid formal definition. Make your conception of the term clear by describing the subject as fully as you can. By the time readers finish the paper, they should understand what the term means to you.

As with formal definitions, you can use any method or combination of methods of development that you have studied to create an informal definition. Examples and anecdotes are especially good for explaining a term. So are comparison, process, classification, and cause and effect. The idea is to use whatever techniques come in handy to put the idea across.

STRATEGY CHECKLIST: Writing and Revising Your Definition Paper

| Plan the paper. | ❑ Have I selected a word or phrase that lends itself to an extended definition? |

❑ Is the word I've chosen too broad or too narrow, and how can I correct either of these two limitations?

❑ Have I used one of the prewriting strategies to stimulate my thoughts?

❑ Have I identified details and examples that support my understanding of the word?

❑ Have I paid attention to peer comments about my prewriting?

❑ Have I considered my audience and purpose?

❑ Have I considered using an outline to plan my presentation?

| Write a first draft. | ❑ Have I written a thesis that expresses an opinion about the word I am defining? |

❑ For an extended formal definition, have I included a one-sentence definition with three major parts?

• Term
• Class
• Differentiation

❑ Have I written an introduction that states the term and provides some idea of why I'm choosing to define it?

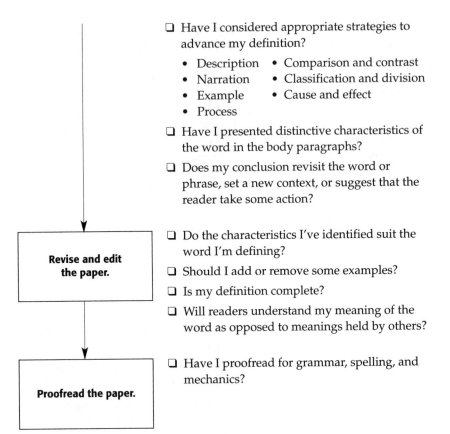

❑ Have I considered appropriate strategies to advance my definition?

- Description
- Narration
- Example
- Process
- Comparison and contrast
- Classification and division
- Cause and effect

❑ Have I presented distinctive characteristics of the word in the body paragraphs?

❑ Does my conclusion revisit the word or phrase, set a new context, or suggest that the reader take some action?

Revise and edit the paper.

❑ Do the characteristics I've identified suit the word I'm defining?

❑ Should I add or remove some examples?

❑ Is my definition complete?

❑ Will readers understand my meaning of the word as opposed to meanings held by others?

Proofread the paper.

❑ Have I proofread for grammar, spelling, and mechanics?

Writing Topics

Consider these words and terms as possible topics for your extended definition paper. Do library or online research, as needed.

1. Evolution
2. Happiness
3. Homelessness
4. Affirmative action
5. Shopping malls
6. Laziness
7. Wealth
8. Leadership
9. Astrology
10. Religion
11. Success
12. Political correctness
13. Depression
14. Hope
15. Virus
16. Friends
17. White-collar crime
18. America
19. "Wannabes"
20. Fun

20

Argumentation

An **argumentation** paper attempts to strengthen or change an attitude of the reader, or to persuade the reader to a particular point of view by means of logic. Although writers of argumentation papers may use emotional appeals, they place their principal faith in appealing to the intellects of their readers.

Argumentation has probably too often appeared in the combative context of a courtroom or debating society: Right and wrong confront each other; one side wins, and one side loses. The victors gloat over the demolished points of their opponents or graciously accept their opponents' concessions of defeat and apologies for being so wrong. Many writers still do strive for total victory of this sort, of course, but argument also can be a matter of bringing opposing parties together, of showing the strengths and weaknesses of all points of view, of building consensus among former enemies. Argumentation can involve making peace as much as waging war.

USING LOGIC

To check your own logic and that of others, a knowledge of the two kinds of logical thinking, *induction* and *deduction*, and of the errors in logic, the *fallacies*, will be helpful.

Induction

Induction is the process of reasoning from the particular to the general. It is the process of arriving at a general conclusion about all the members of a group or class. Induction is a useful tool because it isn't always practical or possible to check every member of a group before drawing your conclusion. If, for example, you've noticed that for three Fridays in a row, Professor Hadley has given a pop quiz, you may draw the useful conclusion that Professor Hadley is likely to give pop quizzes on Fridays. You don't have to wait until the end of the term to see if you're right.

But induction is useful only if the conclusion about a class is drawn from a fair sampling of that class. What's fair depends on the class. You needn't stick your hand into twenty fires to conclude that fire burns; one or two fires will do. You should sample other classes more broadly. You should draw conclusions about groups of people, for example, from a large representative sampling and even then you should usually qualify statements with words like *tend, may, are likely,* and so on. (See "Hasty Generalization" and "Overgeneralization," page 142; see also Chapter 14, "Example.")

Deduction

Deduction is the process of reasoning from the general to the particular. You apply a generalization already established—by yourself or by someone else— to a specific case. You've concluded, for example, that Professor Hadley is likely to give pop quizzes on Fridays. When your roommate suggests one Friday morning that you cut classes and spend the day in the park, you say, "No, I can't go today. Professor Hadley may give a pop quiz, and my average can't stand a zero." You've applied your generalization (Fridays are likely days for quizzes) to a specific case (this Friday) and just may have assured yourself a passing grade in Professor Hadley's class.

The Syllogism

In its simplest form, the deductive process is stated as a *syllogism*: an argument consisting of a major premise, a minor premise, and a conclusion.

Major premise:	Fridays are likely days for pop quizzes.
Minor premise:	Today is Friday.
Conclusion:	Therefore, today is a likely day for a pop quiz.

Perhaps a more sophisticated example is the syllogism implicit in the Declaration of Independence:

Major premise:	Rulers who violate basic human rights should be overthrown.
Minor premise:	King George III has violated basic human rights.
Conclusion:	Therefore, King George III should be overthrown.

Syllogisms rarely appear in writing or conversation in their pure three-part form. It is far more common to find *enthymemes,* condensed syllogisms in which one or more parts are missing, the writer assuming that the missing parts are clearly understood and don't need to be stated directly.

It's Friday, so I'd better go to Professor Hadley's class. (*Missing premise*: Fridays are likely days for quizzes in Professor Hadley's class.)

I don't trust him because he's sneaky. (*Missing premise*: Sneaky people should not be trusted.)

I hate movies with violence, and this movie is teeming with violence. (*Missing conclusion*: Therefore, I hate this movie.)

For a valid syllogism, both premises must be true. It's hard to imagine a syllogism that begins with the premise "The earth is flat" leading to any valid conclusion. But even if both premises are true, the reasoning process itself may be faulty and the conclusion invalid. Consider this syllogism:

Major premise: English majors read lots of books.

Minor premise: David reads lots of books.

Conclusion: Therefore, David is an English major.

Despite the true premises, the conclusion still doesn't follow. The major premise merely says, "English majors read lots of books"; it says nothing about other people who may also read books. Logically, David may be an English major, but he may also be a merchant marine who spends time on shipboard reading, an invalid who doesn't enjoy television, a desk clerk whose job is boring, or just someone who likes to read for no particular reason. The logical structure of the argument makes no more sense than this syllogism: Grass is green; her hat is green; therefore, her hat is grass.

Using Induction and Deduction

Induction and deduction are not mutually exclusive. You will seldom engage in one kind of thought without using the other. When you use induction, you usually have a hunch about what generalization the facts will add up to. If you didn't, you wouldn't have a guideline for handling the facts. Consider, for example, that observation about Professor Hadley's quiz-giving tendency. If you hadn't already suspected that Hadley was a Friday quiz-giver, you might not have noticed that the pop quizzes did occur on Friday. Some deduction, therefore, was involved in the process of reaching the generalization about pop quizzes on Friday.

Similarly, in deductive reasoning you must also use induction. To ensure sound premises, you must be sure that your evidence is both adequate and fair, and that involves induction. Even if yours is the best of syllogisms, you probably won't convince a reader of its worth unless you offer support for it—reasons, statistics, facts, opinions of authorities, examples. The reader's agreement or approval depends on the case you build; it depends on evidence. In the Declaration of Independence, for example, Thomas Jefferson supported his case against George III by citing twenty-eight instances in which the king had violated basic human rights. The instances came from induction.

Avoiding Logical Fallacies

Whether your primary tool is induction or deduction, you need to make certain that the evidence you offer isn't based on errors in logic. In other words, you should avoid the following fallacies.

Post Hoc, Ergo Propter Hoc

This impressive Latin phrase means, "after this, therefore because of this." This fallacy takes for a cause an event that merely happened earlier: For example, *A black cat crossed my path and ten minutes later I broke my ankle; therefore, the black cat caused my broken ankle.* Unless the speaker tripped over the cat, such a statement is as unreasonable as *Night follows day; therefore, day causes night.*

Card Stacking

Card stacking means using only the evidence that supports a thesis and ignoring that which contradicts or weakens it. Card stacking is dishonest and can sometimes do serious damage. Suppose, for instance, that a popular newspaper columnist dislikes the mayor of the city. The columnist could prevent the mayor's reelection simply by emphasizing the administration's mistakes and playing down its accomplishments. Soon, the readers of the newspaper would begin to think of the mayor as a bungler who shouldn't be reelected.

Unfair? Of course. It's also unnecessary. A reasonable thesis doesn't require card stacking. A writer can make concessions and still advance the argument: *Although the mayor has made some attempts to attract convention business, the efforts have been too few and too late,* for example. If a thesis isn't reasonable, if it requires card stacking for support, it probably isn't worth defending and the writer should change it.

Slanting

A variation of card stacking is **slanting**, systematically using words whose connotations suggest extreme approval or disapproval of the subject. A person may be "a bag of bones" or have "a model's figure." In either case, the weight is the same, but one term suggests scorn and the other approval. The conscious use of slanting to sway opinion usually occurs when a writer lacks enough logical evidence to support the thesis. Used this way, it is, like card stacking, quite dishonest. But slanting should not be confused with a writer's legitimate efforts to convey admittedly personal impressions and emotions.

Hasty Generalization

One snowflake doesn't make a blizzard, nor does one experience make a universal law. That one student has cheated on the last five psychology quizzes doesn't mean that all psychology students in the school are cheaters; to say so is to make a **hasty generalization**, to draw a conclusion about a group that is based on insufficient evidence.

Overgeneralization

Overgeneralizations are similar to hasty generalizations. A hasty generalization results from drawing a conclusion about a large number on the basis of very limited evidence. Overgeneralization occurs, regardless of how much "evidence" is available, when one assumes that all members of a group, nationality, race, or sex have the characteristics observed in some members of that group: "all feminists hate housework"; "the English are always cold and reserved"; "never trust a used-car salesperson." Surely it's possible that some feminists like to cook, that some English people are volatile, and that at least one or two used-car salespersons are trustworthy. Words such as *all, never, always, every, true,* and *untrue* are seldom justified when dealing with the complexities of human beings and human institutions. You would do well in writing your papers to qualify potentially troublesome generalizations with words such as *some, seldom, tend, sometimes, frequently, seem, appear, often, perhaps,* and *many.* Both hasty generalizations and overgeneralizations lead to prejudice and superstition and to theses that cannot be developed logically or effectively.

Non Sequitur

Meaning "it does not follow," a *non sequitur* is a conclusion that does not follow from the premises. For example:

> I was a volunteer worker this summer so now I am saving to go to medical school.

Usually, *non sequiturs* occur because the writer or speaker neglects to make the connection between the premise and the conclusion clear to readers. In the preceding example, the writer's thinking probably resembles this:

- I worked as a volunteer this summer for an organization that served men and women with serious diseases.
- These people suffered greatly.
- I felt that I was able to bring them some comfort from their pain and that this work gave me great satisfaction.
- I'd like to be able to help ill people.
- Therefore, I am saving to go to medical school so that I can become a physician and bring even more comfort to the sick.

Although the writer sees the connection easily, he has to reveal thought processes so that the audience may also see the connection.

Another kind of *non sequitur* occurs because the writer or speaker draws an incorrect or debatable conclusion:

> Jack is 6 feet, 7 inches tall; I want him on my basketball team.

The unstated syllogism that leads to the conclusion is

> Successful basketball players tend to be very tall.
> Jack is very tall.
> Therefore, Jack will be a successful basketball player.

Although both the major premise and the minor premise are true, the conclusion does not necessarily follow. Jack may be so awkward that he trips over his own feet; thus, not all tall people make good basketball players. The writer's conclusion is, therefore, questionable and perhaps should be rejected.

Ignoring the Question

In **ignoring the question**, the writer or speaker deliberately or unintentionally shifts emphasis from the topic under discussion. You can (but should not) ignore a question in several ways.

Ad Hominem *Argument*

Arguing *ad hominem* (literally, "against the man") means making an irrelevant attack on a person rather than dealing with the actual issue under discussion. Suppose, for example, that Senator Goodfellow, who has admitted to cheating on his income tax for the past five years, proposes a bill for welfare reform. It would be a fallacy to attack the bill by arguing that its proponent is guilty of tax evasion. The bill may be logical, humane, and in the best interest of the country. If it is not, what are its weaknesses? The bill, not Senator Goodfellow's problems with the Internal Revenue Service, should be the subject of discussion.

Not all personal attacks, of course, are necessarily irrelevant. If Senator Goodfellow were seeking reelection, one could logically approve of his ideas and still vote against him because his character defects indicate the danger of trusting him in a position of power and responsibility.

Inexperienced writers sometimes employ the *ad hominem* fallacy in discussing literary works by rejecting a work whose author does not fulfill their idea of a good person:

> One cannot be expected to take "Kubla Khan" seriously. Coleridge admitted to writing it after he had taken drugs.

> Hemingway was a notorious womanizer. How can we value any of his ideas on morality and fidelity?

Such a practice indicates little understanding of the artistic process or of human nature. Writers, like all people, have human quirks and illnesses; yet such writers have produced inspiring works that affirm the highest values of civilization, and those affirmations deserve consideration. After all, most of us are a mixture of good and evil, wisdom and folly, generosity and greed; if we waited until we found a good idea proposed by a perfect person, we might wait forever.

Straw Man Argument

The writer or speaker attributes to the opposition actions or beliefs of which the opposition is not guilty and then attacks the opposition for those actions or beliefs.

> Parents who boast of never having to spank their children should feel shame instead of pride. Discipline and socially responsible behavior are vitally important, and people who sneer at such things deserve the condemnation of all concerned citizens.

Some parents might very well be able to boast of not having to spank their children and yet also demand of their children discipline and socially responsible behavior.

Begging the Question

The writer or speaker assumes in the thesis something that really needs to be proved.

> Since students learn to write in high school, the college composition course is a waste of time and should be replaced by a more useful and stimulating course.

One who chooses to write a paper with that thesis has the obligation to prove that students do learn how to write in high school—a source of great controversy in all discussions of American education.

Shifting the Burden of Proof

Logic requires that *whoever asserts must prove*. It is not logical to say,

> I believe the flu epidemic was caused by a conspiracy of large drug companies, and you can't prove it wasn't.

For the assertion to be taken seriously, reasonable proof of a conspiracy must be offered.

Circular Argument

Arguing in a circle means simply restating the premise instead of giving a reason for holding the premise.

> I like detective novels because mystery stories always give me great pleasure.

All that sentence says is, "I like detective novels because I like detective novels." Of greater interest would be the characteristics of the detective novels the speaker does like. In other words, one needs a reason for liking detective novels, and to say that one likes them because they give pleasure is not to give a reason. Why do the novels give pleasure? An honest answer to that question will provide a workable thesis and prevent a circular argument.

Either/Or

In the **either/or fallacy**, the writer or speaker suggests that there are only two alternatives when, in fact, there may be more.

> Although I am quite ill, I must turn my term paper in tomorrow, or I will fail the course.

The writer presents only two alternatives; however, it is also possible that the instructor, recognizing the student's illness, might accept a late paper. Of course, if one is cursed with a professor who does not accept late papers, regardless of circumstances, then one actually has only two alternatives, and no fallacy exists.

Argument by Analogy

An **analogy** is an extended comparison. It can clarify a difficult concept or dramatize an abstraction by comparing the unfamiliar with the familiar. But an analogy doesn't prove anything because, regardless of the number of similarities between two things, there are always some differences. One can't assume that because two things are alike in some respects, they are alike in all respects. Consider the following example.

> Learning to write a good essay is like learning to drive a car. Beginning drivers feel overwhelmed by the number of operations they must perform to keep a car moving—controlling the brake and the accelerator, staying in their lane, watching the cars in front of them while keeping an eye on the rear-view mirror. In addition, they must observe all traffic laws. The tasks seem insurmountable. Yet, in time, some of the operations become almost automatic and the drivers relax enough so that they can even look at the scenery now and then. So it is with beginning writers. At first, they wonder how they can make an outline for a paper, write clear topic sentences, develop paragraphs, provide transitions, write good introductions and conclusions, and still observe all the rules of English grammar. As with driving, part of the process eventually becomes automatic, and the writers relax enough to concentrate primarily on the ideas they wish to develop.

The comparison deals only with the similarities of feelings in the two experiences and is a successful analogy because it clarifies the experience of writing for the beginner. But if one extends the comparison to encompass other demands on drivers—checking antifreeze, acquiring new windshield wipers, renewing license plates, repairing flats, maintaining brake fluid—the analogy falls apart.

Historical analogies present a similar problem. We can't assume that because two historical events are alike in some respects, the outcomes will inevitably be the same. You have probably heard the argument that the United States is on the verge of collapse because some conditions here—relaxed sexual mores, widespread demand for immediate pleasure, and political cynicism and corruption—parallel those of the Roman Empire just before its fall. The argument doesn't consider, among other things, that the forms of government differ, that the bases for the economy differ, or that the means of educating the population differ. The two societies are not alike in every respect, and one cannot assume that because one society fell, the other also will fall.

Analogy can be useful for clarifying an idea, but argument by analogy can be dangerous.

EXERCISE

Following are examples of logical fallacies. Read them, and determine what type of fallacy each most strongly represents.

1. I lost my wallet yesterday. I knew that walking under that ladder in the morning would be trouble!
2. Yesterday, my neighbor's sixteen-year-old son zoomed out of the driveway in his new car and barely missed my daughter, who was riding her tricycle on the sidewalk. Last week, a seventeen-year-old girl hit the rear of my car when I had to stop suddenly for a traffic light. When are we going to come to our senses and raise the legal driving age to twenty-one?
3. How can she be guilty of that crime? She has such a lovely family—they go to church regularly and are such friendly people.

4. Of course she's poor. Look at that old torn coat she's wearing!
5. How can Senator O'Malley speak for labor? What does he know about the needs of the average worker? He was born rich.

WRITING YOUR ARGUMENTATION PAPER

Argumentation papers must draw on controversial subject matter—that is, the possibility for a difference of opinion on the subject must exist. Otherwise, there would be no need to argue. That does not mean, however, that the subject matter need be earthshaking. Writers differ on how to interpret poems or on how to bake cakes. In the sense that the purpose of an argumentation paper is to persuade a reader to a point of view, you have written argumentation papers since you began your study of English composition. In every paper, you have taken a position on a subject and have offered logical reasons for holding that position.

Writing a Formal Argument

A formal argumentation paper has its own specific requirements. In a formal argument, the writer should follow certain guidelines.

TIPS **FOR WRITING A FORMAL ARGUMENT**

- State the problem or issue, sometimes tracing its causes.
- In some cases, state the possible positions to be taken on the problem.
- State the position that the paper will take.
- Offer supporting detail that the position taken is the reasonable one to hold.
- Anticipate objections to the position and acknowledge or refute them.
- Affirm the position and make a final appeal.

All these requirements are important, but we want especially to note the importance of the next to the last point. Anticipating objections to your position, presenting them in your paper, and admitting or refuting them are key features of the strong argumentative essay.

Developing a Debatable Position

You know all about limiting a topic to suit the time and requirements of the assignment, but in an argumentation paper, there's another key element in regard to selecting your topic. Your topic and thesis must lend themselves to debate. If people can take sides on the issue, you've probably chosen a good topic. Of course, you have to know it well and be able to argue it convincingly. To check on whether your thesis is a good one, always ask yourself this question: Would anyone care to debate it?

Possible Thesis	Is It Debatable?
The scientific community should work hard to find a cure for cancer.	**No.** Who would dispute this statement? It's not a good topic for an argument paper.
We should stop using live animals for scientific testing.	**Yes.** Many disagree and feel that animal testing is essential if we are to make advances in medicine.
Gay couples should have the same marital rights as heterosexual couples.	**Yes.** This is a heated topic in today's society, and many people believe that laws should prevent gay marriage.
People who own pets should clean up their animals' mess from city streets.	**Possibly but not probably.** Few would disagree that someone must clean up after pets; unless the argument is that someone other than the owners should address the problem, or that city-dwellers should not be allowed to own pets at all, this is not a viable argument.
We should provide high quality schools for our children.	**No.** No one would debate this assertion.
I believe in a citizen's right not to vote.	**Yes.** Clearly this is a contrarian position, and many people would be happy to debate it.

STRATEGY CHECKLIST: Writing and Revising Your Argumentation Paper

Plan the paper.

❏ Have I identified a topic and a debatable position? Is there clearly one or more positions that might oppose mine?

❏ Have I used prewriting to stimulate my thoughts?

❏ Have I paid attention to peer comments about my prewriting?

❏ Have I weighed my audience and purpose?

❏ Have I done any necessary research at the library and online?

❏ Have I considered using an outline to lay out my argument and the specific details to support it?

Write a first draft.	❏ Have I written a thesis that expresses my position on the debatable topic?
	❏ Have I developed an introduction to set the context for my position?
	❏ Have I used a tone suitable to my position on the topic?

- Calm and reasonable
- Emotional
- Ironic
- Humorous
- Angry
- Other tone

❏ Have I used appropriate strategies to advance my argument?

- Description
- Narration
- Example
- Process
- Comparison and contrast
- Classification and division
- Cause and effect
- Definition

❏ Have I used induction and deduction to make my points?

❏ Have I presented supporting details in the body paragraphs of my essay?

- Relevant
- Sufficient
- From credible sources
- Documented if necessary

❏ Have I anticipated and refuted opposing positions?

Revise and edit the paper.

❏ Do my examples and details properly support my argument?

❏ Will the manner in which I've argued my position suit the audience I have in mind?

❏ Are my inductions and syllogisms logical?

❏ Are there any logical fallacies that I should revise?

❏ Have I considered my opponents thoughtfully and courteously?

❏ Have I made the argument successfully in the space and time I have available, or should I limit my topic further?

❏ Should I add or remove supporting evidence?

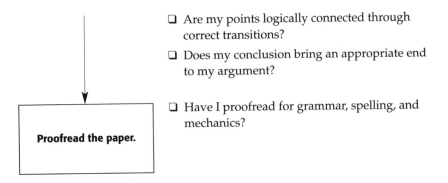

❏ Are my points logically connected through correct transitions?

❏ Does my conclusion bring an appropriate end to my argument?

❏ Have I proofread for grammar, spelling, and mechanics?

Proofread the paper.

Writing Topics

If you are having difficulty deciding on a topic for your argumentation paper, you might find help simply by choosing one of the following statements and arguing for or against that statement.

1. The media unfairly hound celebrities accused of crimes.
2. The United States government should reinstitute the draft for all men and women eighteen years and older.
3. Reality TV should really be called unreality TV.
4. The sale of tobacco should be made illegal.
5. Among the groups most unfairly discriminated against are over-weight people.
6. If we require people to pass a driving test before licensing them to operate a car, we should require people to pass some kind of parenting test before allowing them to have children.
7. Marijuana should be legal for medicinal purposes.
8. As an exercise, swimming far exceeds running as a means to health and fitness.
9. The pollution of the world's oceans is a major threat to humanity.
10. Random drug tests of high school students are a violation of human rights.

21

Doing Research

A research paper (or research essay or library paper or term paper) is a nearly universal assignment in your first-year English course and in many other courses.

CHOOSING YOUR SUBJECT

As you think about formulating a subject for your research paper, follow some of the prewriting strategies you explored in Chapter 3. Surf the Web to explore a range of approaches to your subject. Make a rough list. Use free association. Brainstorm on a topic that seems even remotely interesting. Talk at length with roommates, friends, teachers, relatives, employers, coworkers—with anyone who will listen. Watch television talk shows or documentaries related to your subject. Browse in libraries and bookstores. Study newspapers, magazines, and journals; a word or two in a headline or title may catch your eye and get you thinking. Some background reading in a general encyclopedia like the *Encyclopaedia Britannica* may provide a useful overview of your topic.

Once you have even a vague notion of a topic that interests you, think about it for a while. Consider whether it's too broad. Remember the importance of limiting your subject. "Custer's Last Stand" and "The Lizzie Borden Murder Case" might make good papers, but you could not write a good paper of reasonable length on a topic like "Famous Battles" or "Great Trials" because it's too broad.

One final suggestion: Don't be too eager to settle on any single topic immediately. If you have two or three possibilities in mind, so much the better. There may not be as much information available on your first choice as you had hoped, and it's comforting to have something ready to fall back on.

DEVELOPING YOUR THESIS

Virtually every research paper requires that you gather facts and opinions (sometimes conflicting) from a variety of sources and that you organize and present them in your own words and style through your own hard work. Every research paper also requires that you document whatever sources you have used. When you document a source, you tell the reader where you found information taken from someone else's writing. Typical documentation includes the author's name, the title of the selection, and important publication data. You'll read more about documentation in Chapter 23.

However, the most important kind of research paper does more than cite sources—it has as its basis a **thesis**. Most teachers want students to use research in order to develop opinions of their own and to present those opinions in a carefully documented paper. Hence, in a research paper with a thesis, you do extensive investigation to find facts, but you also interpret those facts and you try to persuade the reader that your interpretation or opinion is correct. Rather than merely stating the facts, you use them to support your opinion. The thesis drives the research you present to your readers.

Developing a thesis is critical to writing a successful research paper. For the sample paper "The Banning of the Polygraph," which appears in Chapter 23, student writer Elizabeth Kessler arrived at this thesis sentence after conducting some research on her topic.

Thesis 1

Many employers have used polygraph testing as a means for determining the honesty of future employees.

As Kessler considered this thesis sentence, she realized that it makes a simple assertion of fact but offers no opportunity for interpretation or judgment. She then revised her thesis sentence as follows:

Thesis 2

Supporters and critics battle the merits and drawbacks of lie detector tests.

We see a clear topic statement in this sentence and, on the surface, what seems to be strong opinions about the topic. Yet the more Kessler thought about the topic, the more she realized that her own opinion was absent from the thesis statement. She again had made an assertion of fact: Some people supported the polygraph test and others opposed it. As she pondered the question "How do I feel about using the polygraph test in job-related situations?" and started shaping an early draft, Kessler wrote this thesis sentence:

Thesis 3

My own research indicates that the polygraph test as a condition for employment is highly unfair.

Here Kessler's interpretation of the topic is clear: Required polygraph testing for a job is not fair. As you will see when you examine her paper, as Kessler continued her research, she changed her thesis again.

DOING PRELIMINARY READING

Once you have an idea of the topic or topics you're interested in, it's time for a close look at reliable Web sites and a trip to the library. Your purpose now is to do some fairly easygoing "reading around." You want to make sure that the subject that seems so interesting when you think about it is still interesting when you read about it. You want to acquire enough of a general perspective on your subject to be able to respond thoughtfully when you begin more serious and detailed reading.

Your librarian will direct you to general encyclopedias for an overview of your topic and will also show you where to find any specialized reference works that can help you get started. You'll no doubt want to "Google" your subject to identify useful Web sites. When you do, you should note the overwhelming number of potential resources (sometimes millions) that appear for your topic. Next, even on the first page of entries, you face an incredible mix of links to examine for further information. You no doubt will find a column with the heading "Sponsored Links," which is a list of advertisers, people, and companies who pay to have their sites listed and have commercial services to offer. They want you to buy something from them.

As for the other entries, you have to judge the quality of the site before you can rely on it as a valid resource. In some cases you can tell the nature of the site from the descriptions below the highlighted link and can reject any that seem irrelevant to your purpose; or you can go immediately to any that seem useful. Review pages 14–16 on "Reading and Evaluating Web Sites."

PREPARING YOUR PRELIMINARY OUTLINE

If all goes well in your preliminary reading, you should be in a position to draw up a **preliminary outline**, or **rough outline**, indicating the major divisions of your paper.

Here is Elizabeth Kessler's rough outline for her research paper:

Topic/Thesis: Polygraph Testing on the Job

1. Cost
2. Reliability
3. Accuracy
4. Relation between guilt and physical measures from test
5. Consequences of test on person's life

This outline, based on preliminary reading, guided Kessler's deeper probing into sources related to her topic and her ultimate writing of drafts for the paper. The outline changed many times—compare it with the items in her formal outline on pages 168–169. At this stage, a preliminary outline is a useful guide to further thinking about your topic.

FINDING SOURCES AND DEVELOPING A WORKING CITATIONS LIST

When you complete your rough outline, it's time for serious research and reading, and that brings us to the subject of your sources. When you write the final draft of your research paper, you'll have to include a list of works cited, which is an alphabetical list of the books, articles, Web sites, and other sources that you refer to in the text of your essay. To prepare for that effort, you want to develop a **working citation list** that records key information about each source. For each book, article, and Web site you find, you will need to note authors' names, titles, and publication data. Since you cannot know in advance which sources will contain useful information, you should record information for all the sources that you consult.

Evaluating Your Sources

In an age of information overload, facts and opinions bombard us from more sources than we could ever imagine. Newspapers, magazines, journals, Web sites, broadcast and cable television, pamphlets, newsletters, advertisements—everywhere someone is trying to influence the way we think and act. As you explore your research topic, you need to be sure that the sources you are using are valid and appropriate to serve as support for your paper. Not everything in print is legitimate enough to use as a resource, and you have to learn to evaluate the sources that you consider using.

TIPS **FOR EVALUATING SOURCES**

- **Identify the author and publisher.** Find out what you can about the person or entity that produced the material. What credentials do they offer? Some publishers lean toward publishing only those books that reinforce their own views. Sometimes a book or Web site has a corporate author; sometimes a professional organization will produce a source. You need to know about the producer of the source.
- **Check the date that the source was published.** Information is often outdated by new research and developments in a field. By checking the date of publication, you will know how recent the work is and whether the facts are still valid. Authors and publishers sometimes revise books to bring facts into line with current data.
- **Find out what other experts say about your source.** Many scholarly journals regularly review books in their field, and you want to know what others think of the source or writer that you have chosen. Does the writer have a

reputation as a particular kind of thinker—liberal or conservative, democrat or republican, radical or reactionary or progressive?

- **Weigh the evidence provided.** Be sure that the writer's logic is clear and supported by the facts at hand. Does the writer draw upon reliable data and identify the sources of those data? Does the writer avoid any relevant issues or treat them too lightly?
- **Have a reason for choosing one source over another.** Be sure that you can justify your selection of a source. If your professor or a librarian recommended it, so much the better. Often, many books are available on a topic; clearly, you can't choose them all. But you should have a reason other than simple convenience for choosing one book instead of another.
- **Be aware of the purpose of the source.** Your source may want to entertain, inform, shape opinion about an issue, supply information, publish new and dramatic research—there are other reasons certainly. The writer's purpose always contributes to the validity of the source material. And you want to know just what point of view your source takes.
- **Be especially cautious about any Web-based material that you want to use.** Always check the date, author, sponsor, philosophical position, and intent of any Web site or other Internet sources.

Keeping Records for Your Sources

As you find each source for your paper, you should record the information you will need to prepare your source list (called a Works Cited list in MLA format papers and a References list in APA format papers). There are many ways you can record source information. You can use index cards, Word files on a computer, a notebook, or even a software program that prepares citations.

An efficient way to prepare your working list is with **index cards**. For each promising title you find, make out a 3 × 5-inch card. Obviously, you will not use all the sources for which you make cards, but it saves time to make cards for any title that might be useful before you begin your reading. Cards are easy to handle, and they permit you to add new sources and to delete sources that turn out to be useless. Cards can also be alphabetized easily, which will save you time when you make up your final list of works cited.

Whether you use cards or another method, each source record should include all the relevant data that you will need to write a proper entry for your list of works cited. Take time to prepare complete source records as you go along because, again, following the appropriate procedure now will save time and frustration when you write your paper later on. Follow the format of the samples that follow as you prepare your own source records.

Source Records for Books

Source records for books should include the following information. A sample record appears below.

- The author's name
- For an essay, a poem, a short story, or a play in a collection, the title of the relevant selection, enclosed in quotation marks
- The title of the book
- The city in which the book was published
- The name of the publishing company
- The copyright date
- The complete call number of the book. If you do not have the correct call number, you will not be able to locate the book.
- Edition and revision information, if any
- For multivolume works, the overall number of volumes and the specific number used
- If the book is edited, the editor's name
- If the book is translated, the translator's name

Source Record for a Book

Call number ————————➤	363.254 ALD
Author ————————➤	Alder, Ken
Title ————————➤	*The Lie Detectors: The History of an American Obsession*
Place of publication ————➤	New York
Publisher ————————➤	Free Press
Year of publication ————➤ (copyright date)	2007
Medium of publication ————➤	Print

Corresponding MLA Citation in Works Cited List

Alder, Ken. *The Lie Detectors: The History of an American Obsession*. New York: Free P, 2007. Print.

Look ahead to pages 176–178 for the various works cited formats required for a wide variety of books that you might find in your research. These formats tell you what information to include in your preliminary citation records.

Source Records for Periodical Articles

Source records for periodicals should include the following information. A sample record appears below.

- The author's name, if one is given
- The title of the article
- The name of the magazine, journal, or newspaper
- The publication date
- The inclusive page numbers
- For a newspaper, the section number or letter and the edition, when given on the masthead
- For a scholarly journal article, the volume and issue numbers, when given
- For a scholarly journal article from an online database, the database name and date of access
- For APA style citations, record the DOI (digital object identifier) when given

Source Record for a Journal Article from an Online Database

Authors ----------------------------------➤ Grubin, Don, & Madsen, Lars

Title of article ------------------------➤ "Lie Detection and the Polygraph: A Historical Review"

Periodical name ---------------------➤ *Journal of Forensic Psychiatry & Psychology*

Date of publication ----------------➤ June 2005

Volume and issue numbers ------➤ Vol. 16, Issue 2

Page numbers -------------------------➤ 357–69

Database name ----------------------➤ ContentSelect Research Navigator

DOI (needed for APA ---------------➤ 10.1080/14789940412331337353
style citations)

Medium of publication -------------➤ Web

Date accessed -------------------------➤ 17 Mar. 2008

Corresponding MLA Citation in Works Cited List

Grubin, Don, and Lars Madsen. "Lie Detection and the Polygraph: A Historical Review." *Journal of Forensic Psychiatry and Psychology* 16:2 (2005): 357–69. *ContentSelect Research Navigator*. Web. 17 Mar. 2008.

Pages 175–176 provide examples of the different formats used for citing articles in the list of works cited. Examine these examples carefully as you prepare your source records.

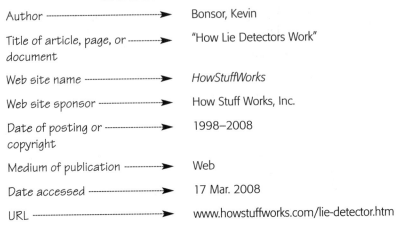

Source Record for World Wide Web Source

Author ————————————➤ Bonsor, Kevin

Title of article, page, or ————➤ "How Lie Detectors Work"
document

Web site name ————————➤ *HowStuffWorks*

Web site sponsor —————————➤ How Stuff Works, Inc.

Date of posting or —————————➤ 1998–2008
copyright

Medium of publication ————➤ Web

Date accessed ————————————➤ 17 Mar. 2008

URL ——————————————————➤ www.howstuffworks.com/lie-detector.htm

Corresponding MLA Citation in Works Cited List

Bonsor, Kevin. "How Lie Detectors Work." *HowStuffWorks*. HowStuffWorks, 1998–2008. Web. 3 Mar. 2008.

Source Records for Worldwide Web Sources

If you are taking material from the general access World Wide Web portion of the Internet, record information using the format in the sample above. The following list indicates most parts of an entry for an Internet publication as well as their order in an entry. Some information you record may not appear in the works cited entry but will help you find your source again.

- Author's name—or the name of the editor, compiler, or translator
- Document title (article, poem, essay, or other short work) *or* title of posting to discussion list or forum (taken from subject line)
- Title of book or periodical, if any
- Name of editor, compiler, or translator of text, if relevant
- Publication information of the print version of the source, if any
- Title of Internet site—online periodical, scholarly project, or personal or professional site (italicized)—or, if a personal or professional site without a title, some description such as *Home page*
- Name of site's sponsor
- For an article, volume and issue numbers, or the version number of the source if not part of the title
- Date of electronic publication, latest update, or posting
- For a posting to a discussion list or forum, name the list or forum

- Number range or total number of pages, sections, or paragraphs, if numbered
- Medium of publication (Web)
- Date when the researcher accessed the source
- The URL for the source

An important caution: URLs can be long and complicated in their use of letters and symbols. Record them carefully and accurately. Use the copy and paste function in your word processing software to ensure the accuracy of the URL.

STRATEGY CHECKLIST: **First Steps in Doing Research**

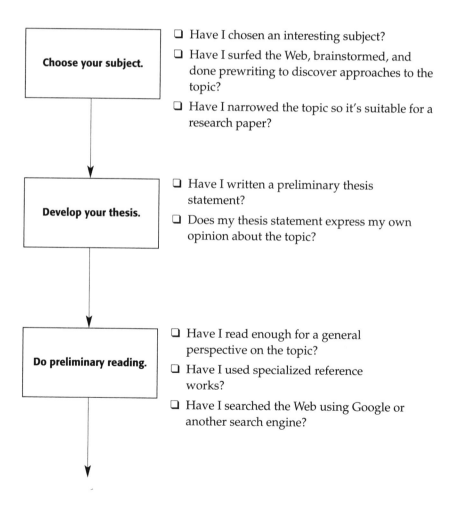

Choose your subject.

- ❏ Have I chosen an interesting subject?
- ❏ Have I surfed the Web, brainstormed, and done prewriting to discover approaches to the topic?
- ❏ Have I narrowed the topic so it's suitable for a research paper?

Develop your thesis.

- ❏ Have I written a preliminary thesis statement?
- ❏ Does my thesis statement express my own opinion about the topic?

Do preliminary reading.

- ❏ Have I read enough for a general perspective on the topic?
- ❏ Have I used specialized reference works?
- ❏ Have I searched the Web using Google or another search engine?

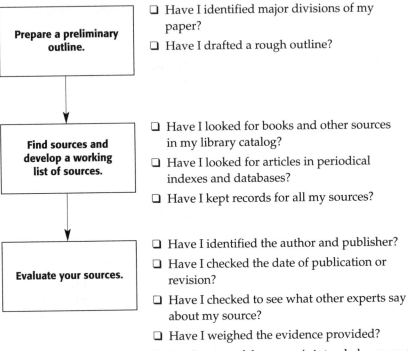

Prepare a preliminary outline.

❏ Have I identified major divisions of my paper?

❏ Have I drafted a rough outline?

Find sources and develop a working list of sources.

❏ Have I looked for books and other sources in my library catalog?

❏ Have I looked for articles in periodical indexes and databases?

❏ Have I kept records for all my sources?

Evaluate your sources.

❏ Have I identified the author and publisher?

❏ Have I checked the date of publication or revision?

❏ Have I checked to see what other experts say about my source?

❏ Have I weighed the evidence provided?

❏ Am I aware of the source's intended purpose?

❏ Was I especially careful about Web-based sources?

22

Selecting, Organizing, and Integrating Source Material in Your Writing

What do you look for when taking notes? You should look for any fact, idea, or opinion not generally known that appears to relate to your topic. It's easier to take a few extra notes than it is to go back to the library and reread a book or an article or to an electronic source when you discover, after you start writing the paper, that you don't have enough evidence to make a point.

TAKING NOTES

Be certain to not simply take notes at random. You have begun your research with at least a vague idea of what you want to say. The sooner the idea becomes definite, the more directed and less time-consuming your note taking will become. But don't worry if you find yourself taking many notes from the first sources you read. After all, the subject is fairly new to you, and everything about it may seem important. You should soon get a focus on the material, and then you can become more selective in the notes you take.

Limit your subject and your approach to it as soon as you can, so you can perform the job of note taking efficiently.

Recording Quotations

When you **quote** a source, you use the exact wording from that source to convey facts or ideas contained in it. Quotation marks must enclose the material that you quote. Be certain that you copy the quotation *exactly* as it appears in the original. If the original contains an obvious error, copy the error and follow it with *sic* (the Latin word for "thus") in brackets.

Occasionally, you may want to quote only parts of an entire passage. If you leave out a whole paragraph or more, indicate the omission by placing spaced dots all the way across the note. If you leave out a part of a sentence or one or two sentences, use three spaced dots (an *ellipsis*) to indicate the omission. For an ellipsis within a sentence, use a space before the first period and after the last period as well. If you omit the beginning of a sentence, place the quotation marks before the ellipsis. If you omit the end of a sentence, place the quotation mark after the ellipsis and the end punctuation (period, question mark, or exclamation point).

A few words of caution about using the ellipsis: Never alter the meaning of the original by using an ellipsis. If the original statement reads, "This is not the most exciting movie of the year," using an ellipsis to omit the word *not* would be dishonest. Second, be sure that you still have a complete sentence when you use the ellipsis. Don't omit from the sentence important elements such as subjects and verbs.

When quoting, you may find it necessary to clarify a word or date in the original quotation because you are taking the words out of context. If you want to insert a word, phrase, or figure into the quotation, do so by putting the information in brackets: "He [Lincoln] suffered extreme hardships." Or the original might read, "in that year, he faced the greatest crisis of his life." The sentence, taken out of context, does not identify the year. You would want to insert it: "in that year [1839], he faced the greatest crisis of his life."

Summarizing and Paraphrasing in Your Notes

Despite this advice on how to use quotations in your research and note taking, you should quote sparingly. In your notes you should summarize or paraphrase most of the original material.

A **summary** is a short restatement of the original source in your own words. A **paraphrase** is a more expanded summary, often contains words taken from the original, and generally follows both the sequence and the logic of the original source. Often, paraphrase and summary work hand in hand.

When Elizabeth Kessler researched her topic, she found the following passage useful (from page 132 of *Science vs. Crime: The Hunt for Truth* by Eugene B. Block).

Original Source

In the first part of the nineteenth century, Cesare Lombroso pioneered in experiments with the heartbeat as a means of detecting lying, an interesting forerunner of today's polygraph, which has now advanced far beyond the early concepts of the distinguished Italian, utilizing not only heartbeats but changes in respiration and blood pressure to determine the truth or falsity of an answer.

In her notes, shown on page 163, she recorded the exact words of the original source, enclosed in quotation marks. The ellipsis—the three spaced dots following the word *polygraph*—indicates that Kessler omitted a portion of the quote from the original (the words "which has now advanced far beyond the early concepts of the distinguished Italian"). Further, she uses an asterisk to flag concerns that she will consider later on, when she reviews her note cards.

Note Containing a Direct Quotation

> *Block,* Science vs. Crime *132*
>
> "In the first part of the nineteenth century, Cesare Lombroso pioneered in experiments with the heartbeat as a means of detecting lying, an interesting forerunner of today's polygraph…utilizing not only heartbeats but changes in respiration and blood pressure to determine the truth or falsity of an answer."
> *Check earlier work on lie detection. 18th century? earlier?

In a paraphrase of the original source, Kessler uses her own language, blending in some of Block's words and enclosing them in quotation marks.

Note Containing a Summary/Paraphrase of the Original Material

> *Block,* Science vs. Crime *132*
>
> In the early 1800s, Cesare Lombroso used heartbeats in experiments to detect lies; his work anticipated the modern polygraph, which measures heartbeats as well as "changes in respiration and blood pressure to determine the truth or falsity of an answer."

Combining paraphrases and direct quotations is a good note-taking strategy. It allows you to capture the writer's main idea in your own language and to record some of the writer's own words for possible quotation in your paper.

QUOTING AND PARAPHRASING YOUR SOURCES IN YOUR PAPER

Your outline is a kind of X-ray of your awaiting paragraphs—only the bare bones showing. Consider how to flesh out the sentences and develop the paragraphs of your research essay. To support the points made in your paper, you need to quote or paraphrase the information you found in other sources. Most important, however, you need to connect your own writing style smoothly with the comments drawn from other writers. Your note cards with quotations and paraphrases from your sources are now your major resource.

Quoting an Original Source

Assume that you want to use selected source material in your paper. You might want to quote your source exactly—using one or more phrases to several sentences to even a whole paragraph, depending on your purpose. In the following example, note the smooth connection between the student Elizabeth Kessler's words and the words of her source.

Agencies of the United States government have relied on lie detector tests in important legal matters:

> The FBI uses polygraphs mostly to probe leads and verify specific facts....The agency also employs highly trained examiners, who usually spend half a day on each session....Attorney General Benjamin Civiletti has ruled that an "adverse inference" may be drawn if an employee of the FBI or any other part of the Justice Department balks at submitting to the machines. (Beach 44)

The writer introduces the long supporting quotation with a sentence of her own. The **block format** is used to set off a quotation of four or more typed lines from the text of the essay. The ellipsis (...) allows the writer to omit a portion of the quotation. Quotation marks are not used in a block quotation; rather, a one-inch indentation at the left margin sets off the quote. However, when quotation marks appear in the original, as in "adverse inference" in the preceding example, the quotation marks are included in the block quotation as well.

In the following example, Kessler uses shorter quotations from the same source to support her point. However, here the quotations are carefully integrated with the writer's own words and are in each case enclosed by quotation marks.

> Not only does private industry use lie detectors but the federal government does also. "The FBI," reports Beach, "uses polygraphs mostly to probe leads and verify specific facts, areas in which, experts concede, the machines are at their best." To assure a higher degree of accuracy than in other testing situations, no doubt, the FBI "employs highly trained examiners, who usually spend half a day on each session (compared with an average of an hour in private industry)" (44).

Paraphrasing an Original Source

You may also choose to paraphrase the source material. In the following example, Kessler skillfully expresses the point made by her source. Quotation marks surround the phrase "balks at submitting to the machines" because it is quoted from the original. Note how Kessler attributes the information to her source and cites the page number for the material she uses.

> As Beach points out, the FBI (as might be expected) uses polygraph testing to aid in major investigations. Yet employees also are expected to take the test. It is clear that the FBI views in a negative light any employee who "balks at submitting to the machines" (44).

Direct Quotations: How Many?

All the rules of good writing that you have learned so far apply to the research paper. But, as you have seen, the research paper presents a special challenge: You must make borrowed material a part of your own statement. You have spent several weeks now taking notes; you have studied them and have decided how to organize them, and that is half the battle. If, however, you simply string quotations together, you will not be writing a research paper; you will be merely transcribing your notes. The paper must be yours—your idea, your organization, and, for the most part, your words. You should use the notes to support your ideas, which means that you should integrate the notes into your own statements. Otherwise, you do not have an honest research paper.

In the following excerpt from a student paper, the writer merely strings quotations together:

> W. E. B. DuBois said in *The Souls of Black Folk* that "the problem of the twentieth century is the problem of the color line" (xiv).
>
> DuBois became aware of racial differences at an early age. He related this experience vividly:
>> The shades of the prison-house closed around about us all: the walls strait and stubborn to the whitest, but relentlessly narrow, tall, and unscalable to sons of night who must plod darkly on in resignation, or beat unavailing palms against the stone, or steadily, half hopelessly, watch the streak of blue above. (16)
>
> When his infant son died, DuBois was depressed, yet he rejoiced because his son would not have to endure life "behind the veil" (155):
>> No bitter meanness now shall sicken his baby heart till it die a living death, no taunt shall madden his happy boyhood. Fool that I was to think or wish that this little soul should grow choked and deformed within the veil!...Well sped, my boy, before the world had dubbed your ambition insolence, had held your ideals unattainable, and taught you to cringe and bow. Better for this nameless void that stops my life than a sea of sorrow for you. (155–56)

The student here has simply copied her notes into the paper. She could make the point more clearly if she phrased it largely in her own words, as in this example:

> W. E. B. DuBois, who said in *The Souls of Black Folk* that "the problem of the twentieth century is the problem of the color line" (xiv), came to believe that dreams of opportunities and fulfillment were reserved solely for whites, and he compared the life of blacks in America with that of prison inmates (16). Indeed, he grew so bitter about the plight of blacks that he rejoiced when his infant son died because the child would never have to experience the prejudice that he had felt (155–56).

In this version, the writer composed a unified paragraph that makes the point clearly without the overuse of quotations. (A good, safe rule of thumb is, unless the subject of your paper is an author's style, quote no more than 10 percent of your paper.)

AVOIDING PLAGIARISM

Unless the material you borrow is as well known as the Gettysburg Address, when you take facts or ideas from someone else, you must credit the source. This does not mean that you will have to credit almost every sentence in your papers.

You should cite all direct quotations that are not well known. You should also cite all facts and opinions that are not common knowledge—*even when you have put the facts or opinions into your own words*. Two kinds of facts or opinions come under the heading *common knowledge*: (1) facts everyone in our culture is expected to know (George Washington was the first president of the United States, for example), and (2) facts that are common knowledge in the field you are investigating. Suppose you are writing a paper on Custer's last stand. You might not have known, when you began reading, the name of the Indian tribe that fought Custer and his men. If every source you read, however, says that it was the Sioux tribe, you would not need to give a citation for that fact. Nor would it be necessary to credit the opinion that Custer blundered; most historians agree that he did. But any theories about why Custer led his men into such a trap should be credited.

If you do not pay careful attention to the techniques of quoting and crediting sources, you run the risk of being accused of plagiarism. **Plagiarism** is the use of facts, opinions, and language taken from another writer without acknowledgment. At its worst, plagiarism is outright theft or cheating: A person has another person write the paper or simply steals a magazine article or section of a book and pretends to have produced a piece of original writing. You're bound to see offers to purchase research papers online: This is another invitation to a plagiarism disaster. Common among students is plagiarism in dribs and drabs—a sentence here and there, a paragraph here and there. For your own safety and self-respect, remember the following rules—not guidelines, *rules*:

- The language in your paper must either be your own or a direct and credited quote from the original source.
- Changing a few words or phrases from another writer's work is not enough to make the writing "your own." Remember rule 1: The writing is either your own or the other person's; there are no in-betweens.
- Documentation acknowledges that the fact or opinion expressed comes from another writer. If the language comes from another writer, quotation marks are necessary in addition to documentation.

Now for a detailed example.

Original Passage

In 1925 Dreiser produced his masterpiece, the massively impressive *An American Tragedy*. By this time—thanks largely to the tireless propagandizing on his behalf by the influential maverick critic H. L. Mencken and by others concerned with a realistic approach to the problems of American life—Dreiser's fame had become secure. He was seen as the most powerful and effective destroyer of the genteel tradition that had dominated popular American fiction in the post–Civil War period, spreading its soft blanket of provincial, sentimental romance over the often ugly realities of life in modern, industrialized, urban America. Certainly there was nothing genteel about Dreiser, either as man or novelist. He was the supreme poet of the squalid, a man who felt the terror, the pity, and the beauty underlying the American dream. (Richard Freedman, *The Novel* [New York: Newsweek Books, 1975], 104–05)

Student version	Comment
There was nothing genteel about Dreiser, either as man or novelist. He was the supreme poet of the squalid, a man who felt the terror, the pity, and the beauty underlying the American dream.	**Obvious plagiarism.** Student version contains word-for-word repetition without acknowledgment.
There was nothing genteel about Dreiser, either as man or novelist. He was the supreme poet of the squalid, a man who felt the terror, the pity, and the beauty underlying the American dream (Freedman 104).	**Still plagiarism.** *The documentation alone does not help.* The language is the original author's, and only quotation marks around the whole passage plus documentation would be correct.
Nothing was genteel about Dreiser as a man or as a novelist. He was the poet of the squalid and felt that terror, pity, and beauty lurked under the American dream.	**Still plagiarism.** The writer has changed or omitted a few words, but by no stretch of the imagination is the student using original language.
"Nothing was genteel about Dreiser as a man or as a novelist. He was the poet of the squalid and felt that terror, pity, and beauty lurked under the American dream" (Freedman 104).	**Not quite plagiarism,** but incorrect and inaccurate. Quotation marks indicate exact repetition of what was originally written. The student, however, has changed some of the original and is not entitled to use quotation marks.
"Certainly there was nothing genteel about Dreiser, either as man or novelist. He was the supreme poet of the squalid, a man who felt the terror, the pity, and the beauty underlying the American dream" (Freedman 104).	**Correct.** The quotation marks acknowledge the words of the original writer. The documentation is also needed, of course, to give the reader specific information about the source of the quote.

Student version	Comment
By 1925 Dreiser's reputation was firmly established. The reading public viewed Dreiser as one of the main contributors to the downfall of the "genteel tradition" in American literature. Dreiser, "the supreme poet of the squalid," looked beneath the bright surface of American life and values and described the frightening and tragic elements, the "ugly realities," so often over-looked by other writers (Freedman 104).	**Correct.** The student writer uses her own words to summarize most of the original passage. The documentation shows that the ideas expressed come from the original writer, not from the student. The few phrases kept from the original passage are carefully enclosed in quotation marks.

PREPARING YOUR FORMAL OUTLINE

Start by reading and rereading all your notes carefully. You have accumulated the notes over a period of weeks, and you may not know precisely what material you have gathered.

Develop a formal outline. Either a topic outline or a sentence outline is acceptable (see Chapter 5). However, if you plan to prove a thesis, it is probably wise to make a sentence outline; doing so will force you to state in a complete thought how each section of your paper contributes to the thesis. Observe all the conventions of good outlining as you write. For a long and complex paper, it's usually a good idea to add a category labeled *conclusion* to your formal outline.

Look at the topic outline for Elizabeth Kessler's paper, which appears below and on the next page. After her thesis statement, which is a complete sentence, note the three major divisions, each labeled with a roman numeral—I, II, III. First-level sub-divisions appear beside uppercase letters—A, B, C, and so on. Second-level divisions appear beside arabic numbers—1, 2, 3. Note, too, the full-sentence statement of a conclusion here. For Kessler, the outline served as a starting point for the paragraphs she developed in an early draft. Ultimately she made many changes in the order of the elements and in the language of the various outline points. Like your thesis, your outline will change as your thoughts develop on your topic.

Keep in mind that your formal outline should serve as a guide as you develop and refine the various drafts of your paper. As new ideas develop, change your outline as necessary. If you find yourself drifting away from the topic, use your outline to draw you back.

Topic Outline: Polygraph Testing

Thesis: The polygraph test should not be used as part of employment decisions.

I. Arguments of polygraph test supporters

    A. Inexpensive and valid way to identify potential thieves on the job

    B. Reliable findings

    C. Well-trained examiners

II. Arguments of those who oppose polygraph tests

    A. "Toothless" laws

    B. Examiners poor

    C. Inaccurate readings

    D. Physiological displays of guilt not measurable

    E. Human rights violations

        1. Loss of employment

        2. Invasion of privacy

        3. Reputations destroyed

III. Federal legislation against polygraph testing

    A. No polygraph screening for employment

    B. Defined testing procedures

    C. Employee rights

<u>Conclusion</u>—In spite of a recent national law, polygraph testing should be banned in the workplace.

STRATEGY CHECKLIST: Selecting, Organizing, and Integrating Source Material

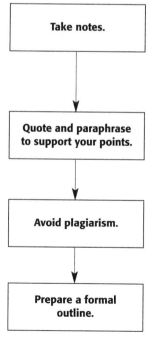

Take notes.

❏ Have I taken notes selectively but adequately for my topic?

❏ Have I recorded quotations accurately?

❏ Have I used summary and paraphrase wisely in my notes?

Quote and paraphrase to support your points.

❏ Have I made smooth connections between my writing and words from my source?

❏ Was I careful not to overuse quotations in the paper?

Avoid plagiarism.

❏ Did I cite all quoted sources?

❏ Did I cite all facts and opinions that are not common knowledge, even if I state them in my own words?

Prepare a formal outline.

❏ Have I observed the conventions of outline format?

❏ Have I used my outline as a flexible guide to writing my drafts?

23

Writing Your Research Paper and Citing and Documenting Sources

WRITING YOUR RESEARCH PAPER: AN OVERVIEW

Writing a research paper involves all the same challenges as writing an essay, and a few additional challenges as well. In writing the paper, you will have to document your sources according to MLA or APA style and prepare the final copy using conventional MLA or APA formats. It's time to set your notes aside, put your outline in front of you, and start writing.

The First Draft

In the first draft, the point is to get your ideas down on paper. Don't worry about grammar or punctuation. Don't try to work in quotations from your sources. You should be familiar enough with the contents of your notes by now to remember the general ideas they contain. Just write.

Subsequent Drafts

Now, write the paper again. Consult your notes to add quotations where appropriate and to fill in facts you might not have remembered when writing the first draft (see pages 23–26). Use blank lines for your draft additions and changes. You should check your notes, too, to be sure that the facts, ideas, or opinions you have reported are accurate. And, in this second effort, you should make some attempt to correct any grammar or punctuation errors you made in the first draft and to rephrase awkward sentences. Then you should add documentation (see pages 171–185).

Once you have completed this draft, go back through it several times to make certain that you have quoted accurately, that you have documented every source properly, and that you have polished your language as well as you can.

Using Explanatory Notes

If you need to explain some point or add information but feel that what you want to say really doesn't fit smoothly into the text of your paper, use a footnote or an endnote. Place a raised number (superscript) after the word where you'd like the reader to consider this additional material. Then, on a separate page called "Notes," use the corresponding number and provide the necessary information. If you use a footnote, place it at the bottom of the page on which your superscript appears. Or, place the supplementary information at the end of your paper in an endnote.

Look at the next example, from the essay "Nathaniel Hawthorne, Una Hawthorne, and *The Scarlet Letter*," by T. Walter Herbert, Jr.

> It would be an oversimplification to say that Una became merely a creature of her father's imagination, no more than the embodiment of his gender conflicts, as projected onto her. Yet her character, like his, was a cultural construction, and it was one in which Hawthorne had a hand.
>
> This is not the occasion for a detailed treatment of the pattern of solicitude and discipline that the Hawthornes organized about their baby daughter,[3] but crucial issues of the selfhood they sought to impart are disclosed in their naming her Una, after Spenser's maiden of holiness. This decision provoked a controversy among family and friends that illuminates the large cultural processes of gender definition that were then taking place.
>
> [3]A discussion of Sophia Hawthorne's role in the formation of Una's mental life lies beyond the scope of this essay. Sophia's exceptional response to the emerging norms of gender, the marriage she made to Nathaniel, and her place in the constellation of family relations are complex subjects that bear on this question, which I will treat in a forthcoming book.

The footnote here discusses Sophia's role in Una's mental life—additional information that the writer chose not to include in the text of his essay.

Toward the Final Copy

If you think you have polished the paper as much as you can, make yet another copy, complete with quotations and appropriate documentation (see pages 171–185). Many instructors will not accept a final copy of a paper unless they have seen and approved a draft. If your instructor falls into this category, this draft is the one you should submit. Your instructor will make suggestions, point out stylistic problems, and indicate the parts of your paper that are not developed as fully as they might be. Conscientious students heed their instructors' suggestions and make the appropriate changes on the submitted draft before preparing the final paper.

Also, before printing your final copy, pay attention to editing details. Proofread carefully. By now you should be familiar with your characteristic errors, and you should comb your paper to find and correct them before submitting your work for evaluation.

DOCUMENTING SOURCES IN THE HUMANITIES: MLA STYLE

The Modern Language Association (MLA) style documentation guidelines presented here follow the *MLA Handbook for Writers of Research Papers*, 7th ed. (2009).

Parenthetical Citations

Documenting or **crediting** or **citing** a source simply means letting the reader know where you found another writer's quotation, fact, idea, or opinion that appears in your paper. Most current style manuals, including the influential Modern Language Association's *MLA Handbook for Writers of Research Papers*, Seventh Edition (2009), recommend the efficient method of **parenthetical documentation**.

In this method, the last name of the author and the page number on which the material appears are placed within parentheses immediately after the information or quotation. Or, if you can integrate the author's name conveniently into the text itself, only the page number appears in parentheses. (If you refer to a whole work, however, no page reference is necessary.) Readers interested in finding the work cited then consult the bibliography, titled "Works Cited," at the end of the paper, for further information about the source. In parenthetical documentation, footnotes and endnotes are used only to provide additional information or commentary that might otherwise interrupt the flow of the text.

The following examples of parenthetical documentation reflect the Seventh Edition MLA style, used widely in the humanities and in other disciplines as well.

Work by One Author

The most common citation is for a work written by a single author. It contains the author's last name and the page number from which the material is taken, unless the citation is of an entire work.

"The problem of the twentieth century is the problem of the color line" (DuBois xiv).

Indeed, he grew so bitter about the plight of blacks that he rejoiced when his infant son died because the child would never have to experience the prejudice that he had felt (DuBois 155–56).

In *The Souls of Black Folk*, DuBois shows in dramatic personal terms the effects of prejudice in America.

Work by Two or More Authors

If the work has two or three authors, use the last names of all the authors as they appear on the title page.

If the work has more than three authors, name them all in the order in which they appear on the title page, or use the last name of only the first author and follow the name with *et al.*, the abbreviation for the Latin *et alia*, "and others." Note the period after *al.*, which is an abbreviation for *alia*; and note that no period follows *et* because it is not an abbreviation. (*Et* means *and*.)

A wide range of job opportunities is available to adventurous travelers (Krannich and Krannich 1–3).

The preceding example refers to the book *Jobs for People Who Love to Travel* by Ronald L. Krannich and Caryl Rae Krannich.

Heller, Heller, and Vagnini see carbohydrates as part of a healthy diet (2).

The work cited, *The Carbohydrate Addict's Healthy Heart Program,* is by three authors, Richard F. Heller, Rachael F. Heller, and Frederic J. Vagnini.

Teachers in all courses should determine the writing skill levels of their students (Anderson et al. 4).

Anderson and her coauthors insist that teachers in all courses determine the level of writing skills for their students early in the semester (4).

Anderson and three coauthors wrote *Integrated Skills Reinforcement.* A full reference for this book appears on page 177.

More Than One Work by the Same Author

He learned as a child that he could be rejected simply because of the color of his skin (DuBois, *Souls* 16).

Because the researcher cites more than one work by DuBois in the paper, an abbreviation of the title, *The Souls of Black Folk,* serves to distinguish this work by DuBois from other works by the same author.

More Than One Volume of a Work

Although he had urged conscientious objection during World War I, his views changed gradually, and by 1940, he concluded that he must support the war against the Nazis (Russell 2: 287–88).

The Autobiography of Bertrand Russell has more than one volume; thus, the information cited comes from the second volume, pages 287–288.

Work for Which No Author Is Given

Frequently, the author of a work is not given or is not known. In such a case, do not use the word *anonymous* or its abbreviation, *anon.* Instead, put in parentheses the title or an abbreviated title and the page number, as in this example:

Supporters of the polygraph test point out that to help alleviate possible nervousness, the subject is given access to the questions he will be asked during the test for as long as he desires ("What's It Like" 8).

Information About a Work or Author Already Given in Sentence

Many of your sentences may already contain enough information about a work that the parenthetical documentation can be made even shorter than in the examples given so far.

W. E. B. DuBois said in *The Souls of Black Folk* that "the problem of the twentieth century is the problem of the color line" (xiv).

Because the writer names the author and title in the sentence, only the page number appears in parentheses.

The following sentence is from a paper that cites more than one work by DuBois. Since the author's name is used in the sentence, you need not repeat it in the documentation. However, an abbreviated title of the book distinguishes this work by DuBois from other works by the same author.

W. E. B. DuBois, who believed that "the problem of the twentieth century is the problem of the color line" (*Souls* xiv), learned as a child that he could be rejected simply because of the color of his skin.

There are even times when you don't need to use parenthetical documentation. For example, if a writer says, "DuBois devotes his entire *Souls of Black Folk* to the subject," a reader need simply turn to the Works Cited list to find the remaining facts of publication. However, if you need to cite a section of a work, rather than the entire work, use one of the following forms:

This point has been made before (DuBois 16–156).

or

DuBois has made this point before (16–156).

If the section is in a work of more than one volume, you might write

Russell has detailed the kind of opposition to the war made by pacifists in England (2: 3–128).

or

In the second volume of his work (3–128), Russell has detailed the kind of opposition to the war made by pacifists in England.

In other words, the more skillfully you construct your sentences, the less information you need to include in your parenthetical documentation.

A List of Works Cited

Parenthetical documentation requires a **list of works cited**, an alphabetical, double-spaced listing of the sources cited in the paper. This list appears on a separate page at the end of the paper and is headed "Works Cited." The list of works cited contains full references to all sources used in the paper.

Different types of sources require somewhat different treatment. The examples that follow are typical MLA-style entries for the list of works cited. For entries that do not appear here, consult the *MLA Handbook for Writers of Research Papers*, 7th ed. (2009) or some other research style manual that your instructor recommends.

Standard Periodical Entries for the Works Cited List

Article with one author

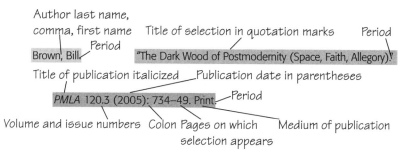

Author last name,
comma, first name   Title of selection in quotation marks   Period
       Period
Brown, Bill.   "The Dark Wood of Postmodernity (Space, Faith, Allegory)."

Title of publication italicized   Publication date in parentheses
    PMLA 120.3 (2005): 734–49. Print.   Period

Volume and issue numbers   Colon   Pages on which   Medium of publication
                     selection appears

Many journals use continuous pagination throughout the year—for example, if the first issue ends on page 280, the second issue will begin on page 281. To cite journals that use continuous pagination, place the volume and issue numbers before the year of publication, which is given in parentheses. The month is not needed. A colon precedes the inclusive page numbers on which the selection appears.

Article in a journal that numbers pages in each issue separately

Bernard, Emily. "Fired." *American Scholar* 76.1 (2007): 101–07. Print.

The issue number follows the volume number, and a period separates them (76.1 in the preceding example refers to volume 76, issue 1). If only an issue number appears, include it as you would a volume number.

Selection in a monthly (or bimonthly) magazine

Le Guin, Ursula. "Staying Awake." *Harper's* Feb. 2008: 33–38. Print.

The entry includes the month (abbreviated) instead of a volume number. Do not abbreviate the months May, June, and July.

Selection in a weekly (or biweekly) magazine

Yousafzai, Sami, and Ron Moreau. "Suicide Offensive." *Newsweek* 3 Apr. 2007: 24–36. Print.

Unsigned selection in a magazine

"The Bible in First Person." *Christian Century* 3 Apr. 2007: 5. Print.

When no author is given, the entry begins with the title of the article. Do not use the word *anonymous* or its abbreviation, *anon.*

Unsigned article in a daily newspaper

"A Suburb Looks Nervously at Its Urban Neighbor." *New York Times* 17 Jan. 2008, late ed.: A20. Print.

Give the name of the newspaper, but omit any introductory article, such as *The* from *New York Times* in the example. If the name of the city is part of the title of the newspaper, as in the *New York Times*, italicize it. However, if the name of the city is not part of the newspaper's title, include the city in brackets and do not italicize it: *Star-Ledger* [Newark].

Some newspapers print more than one edition a day, and the contents of the editions may differ. In such cases, include the edition you used. In addition, newspapers often indicate section numbers, and you should include them in the citation. In the preceding example, A20 refers to section A, page 20.

Use a plus sign after the page number when the entire selection does not appear on consecutive pages.

Review in a periodical

Rev. of *Love and War in California*, by Oakley Hall. *New Yorker* 14 May 2007: 149. Print.

Flanagan, Caitlin. "The Age of Innocence." Rev. of *College Girls: Bluestockings, Sex Kittens, and Coeds, Then and Now*, by Lynn Peril. *Atlantic* Apr. 2007: 107–11. Print.

In the first example, the book review is unsigned. In the second, the review is both signed and titled: Flanagan's review of the book *College Girls: Bluestockings, Sex Kittens, and Coeds, Then and Now* is called "The Age of Innocence."

Standard Book Entry for the Works Cited List

Book with one author

Author last name, comma, first name, period   Title of book italicized

Alder, Ken. *The Lie Detectors: The History of an American Obsession.*—Period

City of publication   Publisher   Publication date

New York: Free P, 2007. Print.—Period

Colon   Comma   Medium of publication

Book with two authors

Haynes, William O., and Rebekah H. Pindzola. *Diagnosis and Evaluation in Speech Pathology*. New York: Allyn, 2007. Print.

Invert only the name of the first author. The order of the names is the same as that on the title page of the original source.

Book with three authors

Heller, Richard F., Rachael F. Heller, and Frederic J. Vagnini. *The Carbohydrate Addict's Healthy Heart Program*. New York: Ballantine, 1999. Print.

Book with more than three authors

> Anderson, JoAnn Romeo, et al. *Integrated Skills Reinforcement*. New York: Longman,
> 1983. Print.

You may use the name of the first author only, followed by the notation *et al.*, the Latin abbreviation for "and others." The name given is the first name that appears on the title page. Another option is to provide all names in full in the order in which they appear on the title page.

Anthology

> Wallace, David Foster, and Robert Atwan, eds. *The Best American Essays 2007*. Boston:
> Houghton, 2007. Print.

The editors collected a group of essays in this book. The editors' names appear before the title, with the abbreviation *eds.*

Selection in an anthology

> Driscoll, Mary Erina. "Choice, Achievement, and School Community." *School Choice:*
> *Examining the Evidence*. Ed. Edith Rasell and Richard Rothstein. Washington:
> Economic Policy Inst., 1993. 147–72. Print.

The page numbers given at the end of the entry indicate where the essay appears in the anthology. The editors' names appear after the abbreviation *Ed.* ("edited by").

When you use two or more essays from the same collection, you may *cross-reference* them, as in this example:

> Witte, John F. "The Milwaukee Parental Choice Program." Rasell and Rothstein 69–109.

The reference "Rasell and Rothstein" is to the anthology *School Choice: Examining the Evidence*. A citation for the anthology itself must then be included in the Works Cited list.

Special edition of an author's work

> Thoreau, Henry David. *Walden*. Ed. Jeffrey S. Cramer. New Haven: Yale UP, 2006. Print.

Editions other than the first

> Raimes, Ann. *Keys for Writers*. 5th ed. Boston: Houghton, 2008. Print.

For a revised edition, the abbreviation *Rev. ed.* appears after the title.

Translated work

> Tolstoy, Leo. *War and Peace*. 1869. Trans. Richard Pevear and Larissa Volokhonsky. New
> York: Knopf, 2007. Print.

Multivolume work

> Adams, Wallace E. *The Western World*. 2 vols. New York: Addison, 1968. Print.

Pamphlet

Treat a pamphlet like a book, using the name of the committee or organization that created the pamphlet as the author if no author's name is provided.

> *Helsinki Summer School 2008*. Helsinki: U of Helsinki, 2008. Print.

Selection in an encyclopedia

Kaeliinohomoku, Joanh W. "Hula." *Encyclopedia Americana*. 2006 ed. Print.

When no author is given, the entry begins with the title of the article.

Standard Online Source Entries for the Works Cited List

Source information from an online document

For Web sources, give as much information as you can, including the original publication information if the source was published elsewhere first. If you cannot find the sponsor or publisher of the site, use *n.p.* (for "no publisher given"). If the document does not have a date of posting, use *n.d.* (for "no date"). You do not have to include a URL unless you think readers will have difficulty finding the source by searching. If you must divide a URL at the end of a line, divide it only after a slash mark. If you use a Web source, indicate it with the word *Web* before the date of access.

Document within an information database, a scholarly project, or Web site

"Homer." *Encyclopaedia Britannica Online*. Encyclopaedia Britannica, 2007. Web. 18 Feb. 2008.

Webster, Augusta. "A Castway." *Portraits*. London, 1870. *Victorian Women Writers Project*. Ed. Perry Willett. Indiana U, 24 Apr. 1998. Web. 13 Apr. 2008.

Entire Internet site, such as an online scholarly project, information database, or professional or personal site

Willett, Perry, ed. *Victorian Women Writers Project*. Indiana U, 1995–2003. Web. 13 Apr. 2008.

Boyle, T. C. Home page. N.p., n.d. Web. 19 June 2007.

CBS.com. CBS, 2007. Web. 23 July 2008.

Home page for a course

Wild, Larry. Theater 241: Stagecraft. Course home page. Dept. of Theater, Northern State U, Fall 2006. Web. 12 Aug 2008.

No component of the entry requires italicizing.

Online book

Anderson, Sherwood. *Winesburg, Ohio*. 1919. *Bartleby.com: Great Books Online*. Bartleby.com, 1999. Web. 11 Dec. 2008.

Webster, Augusta. *Portraits*. London, 1870. *Victorian Women Writers Project*. Ed. Perry Willett. Indiana U, 24 Apr. 1998. Web. 20 Apr. 2008.

The Webster example is a book that is part of a scholarly project.

Part of an online book

Anderson, Sherwood. "Hands." *Winesburg, Ohio*. 1919. *Bartleby.com: Great Books Online*. Bartleby.com, n.d. Web. 9 Oct. 2008.

Online article from a scholarly journal

Rist, Thomas. "Religion, Politics, Revenge: The Dead in Renaissance Drama." *Early Modern Literary Studies* 9.1 (2003): 20 pars. Web. 19 June 2008.

The item *20 pars* in the reference indicates the total number of paragraphs in the selection. The online article numbered the paragraphs. If the selection numbers pages or sections instead, indicate the number range or total number of pages or sections.

Online article from a journal database

Grubin, Don, and Lars Madsen. "Lie Detection and the Polygraph: A Historical Review." *Journal of Forensic Psychiatry and Psychology* 16.2 (2005): 357–69. *ContentSelect Research Navigator*. Web. 17 Mar. 2008.

Online article from a magazine

Bowden, Mark. "The Ploy." *TheAtlantic.com*. Atlantic Publishing Group, 24 May 2007. Web. 19 Sept. 2008.

Online article from a newspaper

Schiesel, Seth, and David Leonhardt. "Justice Dept. Acts to Block Proposed WorldCom-Sprint Deal." *New York Times*. New York Times, 28 June 2000. Web. 19 May 2008.

Nonperiodical publication on CD–ROM, diskette, or magnetic tape

Mann, Ron. *Emile De Antonio's Painters Painting*. Irvington: Voyager, 1996. CD-ROM.

Selection from a periodically published database on CD-ROM

"Polygraph." *Encarta Reference Lib. 2007*. CD-ROM. Microsoft, 2007.

Item from a personal subscription service

"Circe." *Compton's Encyclopedia Online*. Vers. 2.0. America Online, 1997. Web. 3 Feb. 2006.

E-mail communication

Kane, Joshua. Message to the author. 2 Aug. 2007. E-mail.

Smith, Johnson C. "Re: Critique of Marx's Views." Message to Ramon Vargas-Llosa. 23 June 2000. E-mail.

Wright, John. E-mail interview. 7–9 Apr. 2008.

The Kane entry illustrates an untitled e-mail message sent directly to the writer of the paper at hand; the Smith entry illustrates a titled e-mail message originally sent to someone else. The entry for Wright shows an e-mail interview over a number of days and indicates the inclusive dates.

Online posting to an e-mail discussion list

McCarty, Willard. "Humanist's 20th!" *Humanist Discussion Group*. N.p., 7 May 2007. Web. 28 Jan. 2009. <http://www.digitalhumanities.org/humanist/Archives/ Virginia/v21/0000.html>.

Synchronous communication on a MUD or MOO

Online Forum for Educational MOO Administrators. LinguaMOO. N.p., 6 July 1995. Web. 20 June 2005. <http://www.pub.utdallas.edu/~cynthiah/lingua_archive/ edumoo-7-6-95.txt>.

MUD is the acronym for multiuser domain; MOO is the acronym for multiuser domain, object oriented. Both are forums for posting synchronous communication.

Other Types of Works Cited Entries Sources

Recordings, tapes, and compact discs

Groban, Josh. *Noel*. Reprise/WEA, 2007. CD.

The entry includes the name of the artist, the title of the recording, the manufacturer, and the date. The recording is a compact disk. If the piece is in another medium, use *LP* (long-playing record), *Audiocassette*, or *Audiotape* (reel-to-reel tape) at the end of the entry.

Films and television (or radio) programs

The Lives of Others [*Das Leben der Anderen*]. Dir. Florian Henckel von Donnersmarck. Perf. Martina Gedeck, Ulrich Mühe, and Sebastian Koch. Sony, 2007. Film.

"Lillian Gish: The Actor's Life for Me." Narr. Eva Marie Saint. Prod. and dir. Terry Sanders. *American Masters*. PBS. WNET, New York, 11 July 1988. Television.

Cartoons

Smaller, Barbara. Cartoon. *New Yorker* 26 Mar. 2007: 65. Print.

Schulz, Charles. "Peanuts Classic." Comic strip. *Daily News* [New York] 21 Nov. 2005: 43. Print.

Interviews

Fraser, Brendan. Interview. *Tavis Smiley*. PBS. WNET, New York, 16 Jan. 2008. Radio.

Hawke, Ethan. Personal interview. 11 Mar. 2008.

Performances

The Homecoming. By Harold Pinter. Dir. Daniel Sullivan. Perf. Ian McShane, Raul Esparza, and Eve Best. Cort Theatre, New York. 9 Jan. 2008. Performance.

Preparing Your Works Cited List

In preparing your list of works cited, follow these guidelines for the correct format.

TIPS FOR PREPARING YOUR WORKS CITED LIST

- **Prepare the list on a separate page headed "Works Cited."** Place the heading about an inch from the top and center it. (Do not underline the heading; use uppercase letters only for the first letter in each word.) The Works Cited page appears at the end of the paper.
- **Double-space before typing the first entry.** Begin each entry flush with the left margin, and indent all other lines of each entry one-half inch. Use double-spacing throughout your list of works cited.
- **Arrange the entries alphabetically, according to the authors' last names.** Do not separate books and periodicals. For entries without authors, use the first word in the title (other than *A*, *An*, or *The*) to determine alphabetical order.
- **When you cite two or more books by the same author, arrange them alphabetically by title.** Give the author's full name only in the first entry. In subsequent entries, replace the author's name with three hyphens. For example:

Geertz, Clifford. *The Interpretation of Cultures*. New York: Basic, 1973. Print.

———. *Local Knowledge: Further Essays in Interpretive Anthropology*. New York: Basic, 1983. Print.

See pages 195–196 for a complete, formatted Works Cited list.

DOCUMENTING SOURCES IN THE SOCIAL SCIENCES: APA STYLE

Writers in the social sciences use the system of documentation set forth in the *Publication Manual of the American Psychological Association* (APA), Sixth Edition (2010). Since your instructors in psychology, sociology, and other courses may require you to follow APA guidelines, you should be familiar with this system. Like the MLA style, **APA-style documentation** uses parenthetical citations supported by a separate list of sources headed "References," which appears at the end of the research paper.

Parenthetical Citations

A typical APA-style text citation includes the author's name and the date of publication, separated by a comma.

> Lower species of animals use only a few signs in their communication systems. For example, the rhesus monkey uses only about 37 different signals (Wilson, 1972).

As with MLA-style documentation, the APA system aims to integrate references smoothly with the text of the paper. Here are some further examples:

In 1972 Wilson showed that the rhesus monkey uses only about 37 different signals in its communication system.

According to Wilson (1972), rhesus monkeys use only 37 signals. Communication systems that rely on only a few signs are typical of lower animal species.

When quoting a passage from a source, the page number on which the passage appears follows the publication date. Note the required use of the abbreviations *pp.* for "pages" and *p.* for "page." Separate the date and the page information by a comma.

Creative people use divergent thinking to their advantage and "prefer complexity and some degree of apparent imbalance in phenomena" (Barron, 1963, pp. 208–209).

When citing more than one work by the same author published in the same year, use an *a* after the date for the first publication, a *b* after the date for the second, and so on. The citations on the references list should also include these letters. In the following example, the reference is to the second 1971 article by Schacter, "Some Extraordinary Facts About Obese Humans and Rats." This reference is marked *b* on the references list. Schacter's first 1971 article, "Eat, Eat," would be marked *a* on the references list (see page 184).

Researchers have identified important similarities for obesity in rats and humans (Schacter, 1971b).

The examples that follow show how to cite multiple authors in the APA system. Note that the ampersand (&) replaces the word *and* between authors' names in the parenthetical citation (see the first example). If the authors' names are not given parenthetically, as in the second example, use the word *and*.

Famous studies of the chimpanzee Washoe demonstrated that animals other than humans could learn and use language (Gardner & Gardner, 1969).

Rumbaugh, Gill, and von Glaserfeld (1973) studied the language skills of the chimpanzee Pan.

When citing works by three or more authors, use all authors' names (followed by the date) for the first reference, but in the second and subsequent text references use the abbreviation *et al.* after the first author's name.

Rumbaugh et al. (1973) have documented certain levels of reading and the ability to complete sentences among chimpanzees.

A List of APA References

APA-style documentation requires that a list of the references cited in the paper appear on a separate page at the end. The heading "References" is typed at the top of the page and is not underlined (see pages 184–185). Titles of books, newspapers, journals, and magazines appear in italics. On the following pages are sample references in the APA format.

Standard Book Entries for the References List

Book with one author

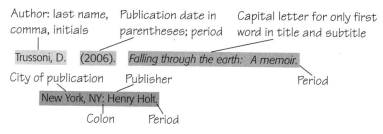

```
Author: last name,    Publication date in    Capital letter for only first
comma, initials       parentheses; period    word in title and subtitle

Trussoni, D.   (2006).   Falling through the earth: A memoir.

City of publication      Publisher                        Period

New York, NY: Henry Holt.
          Colon      Period
```

Book with two or more authors

Hick, S. F., & McNutt, J. G. (2002). *Advocacy, activism, and the Internet.* Chicago, IL: Lyceum.

Standard Periodical Entry for the References List

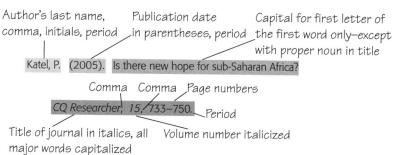

```
Author's last name,      Publication date      Capital for first letter of
comma, initials, period   in parentheses, period   the first word only—except
                                                  with proper noun in title

Katel, P.   (2005).   Is there new hope for sub-Saharan Africa?

             Comma   Comma   Page numbers

CQ Researcher, 15, 733–750.   Period

Title of journal in italics, all    Volume number italicized
major words capitalized
```

When a periodical numbers its pages by volume (year) rather than by issue, use only the volume number.

APA style requires italics for book and periodical titles.

Article in a journal that numbers the pages in each issue separately

Lanza, R. (2007). A new theory of the universe. *American Scholar, 76*(2), 18–33.

The notation refers to volume 76, issue 2.

Article in a monthly (or bimonthly) magazine

Cannon, C. M. (2007, January/February). Untruth and consequences. *The Atlantic, 299,* 56–67.

In a monthly or bimonthly magazine, the month of publication is given after the year in parentheses. A comma separates the year and the month. The volume number follows the magazine title. Use the abbreviation *p.* for page and *pp.* for pages only for newspaper entries.

Article in a daily newspaper

Isaacs, N. (2007, April 5). Exercisers slow it down with Qigong. *The New York Times*, p. G1.

Electronic Sources

Grubin, D., & Madsen, L. (2005). Lie detection and the polygraph: A historical review. *Journal of Forensic Psychiatry & Psychology, 16*(2), 357–369. doi: 10.1080/ 14789940412331337353

Hinshelwood, R. O. (2007). Intolerance and the intolerable: The case of racism. *Journal for the Psychoanalysis of Culture and Society, 12*(1), 1–20. Retrieved from http://palgrave-journals.com/pcs

Sengupta, S. (2008, January 17). Push for education yields little for India's poor. *The New York Times*. Retrieved from http://www.nytimes.com

Legal, ethical, political, and economic concerns. (2008, January 9). Retrieved November 12, 2009, from Flu Wiki: http://www.fluwiki.info

Use the models above to develop citations for a range of electronic sources that you might cite in a paper. If an article is assigned a digital object identifier (DOI) in a database, as in the Grubin entry above, use this number to identify it; a URL is not necessary. If an online article does not have a DOI, as in the Hinshelwood and Sengupta entries, give the publication's home page URL instead. (Do not give a database's URL since readers may find the article in a different database.) Retrieval dates are only necessary for undated sources or sources that are likely to change, as the "Legal" wiki entry shows.

Note that if you need to break a URL from one line to the next, break *before* the slash (/) or other major puncuation mark, but break *after* the double slash (//).

Preparing Your APA References List

If your instructor asks you to prepare your paper in APA format, here is a sample references list for you to examine and some tips for preparing the references list.

References

Chase, A. (2000, June). Harvard and the making of the Unabomber. *Atlantic, 282,* 41–65. Retrieved from http://www.theatlantic.com

Lanza, R. (2007). A new theory of the universe. *American Scholar, 76*(2), 18–33.

Schacter, S. (1971a, November). Eat, eat. *Psychology Today, 5,* 44–47; 78–79.

Schacter, S. (1971b). Some extraordinary facts about obese humans and rats. *American Psychologist, 26,* 129–144.

Seymour, T. L., & Fraynt, B. R. (2009). Time and encoding effects in the concealed knowledge test. *Applied Psychophysiology & Biofeedback, 34*(3), 177–187. doi: 10.1007/s10484-009-9092-3

Trussoni, D. (2006). *Falling through the earth: A memoir.* New York, NY: Henry Holt.

TIPS FOR PREPARING YOUR APA REFERENCES LIST

- **Type the heading "References" at the top of a new page.** On a separate page that will appear at the end of the paper, type the heading centered on the line. Do not underline it; do not enclose it in quotation marks. List all the sources cited in the text. Double-space from the heading to the first entry.
- **Arrange all entries alphabetically.** Without separating books from periodicals, arrange all entries alphabetically according to the author's last name (or, according to publication dates—earliest to most recent—for works by the same author).
- **Double-space within and between all entries.**
- **The first line of each entry is flush with the left margin.** Indent second and subsequent lines of each entry.
- **Number the References page.**

Be sure to check the APA Web site <http://www.apastyle.org> for more information about APA style requirements.

PREPARING YOUR MANUSCRIPT

TIPS FOR PREPARING THE FINAL COPY

- **Use quality bond paper.**
- **Double-space.** Double-space the paper throughout, including long quotations and notes, except as indicated in the following discussion of margins.
- **Use one-inch margins.** Leave margins of one inch at the top, bottom, and both sides of the text. If you are not using a title page, type the centered title two inches from the top of the page, and double-space between the title and the first line of the text. Indent the first word of each paragraph five spaces ($1/2$ inch) from the left margin. Indent a block quotation ten spaces (or 1 inch) from the left margin.
- **Format the title.** MLA guidelines call for a heading on the first page instead of a separate title page. The writer's name, instructor's name, course number, and

(Continued on next page)

date appear flush left on the first manuscript page, spaced as shown in the example below.

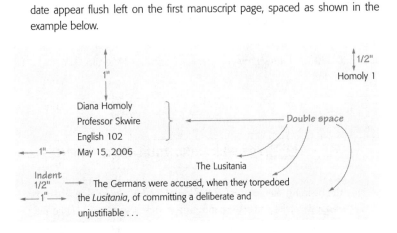

1/2"

Homoly 1

1"

Diana Homoly
Professor Skwire
English 102
May 15, 2006

Double space

1"

The Lusitania

Indent
1/2"   The Germans were accused, when they torpedoed

1"   the *Lusitania*, of committing a deliberate and

unjustifiable . . .

However, many instructors prefer a title page, especially if an outline or table of contents precedes the first page of text. A title page should contain the title of your paper, your name, the course name and number, the name of your instructor, and the date. Neatly center this information on the page, as shown on page 188.

Whichever form you use, remember that you should never put your own title in quotation marks, underline it, or capitalize it in full.

• **Pagination.** Number all pages consecutively (except the title page and any prefatory material) in the upper-right-hand corner. Just type the number; don't punctuate it with a period, hyphens, or parentheses. In addition to putting the number in the upper-right-hand corner, you may also want to type your name right before the page number to ensure against misplaced pages. (See the pagination of "The Banning of the Polygraph," 189–195, for example.) Number prefatory materials, such as your outline, acknowledgments, or preface, with lowercase roman numerals—i, ii, and so on.

STRATEGY CHECKLIST: Writing Your Research Paper

Note: This checklist begins with the first draft. For a research and planning Strategy Checklist, see Chapter 21.

Write the first draft.

❏ Is my thesis clear and limited? Does it state or suggest an interpretation or judgment on the topic?

❏ Does the body of the paper develop the thesis?

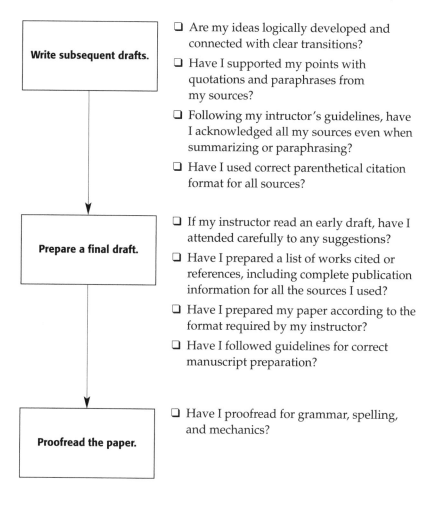

Write subsequent drafts.

❏ Are my ideas logically developed and connected with clear transitions?

❏ Have I supported my points with quotations and paraphrases from my sources?

❏ Following my intructor's guidelines, have I acknowledged all my sources even when summarizing or paraphrasing?

❏ Have I used correct parenthetical citation format for all sources?

Prepare a final draft.

❏ If my instructor read an early draft, have I attended carefully to any suggestions?

❏ Have I prepared a list of works cited or references, including complete publication information for all the sources I used?

❏ Have I prepared my paper according to the format required by my instructor?

❏ Have I followed guidelines for correct manuscript preparation?

Proofread the paper.

❏ Have I proofread for grammar, spelling, and mechanics?

EXERCISE

Using your formal outline as your guide, write the necessary drafts of your research paper. Document all sources. Prepare a list of works cited. Be sure to study the student sample and the accompanying commentary on the following pages.

SAMPLE MLA-STYLE RESEARCH PAPER

The following sample research paper shows how one student, Elizabeth Kessler, managed to blend a variety of elements successfully. The commentary that appears in the margins highlights its key features and calls attention to special issues. The paper uses MLA-style documentation.

TITLE PAGE, IF REQUIRED

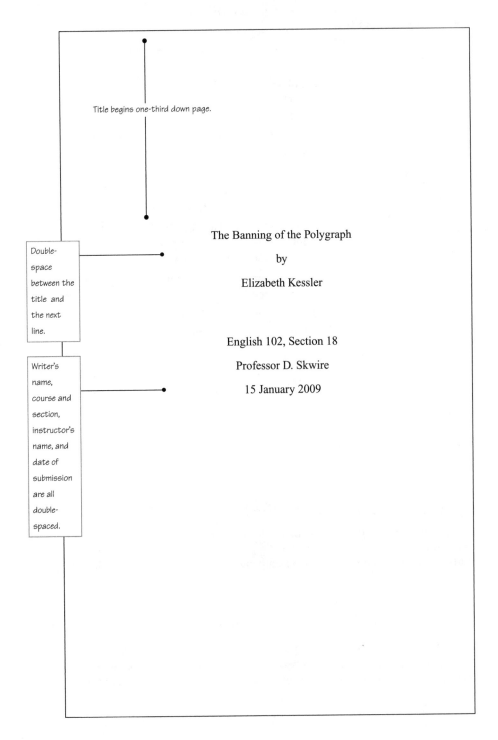

Title begins one-third down page.

Double-
space
between the
title and
the next
line.

Writer's
name,
course and
section,
instructor's
name, and
date of
submission
are all
double-
spaced.

The Banning of the Polygraph

by

Elizabeth Kessler

English 102, Section 18

Professor D. Skwire

15 January 2009

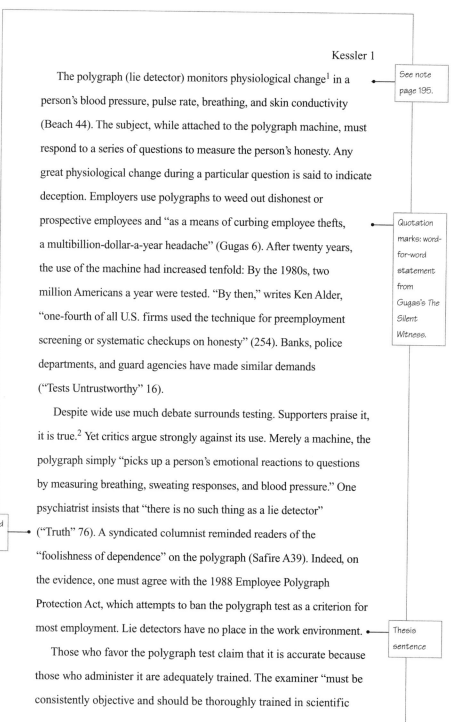

Kessler 1

The polygraph (lie detector) monitors physiological change[1] in a

person's blood pressure, pulse rate, breathing, and skin conductivity

(Beach 44). The subject, while attached to the polygraph machine, must

respond to a series of questions to measure the person's honesty. Any

great physiological change during a particular question is said to indicate

deception. Employers use polygraphs to weed out dishonest or

prospective employees and "as a means of curbing employee thefts,

a multibillion-dollar-a-year headache" (Gugas 6). After twenty years,

the use of the machine had increased tenfold: By the 1980s, two

million Americans a year were tested. "By then," writes Ken Alder,

"one-fourth of all U.S. firms used the technique for preemployment

screening or systematic checkups on honesty" (254). Banks, police

departments, and guard agencies have made similar demands

("Tests Untrustworthy" 16).

Despite wide use much debate surrounds testing. Supporters praise it,

it is true.[2] Yet critics argue strongly against its use. Merely a machine, the

polygraph simply "picks up a person's emotional reactions to questions

by measuring breathing, sweating responses, and blood pressure." One

psychiatrist insists that "there is no such thing as a lie detector"

("Truth" 76). A syndicated columnist reminded readers of the

"foolishness of dependence" on the polygraph (Safire A39). Indeed, on

the evidence, one must agree with the 1988 Employee Polygraph

Protection Act, which attempts to ban the polygraph test as a criterion for

most employment. Lie detectors have no place in the work environment.

Those who favor the polygraph test claim that it is accurate because

those who administer it are adequately trained. The examiner "must be

consistently objective and should be thoroughly trained in scientific

See note page 195.

Quotation marks: word-for-word statement from Gugas's *The Silent Witness*.

Shortened title

Thesis sentence

Kessler 2

interrogation to reduce the inherent human error" ("Polygraph"). In

Electronic source (from Encarta)

fact, many states demand education and other requirements for the

licensing of polygraph examiners ("In Ohio" F4). The training

supposedly enables the examiner to distinguish between nervousness

and actual deception ("What's It Like" F8). Supporters of the test

believe that training equips examiners to make accurate

distinctions.

Advocates of the polygraph further argue that it is "a valuable

tool for an employer in…investigating workplace crime" ("How to

Comply" 36). Each year theft exceeds twenty billion dollars (Beach

44). According to the National Association of Convenience Stores,

the use of the polygraph can reduce employee theft by as much as

50 percent (Flaherty 31). Interestingly, at numerous Chicago banks

during the 1930s, employees who failed lie detector tests and

remained on the payroll became "The banks' most honest

The ellipsis indicates words omitted from the quotation.

employees…. The lie detector become [sic] a psychological

"Thus": writer acknowledges error in source.

deterrent as much as a catcher of thieves" (Alder 124).

Federal support for polygraph testing has added validity to its use.

Agencies of the United States government have relied on lie detector

tests in important legal matters:

> The FBI uses polygraphs mostly to probe leads and verify
>
> specific facts…. The agency also employs highly trained
>
> examiners, who usually spend half a day on each
>
> session…. [A]n "adverse inference" may be drawn if an
>
> employee of the FBI or any other part of the Justice
>
> Department balks at submitting to the machines. (Beach 44)

Quotation more than four lines set off ten spaces from left margin.

Kessler 3

The supporters of the polygraph believe its efficiency and low cost justify its use.

Those who favor the polygraph in the workplace, then, argue that adequately trained examiners produce reliable findings at low cost. These are strong arguments. However, those who oppose the test question the claims made by its supporters, and they are right to do so.

Beach points out that opponents to the test have called attention to regular reports by employees that examiners browbeat them during polygraph testing (44). And "about 90% of the damaging reports made to employers are based not on physiological reactions but on the examiners' assumptions, or on incriminating confessions made during an interview" ("Truth" 76). The quality of operators in the polygraph industry is uneven at best.

Furthermore, critics say that the test is accurate only 60 to 75 percent of the time, and many variants have never been checked for validity ("Lie Detector Tests" 16). Error is more likely to occur when a truthful person is shown to be deceptive (Beach 44). The opposition argues that readings do not always indicate deception and that people who do not believe that the machine can detect dishonesty feel no stress when lying: Therefore, no great physiological response will indicate deception on the readings (Flaherty 32). Clinical tests suggest that tranquilizers can reduce the physiological response that accompanies deception (Ward et al. 74). Also, those who are "really clever… can fool the machines" ("Rights Abuse" 10). One must question the value of readings that may be unreliable.

Transitional paragraph connects two major sections of essay.

Paraphrased statement: source identified

Page number in Beach's article

Shortened title; unsigned newspaper article

Kessler 4

Nor does a clear-cut physiological indication of guilt seem to be as certain as supporters of the test claim. Often, heightened feelings bring about physiological responses that are similar to those caused by deception. According to David Lykken, a psychiatrist and professor of psychology, people who run a special risk include those who get upset if someone accuses them of something they did not do, those with short tempers, and those who tend to feel guilty anyway. Lykken believes that the polygraph machine detects not only the physiological responses that accompany lying but also the nervousness people feel when strapped to a machine. The polygraph confuses guilt with fear, anger, and other emotions that can alter heart rate, breathing, and perspiration. Each person varies in physiological responses to these emotions ("Truth" 79).

Moreover, until now, polygraph laws tended to be "toothless." Some laws prohibit requiring present or prospective employees to submit to a polygraph; however, businesses are still free to make the request (Flaherty 34). Private companies can advertise job-related lie-detection services even now. One company, for example, asserts that its polygraph test "is a valuable 'investigative tool'" for ongoing questions about economic loss and that its expert examiners "can help 'clear' loyal staff members while resolving open issues during a non-accusatory interview and examination process" (Dallas Polygraph Services). If a current or prospective employee refuses to take the test, employers may interpret the refusal as an admission of guilt ("Truth" 79). In fact, refusal may mean the loss of a job (Beach 44). This is unfair: The burden lies entirely on the employee's shoulders.

Title taken from company Web site: www .dallaspoly graph.com/

Further, some laws free only present, not prospective, employees from a polygraph test. Finally, the fines and jail terms for violating these laws rarely have risen above misdemeanor level. Fines, which seldom exceed $1,000, do not hinder "deep-pocketed" employers from using the polygraph (Flaherty 34). Such laws, test opponents argue, have not protected employees.

One must also consider the problem of human rights violation ("In Ohio" F4). Especially in regard to criminal cases, some sociologists and experts in theology say that polygraph testing "unjustly robs suspects of their innermost secrets." Courts have ruled that the test illegally forces people to testify against themselves (Block 131). Several experts claim that the lie detector, with all its apparatus, constitutes a "modern third degree" and may intimidate a subject into blurting out a false confession before the test begins (Beach 44).

> Smooth integration of quote from Block

A further infringement on individual rights, according to opponents of the test, is invasion of privacy. Many examiners have probed into personal affairs of those being tested (Beach 44). The examiners ask questions pertaining to political, sexual, and union matters. Mike Tiner of the Union of Food and Commercial Workers reported that in the 1980s questions involving political, sexual, and union matters were definitely on the increase (Beach 44). As a result, many large nongovernmental employers avoid polygraph testing. A retired director of personnel at Schlumberger Limited, a large multinational corporation, believes that potential employees would prefer to work in organizations that valued "personal impressions and evaluations of candidates

Kessler 6

rather than the 'answer' provided by a machine" (Alexander). Invasions

of privacy are violations of constitutional rights and should not be

tolerated.

Citation for e-mail

Fortunately, the government heeded the chorus of voices

against the lie detector over the years. In 1988, Congress passed

the Polygraph Protection Act, which, according to an article called

"How to Comply with the Polygraph Law" in *Nation's Business,*

finally prohibits polygraphs to "screen job applicants or

investigate employees..." (36). The law defines proper testing

procedures and gives employees a wide range of rights. It also spells

out guidelines for the examiners' qualifications. Some good sense

has prevailed here; many workers now have protection against

offensive testing.

Yet despite restrictions in the 1988 law, many civil rights advocates

are still unhappy. In fact, some are vicious in their attack against poly-

graph use. *AntiPolygraph.org* argues that "Our government's stubborn

reliance on this pseudoscience poses clear and present danger: make-

believe science yields make-believe security." Advertising claims like

those of the James W. Bassett Company in 2008 have not abated

("Polygraph Testing Services"). The polygraph Protection Act allows

too many exceptions. Additionally, federal, state, and local govern-

ments are exempt from the law, as are several private-sector employers,

including security companies and many drug companies. Ultimately,

the poor accuracy record of the tests in general condemns them, no

matter how much they are restricted. As a result of these weaknesses

in the law and of other major issues, polygraphs should have no place

in any employee judgments.

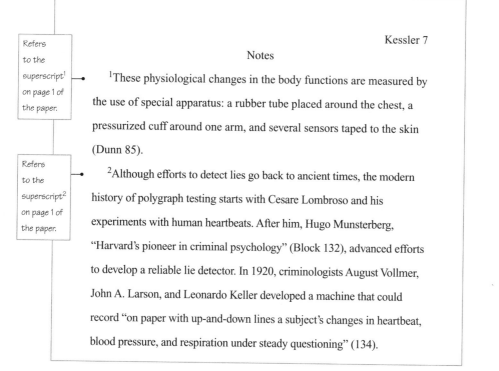

Kessler 7

Notes

Refers to the superscript[1] on page 1 of the paper.

[1]These physiological changes in the body functions are measured by the use of special apparatus: a rubber tube placed around the chest, a pressurized cuff around one arm, and several sensors taped to the skin (Dunn 85).

Refers to the superscript[2] on page 1 of the paper.

[2]Although efforts to detect lies go back to ancient times, the modern history of polygraph testing starts with Cesare Lombroso and his experiments with human heartbeats. After him, Hugo Munsterberg, "Harvard's pioneer in criminal psychology" (Block 132), advanced efforts to develop a reliable lie detector. In 1920, criminologists August Vollmer, John A. Larson, and Leonardo Keller developed a machine that could record "on paper with up-and-down lines a subject's changes in heartbeat, blood pressure, and respiration under steady questioning" (134).

Center "Works Cited" on new page, 1 inch from top.

Kessler 8

Works Cited

Alder, Ken. *The Lie Detectors: A History of an American*
    Obsession. New York: Free P, 2007. Print.

All entries double spaced

Second line of entry indented ½ in.

Alexander, Arthur. "Re: Polygraph Examinations in Employment."
    Message to the author. 15 Oct. 2008. E-mail.

Alphabetize entries by author's last name or, if no author named, by first important word in title.

AntiPolygraph.org. Antipolygraph.org, 2007. Web. 15 Nov. 2008.

Beach, Bennet H. "Blood, Sweat and Fears." *Time* 8 Sept. 1980: 44. Print.

Block, Eugene B. *Science vs. Crime: The Evolution of the Police Lab.*
    San Francisco: Cragmont, 1979. Print.

"Dallas Polygraph Services." *DallasPolygraph.com.* Michael D. Park
    and Associates Polygraph, 2007. Web. 12 Oct. 2008.

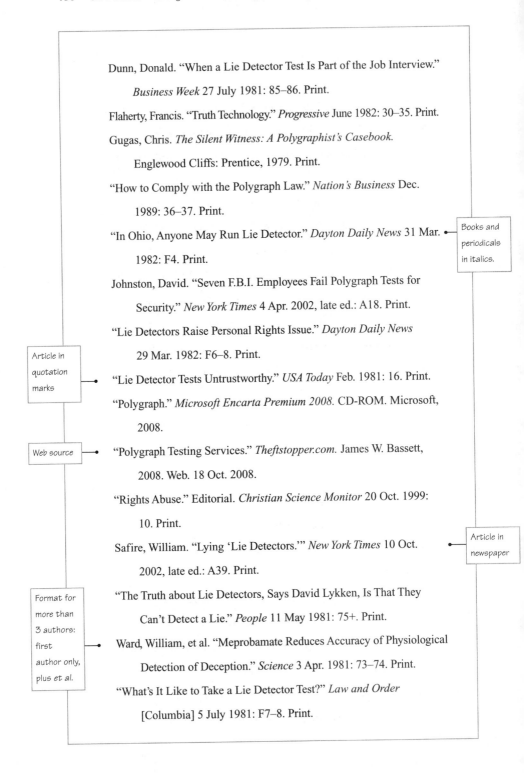

Dunn, Donald. "When a Lie Detector Test Is Part of the Job Interview."

Business Week 27 July 1981: 85–86. Print.

Flaherty, Francis. "Truth Technology." *Progressive* June 1982: 30–35. Print.

Gugas, Chris. *The Silent Witness: A Polygraphist's Casebook.*

Englewood Cliffs: Prentice, 1979. Print.

"How to Comply with the Polygraph Law." *Nation's Business* Dec.

1989: 36–37. Print.

"In Ohio, Anyone May Run Lie Detector." *Dayton Daily News* 31 Mar.

1982: F4. Print.

Johnston, David. "Seven F.B.I. Employees Fail Polygraph Tests for

Security." *New York Times* 4 Apr. 2002, late ed.: A18. Print.

"Lie Detectors Raise Personal Rights Issue." *Dayton Daily News*

29 Mar. 1982: F6–8. Print.

"Lie Detector Tests Untrustworthy." *USA Today* Feb. 1981: 16. Print.

"Polygraph." *Microsoft Encarta Premium 2008.* CD-ROM. Microsoft,

2008.

"Polygraph Testing Services." *Theftstopper.com.* James W. Bassett,

2008. Web. 18 Oct. 2008.

"Rights Abuse." Editorial. *Christian Science Monitor* 20 Oct. 1999:

10. Print.

Safire, William. "Lying 'Lie Detectors.'" *New York Times* 10 Oct.

2002, late ed.: A39. Print.

"The Truth about Lie Detectors, Says David Lykken, Is That They

Can't Detect a Lie." *People* 11 May 1981: 75+. Print.

Ward, William, et al. "Meprobamate Reduces Accuracy of Physiological

Detection of Deception." *Science* 3 Apr. 1981: 73–74. Print.

"What's It Like to Take a Lie Detector Test?" *Law and Order*

[Columbia] 5 July 1981: F7–8. Print.

Books and periodicals in italics.

Article in quotation marks

Web source

Article in newspaper

Format for more than 3 authors: first author only, plus *et al.*

A Minibook of Essential Grammar and Common Errors

Abbreviations.   As a rule, avoid abbreviations. When in doubt, spell it out.

ab

Wrong	Right
NYC and other municipalities can cure their financial ills only by aid from the federal gov't.	New York City and other municipalities can cure their financial ills only by aid from the federal government.
Thanksgiving comes on the fourth Thurs. of Nov.	Thanksgiving comes on the fourth Thursday of November.

In some cases, abbreviations are required or preferred. In general, the trend in abbreviations is not to use periods after letters or spaces between letters, especially when all letters of an abbreviation are capital letters (FBI, CD-ROM, NY).

- *Standard forms of address before a person's name*: Mr., Mrs., Ms., Dr., or St. (for Saint, not street).
- *Titles.* If both a person's surname (last) and given name (first) or initials are used, write *Rev., Hon., Prof., Sen.*

    Rev. John Yip, Prof. A. J. Carr (but not Rev. Yip or Prof. Carr)
- *Degrees.* After a name, abbreviate academic degrees, *Jr.,* and *Sr.* Academic degrees may also be abbreviated when used by themselves.

    Marion Jonas, MD

    He is now studying for a BA after completing his AAS degree.
- *Organizations*:

    NATO   NAACP   OPEC   UN   USA   AFL-CIO   MLA
- *Other.* Traditional footnote references and bibliographical terms (many no longer in common use) are nearly always abbreviated, as are a few familiar words.

etc.	p. 23	DNA
ibid.	pp. 137–40	TNT
et al.	vol.	

Adjective–Adverb Confusion

ad

Adjectives modify nouns (Getting a diploma takes *hard* work).
Adverbs modify verbs, adjectives, or other adverbs (We stepped *carefully*).
Form most adverbs by adding *-ly* to adjectives:

Adjective	Adverb
nice	nicely
strong	strongly
pretty	prettily
nasty	nastily

A few of the resulting adverbs may sound so awkward that an adverbial phrase is the preferred form.

Adjective	Adverbial Phrase
friendly	in a friendly way
lovely	in a lovely way

A few adjectives and adverbs are identical in form:

Adjective:	He is a *better* person for the experience.
	Fast drivers are dangerous drivers.
Adverb:	He did *better* than I.
	I can type *fast*.

Confusion of adjectives and adverbs is among the most common grammatical errors and is likely to turn up from one of the following causes.

- *Misuse of an adjective to modify a verb.*

Wrong	Right
I wish she acted *different*.	I wish she acted *differently*.
Bill did *good* on his examination.	Bill did *well* on his examination.

- *Misuse of an adjective to modify an adverb or other adjective.*

Wrong	Right
The price was *sure* very expensive.	The price was *surely* very expensive.
The patient is *considerable* worse today.	The patient is *considerably* worse today.

- *Misuse of an adverb after a linking verb.* The correct modifier after a linking verb is an adjective. The single most common linking verb is *to be* (*am, is, are, was, were, will be,* and so on). Verbs dealing with the senses—sight, touch, taste, smell, hearing—are often used as linking verbs: *feel, look, sound, taste, appear.* Other verbs frequently serving as linking verbs are *get, seem, remain, become.*

Wrong	Right
The music sounds *beautifully*.	The music sounds *beautiful*.
The food tastes *badly*.	The food tastes *bad*.

Note how an adjective or adverb determines meaning:

I smell bad. (I need to buy deodorant.)

I smell badly. (My sinuses are stuffed up.)

He looks evil. (He looks like a wicked person.)

He looks evilly. (His glances are frightening.)

- *Misuse of comparative or superlative forms.* When comparing entities, be sure to use the correct form:

Positive One item is	Comparative Of two items, one is (add *-er* or use *more*)	Superlative Of three or more items, one is (add *-est* or use *most*)
nasty (adjective)	nastier	nastiest
discrete (adjective)	more discrete	most discrete
friendly (adverb)	friendlier	friendliest
terrible (adverb)	more terrible	most terrible

Some adjectives and adverbs have irregular forms:

Positive	Comparative	Superlative
good	better	best
bad	worse	worst
little	less, littler	least, littlest
some, many, much	more	most
well	better	best
bad, badly	worse	worst
far	farther	farthest

Antecedent. The noun or pronoun to which a pronoun refers.

Richard Yee left *his* lunch at home.

Here, the pronoun *his* refers to its noun antecedent, *Richard Yee.*

Apostrophe. Use the apostrophe to form contractions, plurals, and possessives.

- *Contractions.* The apostrophe means that a letter or letters have been left out.

    it is = it's   she is = she's   who is = who's   you will = you'll

- *Plurals.* Use the *'s* to form the plural of letters: *a's, x's, B's, C's.* Use only an *s* for the plurals of abbreviations and numbers.

    the 1930s   the &s (*or* the &'s)   two *c's* in *occupy*

    DAs   POWs

- *Possessives.* Use an apostrophe to form the possessive of nouns and indefinite pronouns. In speech, *cats, cat's,* and *cats'* all sound identical. The meanings are all different, however, and in writing, those differences show up immediately. *Cats* is a simple plural—add an *s* to the singular without the use of an apostrophe.

    The cats howled all night.

    Purring is a way cats have of showing affection.

Cat's is a possessive singular, another way of expressing the thought *of the cat. Cats'* is a possessive plural, another way of expressing the thought *of the cats.* To determine whether a word with a possessive apostrophe is singular or plural, just look at the part of the word *before the apostrophe.*

Singular	Plural
cat's claws	cats' claws
Mr. Smith's home	the Smiths' home

Note, too, that in a phrase like *of the cats,* the word *of* takes care of the idea of possession, and no apostrophe is used.

Possessives with *of* (no apostrophe)	Possessives with apostrophes
The claws of a cat are sharp.	A cat's claws are sharp.
The hunting abilities of cats are well known.	Cats' hunting abilities are well known.

Possessive pronouns—*my, mine, our, ours, your, yours, his, her, hers, its, their, theirs*—are already possessive in themselves and *never take apostrophes.*

When a possessive apostrophe is required, the rules are relatively simple.

- Singular or plural nouns that do not end in *-s* form their possessives by adding *'s.*

Ivan's car	Arlene's book	Women's Liberation
the teacher's notes	New York's mayor	children's games

- Plural nouns that end in *-s* form their possessives by adding only an apostrophe:

the students' teacher	Californians' freeways
automobiles' engines	the two teachers' classes

- Singular nouns that end in *-s* ordinarily form their possessives by adding *'s.* Some writers make exceptions of words that already have so many s or z sounds in them (for example, *Massachusetts, Jesus*) that pronunciation of a final *'s* is awkward. You can form the possessive of such words by adding only an apostrophe. Both methods are correct, and writers can use their own judgment as long as they are consistent.

Dickens' novels	the business's profits
Charles's bowling ball	Mr. Jones's new roof

- Indefinite pronouns form their possessives by adding *'s:*

nobody's fool	someone's knock
anyone's guess	everybody's business

- In the case of joint possession—possession by two or more—form the possessive by adding an apostrophe or 's, as appropriate, to the last noun:

   the girls and boys' school   Jill and Bob's car

   NOTE: To show individual possession, write "Jill's and Bob's cars" and "the girls' and boys' schools." Here Jill has a car and Bob has a car, the girls have a school and the boys have a school.

Brackets. Use brackets ([ ]) to enclose comments or added information that you have inserted into a direct quotation.

> "While influenced by moral considerations, Lincoln signed it [the Emancipation Proclamation] primarily to further the war effort."

> "The music column had the altogether intimidating title of *Hemidemisemiquavers* [sixty-fourth notes]."

[ ]

Capital letters. Use a capital letter for the following:

cap

- *The first word of a sentence or direct quotation.*

   A popular early television show featured a detective whose most characteristic line was, "We just want the facts, ma'am."

- *The first and all important words of titles of books, movies, radio and television programs, songs, magazines, plays, short stories, poems, essays, and chapters.*

   A Streetcar Named Desire [play]   "Ode to a Nightingale" [poem]
   Time [magazine]   "Gifts" [essay]
   Roget's College Thesaurus [book]   "Basin Street Blues" [song]

- *The first word and all nouns of a salutation.*

   Dear Sir: My dear Ms. Hunt: Dear Bill,

- *The first word of a complimentary close.*

   Sincerely yours,   Yours truly,

- *Some pronouns.*

   1. First-person singular: *I*.
   2. References to the Judeo-Christian deity, where necessary to avoid confusion:

      God told Moses that he must carry out His commandments.

- *Proper nouns.*

   1. Names and titles of persons and groups of persons:
      a. Persons: Martin Luther King Jr., President Barack Obama, Lady Gaga, Hillary Rodham Clinton.
      b. Races, nationalities, and religions: Caucasian, Chinese, Catholic (but *black, white*).
      c. Groups, organizations, and departments: League of Women Voters, Ford Motor Company, United States Senate, Department of Agriculture.
      d. Particular deities: God, Allah, Buddha, Zeus.

2. Names of particular places:
   a. Cities, counties, states, and countries: Cleveland, Cuyahoga County, Ohio, United States of America.
   b. Geographical regions: Europe, Pacific Northwest, the South.
   c. Streets: East Ninth Street, El Cajon Avenue.
   d. Buildings: Empire State Building, Union Terminal.
   e. Heavenly bodies (except the sun and moon): Mars, Milky Way, Andromeda, Alpha Centauri.

3. Names of particular things:
   a. Days and months: Friday, August.
   b. Holidays: Easter, Thanksgiving.
   c. Historical events and periods: the Civil War, the Middle Ages.
   d. School courses: Biology 101, History 102 (but "a *history* course").
   e. Languages: English, Russian.
   f. Schools: Cornell University, Walt Whitman High School (but "I graduated from *high school*").
   g. Brands: Buick, Peter Pan Peanut Butter (but "I had a *peanut butter* sandwich for lunch").

Clause. A group of words with a subject and predicate. A clause can be independent or dependent. An *independent clause* stands alone as a separate sentence.

Maria went home.

A *dependent clause* cannot stand alone; rather, it must depend on an independent clause to complete its meaning.

After I came home, I took a nap. The man *who lived next door* died.

Colon. Use a colon (:) in these situations:

- *List.* A colon appears between a general statement and a list or description that follows:

  We shall never again find the equals of the famous three *B*'s of music: Bach, Beethoven, and Brahms.

NOTE: A colon should appear after a complete statement. Do not use a colon after a form of the verb to be (*be, am, is, are, was, were, been*, etc.) or after a preposition.

Wrong	**Right**
Perennial contenders for the NFL championship are: San Francisco, New England, Dallas, and Buffalo.	Several teams are perennial contenders for the NFL championship: San Francisco, New England, Dallas, and Buffalo.
	or
	Perennial contenders for the NFL championship are San Francisco, New England, Dallas, and Buffalo.

- *Time*. Between hours and minutes: 8:00 p.m.   5:10 a.m.
- *Salutation*.

    Dear Ms. Johnson: Dear Sir:

- *Biblical references*. Genesis 1:8 (chapter 1, verse 8)
- *Title and subtitle*. A colon separates the title and subtitle of a book:

    Johnson's Dictionary: A Modern Selection

- *Independent clauses*. A colon may appear between independent clauses when the second clause explains the first:

    They reared their children on one principle, and one principle only: Do unto others what they would like to do unto you—and do it first.

- *Quotations*. A colon sometimes introduces a short quotation and often introduces a long block quotation:

    Whenever I try to diet, I am reminded of the bitter truth of Oscar Wilde's epigram: "I can resist everything but temptation."

    In commenting on his function as a writer, Joseph Conrad put every writer's dream into words:

    > My task which I am trying to achieve is, by the power of the written word to make you hear, to make you feel—it is, before all, to make you *see*. That—and no more, and it is everything. If I succeed, you shall find there according to your deserts: encouragement, consolation, fear, charm—all you demand—and, perhaps, also that glimpse of truth for which you have forgotten to ask.

    NOTE: No quotation marks surround a block quotation.

Commas. *Never use a comma unless you know it is necessary.* A comma is necessary in the following cases:

A. *Series*. Separate three or more items in a list or series by commas for the sake of clarity.

    The potential buyer should take special care to inspect the roof, basement, and ceilings.

    The three novels in Dos Passos's *USA* trilogy are *The 42nd Parallel, Nineteen Nineteen*, and *The Big Money*.

    NOTE: In both examples, the comma before *and* is optional. However, most experienced writers use the comma.

B. *Independent clauses*. Two independent clauses (a group of words that can stand alone as a complete sentence) joined by a coordinating conjunction—*and, but, or, nor, for, yet, so*—require a comma *before* the conjunction:

    Barack Obama fought hard for votes, and he impressed people all over the country.

    Each writing assignment requires a different kind of organization, and each may require a different length.

Use no comma if there is only one independent clause:

> Barack Obama fought hard for votes and impressed people all over the country.

> Each writing assignment requires a different kind of organization and may require a different length.

C. *Introductory elements.* In general, use a comma after an introductory element:

> *Because the students were having trouble with commas,* they read the section on punctuation.

> *In good writing,* there are few punctuation errors.

When the introductory element is extremely short—one word, for example—you can omit the comma if the meaning remains clear: "*Soon* the term will end."

If you move the introductory element so that it appears *after* the independent clause (and thus no longer introduces anything), do not use a comma:

> No agreement was reached despite the best efforts of both parties.

> He went straight to bed as soon as he had showered.

D. *Interrupting elements.* Use a comma before and after an interrupting element. Interrupting elements are those that break the flow of words in the main thought of a sentence or clause. Interrupting elements may be words such as *indeed, however, too, also, consequently, therefore, moreover, nevertheless,* and phrases such as *as the author says, of course, after all, for example, in fact, on the other hand.*

Wrong	**Right**
Suppose for example that you decide to write about your own life.	Suppose, for example, that you decide to write about your own life.
We must bear in mind too that even the best system is imperfect.	We must bear in mind, too, that even the best system is imperfect.
Punctuation as we can see is not exactly fun.	Punctuation, as we can see, is not exactly fun.

E. *Coordinating adjectives.* Use a comma to separate coordinating adjectives—adjectives of equal rank—that come before the nouns they modify.

Wrong	**Right**
This poet uses concrete believable images.	This poet uses concrete, believable images.
Her warm enthusiastic energetic behavior was often mistaken for pushiness.	Her warm, enthusiastic, energetic behavior was often mistaken for pushiness.

You can identify coordinating adjectives in two ways: (1) the word *and* may be used to join them (concrete *and* believable, warm *and* enthusiastic *and* energetic) or (2) they may be reversed (believable, concrete;

enthusiastic, energetic, warm). Compare these examples to "This poet uses several concrete images." We cannot say "several and concrete" or "concrete several." Therefore, we do not use a comma between them. Note, too, that if the coordinate adjectives had originally been joined by *and*, no commas would have been necessary: "Her warm *and* enthusiastic *and* energetic behavior was often mistaken for pushiness."

F. *Nonrestrictive elements.* A comma should be used before and after a nonrestrictive element.

Nonrestrictive modifiers. A nonrestrictive modifier gives additional information about the noun it modifies but is not necessary to identify or define that noun:

> The Empire State Building, *which I visited last year,* is a most impressive sight.
>
> My father, *who has worked in a steel foundry for thirty years,* has made many sacrifices for me.

A *restrictive modifier* is not set off by commas. It is a necessary part of the meaning of the noun it modifies:

> A person *who is always late for appointments* may have serious psychological problems.
>
> The novel *that Professor Higgins praised so highly* is very disappointing.

Proper punctuation of restrictive and nonrestrictive modifiers often can affect meaning:

The sofa, with those huge armrests, is an eyesore.	(The writer sees just one sofa. The nonrestrictive modifier merely conveys more information about it.)
The sofa with those huge armrests is an eyesore.	(The writer sees more than one sofa. The restrictive modifier is necessary to distinguish this sofa from the others.)

A special type of nonrestrictive element is called the *appositive*—a word or group of words that mean the same thing as the element that precedes it. Commas are used before and after nonrestrictive appositives. A nonrestrictive appositive gives additional information about the noun it follows but is not necessary to identify that noun:

> Ms. Susan Swattem, *my high school mathematics teacher,* was the meanest person in town.
>
> Thomas Jefferson, *third president of the United States,* also founded the University of Virginia.

A *restrictive appositive* is not set off by commas. It is necessary to identify the noun it follows:

> The expression *hitch your wagon to a star* was first used by Emerson.
>
> He spoke to Susan *my sister,* not Susan *my wife.*

As with modifiers, proper punctuation of nonrestrictive and restrictive appositives often can affect meaning.

My brother, George, is a kindly soul.	(The writer has only one brother, so the word *brother* is sufficient identification. *George* is nonrestrictive.)
My brother George is a kindly soul.	(The writer has more than one brother, so the name of the specific brother is a necessary part of the meaning. *George* is restrictive.)

G. *Contrast.* Use commas to set off phrases expressing a contrast.

> She told him to deliver the furniture on Wednesday, not Tuesday.
>
> Hard work, not noble daydreams, is what I believe in.

NOTE: The comma can sometimes be omitted before contrasting phrases beginning with *but*: "We have nothing to fear *but* fear itself."

H. *Direct address, interjections,* yes *and* no.

1. *Direct address:*

> I tell you, ladies and gentlemen, that this strategy will not work.
>
> Jim, you're still not following the instructions.

2. *Interjections:*

> Well, it appears that the committee has finally issued its report.
>
> Oh, I'd say the new car should arrive in about three weeks.

Although commas are generally used with mild interjections, more dramatic interjections may take exclamation points:

> Oh! How could she have made such a contemptible remark?

3. *Yes* and *no:*

> Yes, I plan to vote for Ruppert.
>
> I have to tell you plainly that, no, I cannot support your proposal.

I. *Misreading.* Apart from any more specific rules, commas are sometimes necessary to prevent misreading.

Confusing	**Correct**
High above the trees swayed in the wind.	High above, the trees swayed in the wind.
At the same time John and Arnold were making their plans.	At the same time, John and Arnold were making their plans.

J. *Conventions.* Use commas with the following:

1. *Dates.* Commas separate the day of the month and the year:

> April 24, 1938　　　January 5, 1967

If you write only the month and year, you can omit the comma:

> April 1938　　　*or*　　　April, 1938

If the year is used in midsentence with the day of the month, follow it by a comma. With the month only, you may omit the comma:

World War II began for the United States on December 7, 1941, at Pearl Harbor.

World War II began for the United States in December 1941 at Pearl Harbor.

World War II began for the United States in December, 1941, at Pearl Harbor.

In Works Cited entries, use European or miltary date order, where no commas are necessary (see pages 174–180):

7 December 1941   15 March 2008

2. *Numbers*. Use commas to group numbers of more than three digits to the left of the decimal point:

$5,280.00   751,672.357   5,429,000   5,280

However, commas are not used for page numbers, addresses, or years:

page 4233   1236 Madison Ave.   1989

3. *Addresses*. Use commas to separate towns, cities, counties, states, and districts:

Cleveland, Ohio   Brooklyn, Kings County, New York   Washington, D.C.

NOTE: Do not use a comma to separate the ZIP code from the state.

Pasadena, California 91106

4. *Titles*. A comma often separates a title from a name that precedes it:

Harold Unger, MD   Julia Harding, PhD

5. *Correspondence*. Use a comma after the salutation in informal letters and after the complimentary close:

Dear John,   Dear Jane,

Respectfully yours,   Sincerely yours,

6. *Direct quotations*. Use a comma before and after a direct quote in mid sentence:

He shouted, "Please wait," as I ran off.

Comma splice. Often considered a special kind of *run-on sentence*, a *comma splice* is a punctuation error that occurs when two independent clauses are joined only by a comma. You can correct a comma splice by (1) using both a comma and a coordinating conjunction or (2) replacing the comma with a semicolon or a period.

There are only seven coordinating conjunctions: *and, but, or, nor, for, yet,* and *so.* When you use these between independent clauses, in formal usage, precede them by a comma.

Wrong	**Right**
The boy had been physically disabled since infancy, he still tried to excel in everything he did.	The boy had been physically disabled since infancy, but he still tried to excel in everything he did.

or

CS

> The boy had been physically disabled since infancy; he still tried to excel in everything he did.
>
> *or*
>
> The boy had been physically disabled since infancy. He still tried to excel in everything he did.

It is often tempting to use words such as *however, therefore, nevertheless, indeed*, and *moreover* after a comma to join independent clauses. Don't! The only words following a comma that can join two independent clauses are the seven coordinating conjunctions.

Wrong	Right
We started with high hopes, however, we were disappointed.	We started with high hopes; however, we were disappointed.
She had been hurt many times, nevertheless, she always seemed cheerful.	She had been hurt many times; nevertheless, she always seemed cheerful.

Since the comma splice is created by connecting two independent clauses with a comma, you can change one of the independent clauses into a phrase or dependent clause. Notice how this technique works with the preceding sample sentences.

> Physically disabled from infancy, the boy still tried to excel in everything he did.
>
> Although he had been physically disabled from infancy, the boy still tried to excel in everything he did.
>
> We started with high hopes but were disappointed.
>
> Despite her being hurt many times, she always seemed cheerful.

NOTE: Comma splices can be acceptable in standard English when each clause is unusually short and when the thought of the whole sentence expresses an ongoing process.

> I came, I saw, I conquered.
>
> Throughout the interview, she squirmed, she stammered, she blushed.

Conjunction. A word used to join parts of sentences or clauses. *Coordinating conjunctions* (joining words or clauses of equal importance) are *and, but, or, nor, for, yet, so; subordinating conjunctions* (linking dependent and independent clauses) are *because, while, when, although, until, after*, and so on.

Dash. Use a dash (—) to do the following:

- *To emphasize a parenthetical word or phrase.*

> Only when politicians are exposed to temptation—and rest assured they are almost always so exposed—can we determine their real worth as human beings.

- *To express an afterthought.*

> The only person who understood the talk was the speaker—and I have my doubts about her.

- *In a list or series.*

> The great French Impressionists—Manet, Monet, Renoir—virtually invented a new way of looking at the world.
>
> *The Scarlet Letter, Moby-Dick, Walden, Leaves of Grass, Uncle Tom's Cabin*—these American classics were all published during the incredible five-year span of 1850–1855.

NOTE: Use dashes sparingly, or they lose their force. Do not confuse a dash with a hyphen. In typing, indicate a dash by striking the hyphen key twice (--), leaving no space between the dash and the two words it separates.

Dependent clause. See *Clause.*

Direct object. See *Object.*

Double negative. Always incorrect in standard English, a double negative is the use of two negative terms to express only one negative idea. Negative terms include *no, not, nothing, hardly,* and *scarcely.*

Wrong	Right
I don't have no memory of last night.	I don't have any memory of last night.
	or
	I have no memory of last night.
His mother couldn't hardly express her feelings of pride at his graduation.	His mother could hardly express her feelings of pride at his graduation.
Our troubles had not scarcely begun.	Our troubles had scarcely begun.

Ellipsis. An ellipsis (…) shows omission of one or more words from quoted material. If the ellipsis occurs at the end of a sentence, four spaced dots are used; the first dot is the period for the sentence.

Original	Use of ellipsis
"The connotation of a word is its implicit meaning, the meaning derived from the atmosphere, the vibrations, the emotions that we associate with the word."	"The connotation of a word is its implicit meaning,…the emotions that we associate with the word."
"We had a drought in 1988 and major floods in 1989. Statistics can be deceptive. The two-year statistics for rainfall look totally normal, but the reality was wildly abnormal."	"We had a drought in 1988 and major floods in 1989.…The two-year statistics for rainfall look totally normal, but the reality was wildly abnormal."

End marks. The three end marks are the period, question mark, and exclamation point.

- *Period.* A period is used at the end of complete sentences, after abbreviations, and in fractions expressed as decimals.

1. *Sentences.* If a complete sentence makes a statement, use a period at the end:

> Please give unused clothing to the Salvation Army.
>
> Place pole *B* against slot *C* and insert bolt *D.*
>
> The class wants to know when the paper is due.

2. *Abbreviations.* Use a period after some abbreviations:

> Mr. R. P. Reddish   Mt. Everest   p.m.

NOTE: A period is not used in abbreviations such as UNESCO, NAACP, FCC, MLA, and AARP. See *Abbreviations.*

3. *Decimals.* Use a period before a fraction written as a decimal.

> $\frac{1}{4} = 0.25$ $\frac{1}{20} = 0.05$

NOTE: If you use a decimal point to indicate money, you also need a dollar sign: $5.25, $.67.

- *Question mark.* A question mark indicates a direct question or a doubtful date or figure.

  1. *Direct question.* Use a question mark at the end of a direct question. Do not use a question mark with indirect questions such as "They asked when the paper was due."

     > When is the paper due?
     >
     > Did the teacher say when the paper is due?

     You need to use a question mark when only the last part of a sentence asks a question, and when a quotation that asks a question is contained within a larger sentence.

     > I know I should go to college, but where will I get the money for tuition?
     >
     > The student asked, "When is the paper due?"
     >
     > After asking, "When is the paper due?" the student left the room.

     NOTE: In the last example, the question mark replaces the usual comma inside the quotation.

  2. *Doubtful date or figure.* After a doubtful date or figure, use a question mark in parentheses. This does not mean that if you are giving an approximate date or figure you should use a question mark. Use it only if the accuracy of the date or figure is doubtful.

     > The newspaper reported that the government said it cost $310 (?) to send a person to the moon. (Here a question mark is appropriate because it is doubtful if $310 is the figure. Perhaps there has been a misprint in the paper.)
     >
     > Chaucer was born in 1340 (?) and died in 1400. (Here historians know when Chaucer died but are doubtful of exactly when he was born, even though most evidence points to 1340. If historians were completely unsure, they would simply write, "Chaucer was born in the mid-1300s and died in 1400.")

Never use a question mark in parentheses to indicate humor or sarcasm. It is awkward and childish to write, "He was a good (?) teacher," or, "After much debate and cynical compromise, the legislature approved a satisfactory (?) state budget."

- *Exclamation point.* Use an exclamation point at the end of emphatic or exclamatory words, phrases, and sentences. In formal writing, exclamation points are rare. They most often occur in dialog, and even there they should be used sparingly.

    1. *Word or phrase:*

        My God! Is the paper due today?

        No! You cannot copy my exam.

    2. *Sentence:*

        The school burned down!

        Stop talking!

Fragmentary sentences. A fragmentary sentence (also called a sentence fragment) is a grammatically incomplete statement punctuated as if it were a complete sentence. It is one of the most common basic writing errors.

frag

To avoid a sentence fragment, make sure that your sentence contains at least one independent clause. If it does not contain an independent clause, it is a fragment.

Here are some examples of sentences with the independent clause italicized; sometimes the independent clause is the whole sentence, and sometimes the independent clause is part of a larger sentence.

Jack and Jill went up the hill.

He sees.

If you don't stop bothering me, *I'll phone the police.*

Tomorrow at the latest, *we'll have to call a special meeting.*

Discovering that she had lost her mother, *the little girl started to cry.*

An *independent clause* is a group of words that contain a subject and verb and express a complete thought. There are three major reasons for a missing independent clause:

- *Omission of subject or verb.* This is the simplest kind of fragment to spot:

    There are many events that take place on campus. *Such as plays, concerts, and innumerable other activities.*

    We had many blessings. *Like love, nature, family, God, and television.*

    Simple changes in punctuation will solve the problems. Here are the same sentences with the fragments eliminated:

    There are many events that take place on campus, such as plays, concerts, and innumerable other activities.

    We had many blessings, like love, nature, family, God, and television.

- *Confusion of verb derivatives (verbals) with verbs.* Verbals are words derived from verbs. Unlike verbs, they cannot function by themselves as the predicate of a sentence. Infinitive forms are verbals (*to do, to see, to walk*). So are gerunds and present participles (-*ing* endings: *doing, seeing, walking*). Study the italicized sentence fragments that follow.

> I decided to take her to the game. *Susan enjoying football with a passion.*

> To *make the world a better place. To help people be happy.* These are my goals.

In the second example, the fragments lack subjects as well as verbs.

Inexperienced writers, however, looking at the fragments in the first example, see a subject and what appears to be a verb. They assume, consequently, that the words make up an independent clause. They are wrong. A present participle by itself cannot serve as a verb, and an independent clause must have a verb.

Correct:

> I decided to take her to the game. Susan has been enjoying football with a passion.

> I want to make the world a better place. I want to make people happy. These are my goals.

- *Confusion of a dependent (subordinate) clause with an independent clause.* All clauses contain a subject and a verb. Unlike an independent clause, however, a *dependent* or *subordinate clause* does not express a complete thought and therefore cannot function as a sentence. A subordinate clause at the beginning of a sentence must always be followed by an independent clause. A subordinate clause at the end of a sentence must always be preceded by an independent clause. Subordinate clauses *always begin with subordinating conjunctions.*

Subordinating Conjunctions

after	as soon as	even though	provided that	until
although	as though	how	since	when
as	because	if	so that	whenever
as if	before	in order that	though	wherever
as long as	even if	once	unless	while

NOTE: Except when used as question words, *who, which, when,* and *where* also introduce a subordinate clause.

In the left-hand column below and on the following page, examples of subordinate clauses used as sentence fragments are italicized. In the right-hand column, italics indicate corrections to repair these sentence fragments.

Fragments	**Corrected**
If I ever see home again.	If I ever see home again, *I'll be surprised.*
Keats was a great poet. *Because he was inspired.*	*Keats was a great poet because* he was inspired.

> This is the person who will be our
> next governor. *Who will lead this
> state to a better tomorrow.*

> *This is the person who will be our next governor, who* will lead this state to a better tomorrow.

Sentence fragments should nearly always be avoided. In rare situations, they can sometimes be justified, especially if the writer wants a sudden dramatic effect.

I shall never consent to this law. Never!

Death to the tyrant!

Scared? I was terrified.

Hyphen. A hyphen (-) is used to form some compound words and to divide words at the end of a line.

- *Compound words.*

    1. As a general rule, consult a recent dictionary to check the use of the hyphen in compound words. Many such words that were once hyphenated are now combined. The following are some compound words that are still hyphenated:

        mother-in-law   court-martial   knee-deep   water-cooled

    2. All numbers from twenty-one to ninety-nine (except multiples of ten) are hyphenated:

        forty-three   one hundred fifty-six

    3. A hyphen joins two or more words that form an adjective before a noun:

        a well-known teacher

        but

        The teacher is well known.

        a first-rate performance

        but

        The performance was first rate.

- *Divided words.* Divide words at the end of a line by consulting a dictionary and following accepted syllabication. Do not divide one-syllable words. Do not separate a single letter from the rest of the word; for example, *a-bout* for *about* would be incorrect. The hyphen should come at the very end of the line, not at the beginning of the next line.

Independent clause. See *Clause.*

Indirect question. See *End marks.*

Infinitive. Simple form of a verb preceded by the word *to*—for example, *to come, to go.*

Italics (underlining). In handwriting, underlining represents printed italics. The rules for underlining and italics are the same. Underline or italicize titles of complete works; most foreign words and phrases; words used emphatically;

and letters, words, and phrases pointed to as such. If you are preparing an essay based on MLA or APA style, use italics.

Handwritten:	Print generated:
I love Star Wars.	I love *Star Wars*.

NOTE: When a word or phrase that would usually be italicized appears in a section of text that is already italicized, the word or phrase is typed or written with no italics.

- *Titles of complete works.*
  - Books: *The Great Gatsby, Paradise Lost, The Hitchhiker's Guide to the Galaxy*
  - Newspapers and magazines: *New York Times, Chicago Tribune, Newsweek*
  - Plays and movies: *A Raisin in the Sun, Macbeth, The Hurt Locker, Sleepless in Seattle*

Enclose the titles of poems in quotation marks, except for book-length poems such as Milton's *Paradise Lost* and Homer's *Iliad*. Use quotation marks to enclose the titles of small units contained within larger units—such as chapters in books, selections in anthologies, articles or short stories in magazines, and individual episodes of a television series. (See *Quotation marks.*)

- *Foreign words and phrases not assimilated into English.*

vaya con Diós	*paisano*	*auf Wiedersehen*	
but			
cliché	genre	laissez-faire	taco

- *Words used emphatically.*

  Ask me, but don't *tell* me.

  Under *no* circumstances can we permit this to happen.

Except in special situations, good word choice and careful phrasing are far more effective than italicizing or underlining to show emphasis.

- *Letters, words, and phrases pointed to as such.*

  Do not use words such as *however* and *therefore* as coordinating conjunctions.

  The letter *x* is often used in algebra.

Check with your instructor about his or her preference for italics or underlining.

Modifiers. The most frequent errors involving modifiers are dangling modifiers and misplaced modifiers.

dm

- *Dangling modifiers. A dangling modifier* is a group of words, often found at the beginning of a sentence, that do not refer to anything in the sentence or that seem to refer to a word to which the dangler is not logically related. Dangling modifiers usually include some form of a verb that has no subject, either implied or stated. This construction results in statements that are sometimes humorous and always illogical. To correct a dangling modifier, either change the modifier into a subordinate clause, or change the main clause so that the modifier logically relates to a word in it. On occasion, you may have to change both clauses.

Incorrect	**Correct**
Climbing the mountain, the sunset blazed with a brilliant red and orange. (This sentence says that the sunset is climbing the mountain.)	As we climbed the mountain, the sunset blazed with a brilliant red and orange. (Subordinate clause)

or

Climbing the mountain, we saw the sunset blazing with a brilliant red and orange. (Main clause)

To become an accurate speller, a dictionary is very helpful. (In this sentence, the dictionary is becoming an accurate speller.)	If you want to become an accurate speller, a dictionary is very helpful.

or

To become an accurate speller, you should use a dictionary.

- *Misplaced modifiers.* Be sure that you place phrases serving as modifiers and adverbs such as *only, always, almost, hardly,* and *nearly* in the position that will make the sentence mean what you intend. *Misplaced modifiers,* unlike dangling modifiers, can almost always be corrected simply by changing their positions.

  mm

  1. Phrases serving as modifiers:

     The teacher found the book for the student in the library.

     This sentence indicates that the student was in the library. If, however, the writer meant that the book was found in the library, then the modifier *in the library* is misplaced. The sentence should read:

     In the library, the teacher found the book for the student.

     The writer of the following sentence seems to be saying that the college is near the lake:

     His parents met his friend from the college near the lake.

     If, however, the writer meant that the meeting took place near the lake, the modifier is misplaced and the sentence should read:

     Near the lake, his parents met his friend from the college.

  2. Adverbs like *only, always, almost, hardly,* and *nearly* usually qualify the word that comes after them. Therefore, the position of these words depends on what the writer wishes to say.

The adverb *only* is a notorious troublemaker. Observe how the sentence *"I want a son"* changes meaning significantly with the change in position of *only*:

I *only* want a son.	(I don't yearn for or long for a son; I only want one.)
I want *only* a son.	(I have no other wants.)
I want an *only* son.	(One son is as many as I want.)
I want a son *only*.	(I do not want a daughter.)

Noun.   Traditionally defined as the name of a person, place, thing, or concept, nouns are generally used as the subject, object, or complement of a sentence: *Roosevelt, Bill, accountant, California, Lake Ontario, Boulder Dam, desk, car, freedom, love.*

Numerals.

- *Numerals are used to indicate dates, times, percentages, money, street numbers, and page references.*

  On January 21, 2003, at 5:00 a.m., a fire broke out at 552 East 52nd Street, and before the Lincoln Fire Department brought the flames under control, the fire had destroyed 75 percent of the building.

- *In other cases, if a number is one or two words, spell it out; if it is over two words, use the numeral.*

  In the big contest forty-five young boys won ribbons. William ate 152 hot dogs.

- *Opt for ease and consistency when you refer to different numbers in one sentence.*

  In the big contests yesterday, 45 young boys won ribbons and William ate 152 hot dogs in 2 minutes.

- *Spell out all numbers that begin a sentence.*

  Four thugs assaulted an old woman last night.

  Three hundred thirty-one traffic deaths happened nationwide during the Labor Day weekend.

Object.   The object is the person, place, or thing that receives the action of a verb, or the noun or pronoun after a preposition.

George shot *Joe*.

Florence kissed *him*.

All motives are suspect to *them*.

You'll find your *gloves* in the car.

Parallelism.   Express ideas and facts of equal importance in the same grammatical form. See pages 74–75 for a fuller treatment of parallelism.

Parentheses.   Use parentheses in the following instances:

- *Incidental comments.*

  The movie *The Killers* (its plot had little resemblance to Hemingway's short story) won an award.

- *Explanation of details.*

  The cornucopia (the horn of plenty) is a Thanksgiving symbol.

- *Enumerated points.*

  This essay has four main pieces of advice: (1) know your professors as people, (2) attend college-sponsored events, (3) attend student-sponsored events, and (4) use the library.

- *Citation of sources.*

  In fact, refusal may mean the loss of a job (Beach 44).

( )

Period.   See *End marks.*

Person.   The form of pronouns and verbs that indicates the speaker (*first person*), the person or thing spoken to (*second person*), or the person or thing spoken about (*third person*).

	Pronoun	Verb
First person	I, we	go
Second person	you	go
Third person	he, she, it	goes
	they	go

Predicate.   The part of a clause that tells what the subject does, or what is being done to the subject.

Sal *went home.*
The child *will be punished.*

Preposition.   A connecting word such as *in, by, from, on, to,* or *with* that shows the relation of a noun or a pronoun to another element in a sentence.

The man *with* the gun shot the deer.

Pronoun.   A word that takes the place of a noun. It may be personal (*I, you, he, she, it, we, they, me, him, her*), possessive (*my, mine, your, yours, his*), reflexive or intensive (*myself, yourself, herself*), relative (*who, which, that*), interrogative (*who, which, what*), or indefinite (*anyone, somebody, nothing*).

Pronoun agreement.   A pronoun must agree with its antecedent both in gender (masculine, feminine, or neuter) and number (singular or plural). The antecedent of a pronoun is the word or words to which the pronoun refers. For example, in the sentence "Jason lost his book," the pronoun *his* refers to

agr

the antecedent *Jason*. Another example is "Jason could not find his book. He had lost it." In the second sentence, there are two pronouns—*he* and *it*. The antecedent of *he* is *Jason*, and the antecedent of *it* is *book*. With the exception of constructions such as *it is nearly eight o'clock*, in which *it* has no antecedent, all pronouns should have antecedents.

sexist

- *Gender*. When the gender of a singular antecedent is unknown, irrelevant, or general (as in *student* or *person*, for example), be sure to avoid sexist language. The traditional rule calling for the masculine pronoun to take precedence in such situations is now outdated.

- If you retain the singular antecedent, you can avoid sexist language by using a form of *he or she*, though this phrasing can often be awkward and excessively formal.

  A student needs to turn in his or her work on time.

  A person who truly likes others will find that others will like him or her.

  The most effective way of avoiding sexist language is usually to change the singular antecedent to plural.

  Students must turn in their work on time.

  People who truly like others will find that others will like them.

  (See pages 83–85 in Chapter 10.)

- *Number*. Most pronoun agreement errors occur when the pronoun does not agree with its antecedent in number. If the antecedent is singular, the pronoun must be singular; if the antecedent is plural, the pronoun must be plural.

  1. *Indefinite pronouns*. Words like *anybody, somebody, everybody, nobody,* and *each* are always singular. Others like *few* and *many* are always plural. Indefinite pronouns such as *all, any, most,* and *more* can be either singular or plural, depending on the object of the preposition that follows them: "All of my concern is justified"; but, "All of my concerns are justified."

Incorrect:	Everybody missed the deadline for turning in their paper.
	Each employee was told that they represented the company, not just themselves.
Correct:	Everybody missed the deadline for turning in his or her paper.
	Each employee was told that he or she represented the company, not just himself or herself.

NOTE: Overuse of the *he or she* approach can lead to awkwardness. It's a good idea to see if changing to a plural antecedent can create a more effective sentence.

All the students missed the deadline for turning in their papers.

The employees were told that they represented the company, not just themselves.

2. *Collective nouns.* Some singular nouns refer to more than one thing: *group, youth, family, jury,* and *audience,* for example. If the noun acts as a unit, it takes a singular pronoun. If the individuals within the unit act separately, the noun takes a plural pronoun.

> The jury reached *its* decision.
> The jury divided bitterly on *their* decision.
> The audience rose to *its* feet to show *its* approval.
> The audience straggled to *their* seats through the entire first act.

3. *Antecedents joined by* either...or *and* neither...nor. When two antecedents are joined by *either...or* or *neither...nor,* the pronoun agrees with the antecedent closer to it:

> Either Ruby or Jan lost *her* album.
> Either the mother or the daughters lost *their* albums.
> Either the daughters or the mother lost *her* album.
> Neither the boys nor the girls lost *their* albums.

4. *Compound antecedents.* Except when the words function as a single unit—such as in "Macaroni and cheese *is* my favorite dish"— antecedents joined by *and* take a plural pronoun:

> The owl and the pussycat shook *their* heads sadly.

Pronoun case. *Pronoun case* refers to the change in form of pronouns that corresponds with their grammatical function. There are three cases, and their names are self-explanatory: *subjective* (when the pronoun acts as a subject), *objective* (when the pronoun acts as an object), and *possessive* (when the pronoun acts to show possession). Following is a list of case changes for the most common pronouns:

Subjective	Objective	Possessive
I	me	my, mine
you	you	your, yours
he	him	his
she	her	her, hers
it	it	its
we	us	our, ours
they	them	their, theirs
who	whom	whose

• *Compound subjects and objects (subjects and objects connected by* and*).* Do not be misled by a compound subject or object. Use the pronoun case that shows the pronoun's grammatical role.

Wrong	**Right**
My father scolded Jim and *I.*	My father scolded Jim and *me.*
Betty and *her* had many good times.	Betty and *she* had many good times.

A simple test for getting the right word is to eliminate one of the compound terms and see which pronoun works better. No one would write "My father scolded I"—so "My father scolded me" is correct. No one would write "Her had many good times"—so "She had many good times" is correct.

- *Object of a preposition.* In a prepositional phrase, any pronoun after the preposition always takes the objective case.

Wrong	Right
This match is just between you and *I*.	This match is just between you and *me*.
I went to the movies with Ramona and *she*.	I went to the movies with Ramona and *her*.

- *After forms of* to be (is, am, are, was, were, has been, had been, might be, will be, *etc.*). A pronoun after forms of *to be* is always in the subjective case. This rule still applies rigorously in formal written English. It is frequently ignored in informal English and has all but disappeared from most conversation.

    It was she.   This is he.   The winners will be they.

- *After* as *and* than. In comparisons with *as* and *than*, mentally add a verb to the pronoun to determine which pronoun is correct. Should you write, for example, "Bill is smarter than I," or, "Bill is smarter than me"? Simply complete the construction with the "understood" verb. You could write, "Bill is smarter than I am," but not, "Bill is smarter than me am." Therefore, "Bill is smarter than I" is correct.

Wrong	Right
I am just as good as *them*.	I am just as good as *they*.
Her mother had more ambition than *her*.	Her mother had more ambition than *she*.
Bill liked her more than *I*.	Bill liked her more than *me*. (Meaning *Bill liked her more than he liked me.*)
Bill liked her more than *me*.	Bill liked her more than *I*. (Meaning *Bill liked her more than I liked her.*)

- We *or* us *followed by a noun.* Use *we* if the noun is a subject, *us* if the noun is an object. If ever in doubt, mentally eliminate the noun and see which pronoun sounds right. Should you write, for example, "The professor had us students over to his house" or "The professor had we students over to his house"? Mentally eliminate *students*. No one would write "The professor had we over to his house," so *us* is correct.

Wrong	Right
After the final exam, *us* students were exhausted.	After the final exam, *we* students were exhausted.
The company's reply to *we* consumers was almost totally negative.	The company's reply to *us* consumers was almost totally negative.

- *Gerunds.* A gerund is an *-ing* verb form that functions as a noun. In "Swimming used to be my favorite sport," *swimming* is a gerund. A pronoun before a gerund takes the possessive case.

Wrong	**Right**
Us nagging him did no good.	*Our* nagging him did no good.
His parents do not understand *him* reading so poorly.	His parents do not understand *his* reading so poorly.

Pronoun reference. A pronoun must not only agree with its antecedent, but that antecedent must be clear as well. An ambiguous antecedent is as bad as no antecedent at all. Generally, two types of ambiguity occur: a pronoun with two or more possible antecedents, and one pronoun referring to different antecedents.

- *Two or more possible antecedents.* In the sentence, "When Stanton visited the mayor, he said that he hoped his successor could work with him," the pronouns *he, his,* and *him* can refer to either the mayor or Stanton. Avoid this problem by making the antecedent clear: "When Stanton visited the mayor, Stanton said that he hoped his successor could work with the mayor." Here the pronouns *he* and *his* clearly refer to Stanton. Be particularly careful of the potential ambiguity in vague use of the word *this*.

Ambiguous	**Improved**
I received an *F* in the course and had to take it over again. This was very unfair. (Was the *F* unfair or having to take the course again? Were both unfair?)	I received an *F* in the course and had to take it over again. This grade was very unfair.

- *One pronoun referring to different antecedents.* "Mark received an *F* on his term paper and had to write a revision of it. It took a long time because it had many errors." In these sentences, the first *it* refers to the paper, the second to the revision, and the third to the paper. A reader could easily become confused by these sentences. In that case, simply replacing the pronouns with their antecedents would solve the problem: "Mark received an *F* on his term paper and had to write a revision of it. The revision took a long time because the paper had many errors."

Question marks. See *End marks.*

Questions, indirect. See *End marks.*

Quotation marks. Use quotation marks to indicate material taken word for word from another source; to mark the title of a poem, song, short story, essay, and any part of a longer work; and to point out words used in a special sense—words set apart for emphasis and special consideration, slang and colloquial expressions, derisively used words.

- *Direct quotations.* Quotation marks indicate what someone else has said in speech or writing:

  > The mayor said, "The city is in serious financial trouble if the new city income tax does not pass."

  > "No man is an island," John Donne once wrote.

  > "The world," said the senator, "is growing smaller and smaller."

  If there is a quotation within a quotation, use single marks for the second quote:

  > The mother commented wryly, "I wonder if Dr. Spock and the other great authorities on bringing up kids have ever seen you, calm as can be, say, 'I don't wanna.'"

  Observe the following rules in punctuation of direct quotations.

  1. *Block quotation.* If a direct quotation other than dialog is more than four lines long, it should be blocked. Block quotations *do not* take quotation marks and are indented ten spaces (1 inch) from the left margin.

     > In the section of the text on quotation marks, the authors make the following observation:

     > > Use quotation marks to indicate material taken word for word from another source; to mark the title of a poem, song, short story, essay, and any part of a longer work; and to point out words used in a special sense—words set apart for emphasis and special consideration, slang and colloquial expressions, and derisively used words.

  2. *Periods and commas.* Periods and commas at the end of quotations always go inside the quotation marks.

     > "The city will be in serious financial trouble if the city income tax does not pass," said the mayor.

     > The film was widely considered pornographic although to describe it, the producer used the word "art."

  3. *Other punctuation.* An exclamation point or question mark goes inside the quotation marks if it is part of the quotation. If it is part of a longer statement, it goes outside the quotation marks.

     > The student asked, "Is this paper due Friday?"

     > Did Robert Frost write "Mending Wall"?

     A colon or a semicolon always goes outside the quotation marks.

     > The text says, "A colon or a semicolon always goes outside the quotation marks"; this rule is simple.

- *Titles.* Use quotation marks to indicate the title of a work—a poem, a song, a short story, a chapter, an essay—that is part of a larger whole, or a short unit in itself.

  > John Collier wrote the short story "The Chaser."

  > The chapter is called "Stylistic Problems and Their Solutions."

- *Avoid using quotation marks with words used in a special sense.*
    1. *Words used as words.*

        I can never tell the difference between "affect" and "effect."

        "Really" and "very" are frequently overused words.

    Underlining or italicizing is usually preferable to quotation marks in sentences of this kind. (See *Italics*.)

    2. *Words used as slang and colloquial expressions.*

        The speaker gave me good "vibes."

        I wonder what's on the "tube."

    This usage is almost always undesirable. (See page 83.)

    3. *Words used derisively.* The use of quotation marks to indicate sarcasm or derision is generally a primitive means of showing feelings and, as a rule, should be avoided:

        The "performance" was a collection of amateurish blunders.

        This "dormitory" is unfit for human habitation.

Run-on sentence. A *run-on sentence* or *fused sentence* is two or more sentences written as one, with no punctuation between them. It is most commonly corrected by rewriting the run-on sentence as separate sentences, by placing a semicolon between the sentences, or by placing a comma and a coordinating conjunction between the sentences. A comma alone would create a comma splice, often considered a special kind of run-on sentence. (See *Comma splice*.)

ro/fs

Incorrect	Correct
This rule sounds easy enough putting it into practice is not so easy.	This rule sounds easy enough. Putting it into practice is not so easy.
	or
	This rule sounds easy enough; putting it into practice is not so easy.
	or
	This rule sounds easy enough, but putting it into practice is not so easy.

Semicolon. Use a semicolon between two independent clauses when the coordinating conjunction has been left out and between separate elements in a list or series when the elements contain punctuation within themselves.

- *Between independent clauses.*

    Stating the problem is simple enough; solving it is the tough part.

    Roberta wasn't precisely sure what the bearded stranger wanted; all she knew was that he made her nervous.

Observe that in both of these cases a coordinating conjunction preceded by a comma could be used to replace the semicolon. Under no circumstances could a comma alone be used between these independent clauses. In order to use a comma, you must also have a coordinating conjunction (*and, but, or, nor, for, yet, so*) between independent clauses. (See *Comma splice.*)

- *Between separate elements that contain commas in a list or series.*

   The following American cities have grown enormously in recent years: Houston, Texas; Dallas, Texas; Phoenix, Arizona; and Denver, Colorado.

Sentence. A group of words beginning with a capital letter and ending with a period, question mark, or exclamation point that contains at least one independent clause.

Birds sing.
Do birds sing?
Shut up, all you birds!

(See *Clause; Predicate; Subject.*)

shift

Shifts in tense and person.   Do not unnecessarily shift from one tense to another (past to present, present to future, and so on) or from one person to another (*he* to *you, one* to *I*).

- *Tense shifts.* If you begin writing in a particular tense, do not shift to another unless a change in time is logically necessary. The following paragraph breaks this rule:

   In William Carlos Williams's "The Use of Force," a doctor *was called* to examine a young girl. The doctor *was concerned* about diphtheria and *needs* to examine the girl's throat. The girl *is* terrified and *begins* to resist. As her resistance *continues*, the doctor *is compelled* to use more and more physical force. Though he *knows* the force *is* necessary, the doctor, to his horror, *found* that he *enjoyed* it and really *wanted* to hurt the girl.

Here the writer starts in the past tense (*was called, was concerned*), shifts to the present tense (*needs, is, begins, continues, is compelled, knows, is*), and then shifts back to the past tense (*found, enjoyed, wanted*). Why? There is no reason. No change in time is needed. If writers view the events of a story as happening in the present, they should use the present tense consistently. Writers could also view the events as past actions—over and completed—and write entirely in the past tense. In either case, writers should decide which view they prefer and stick to it throughout.

All verbs in present tense

In William Carlos Williams's "The Use of Force," a doctor *is called* to examine a young girl. The doctor *is concerned* about diphtheria and *needs* to examine the girl's throat. The girl *is* terrified and *begins* to resist. As her resistance *continues,* the doctor *is compelled* to use more and more physical force. Though he *knows* the force *is* necessary, the doctor, to his horror, *finds* that he *enjoys* it and really *wants* to hurt the girl.

All verbs in past tense

In William Carlos Williams's "The Use of Force," a doctor *was called* to examine a young girl. The doctor *was concerned* about diphtheria and *needed* to examine the girl's throat. The girl *was* terrified and *began* to resist. As her resistance *continued,* the doctor *was compelled* to use more and more physical force. Though he *knew* the force was necessary, the doctor, to his horror, *found* that he *enjoyed* it and really *wanted* to hurt the girl.

- *Shifts in person.* Write from a consistent point of view, making sure that any change in person is logically justified. If, for example, you begin expressing your thoughts in the third person (*he, she, it, they, one, the reader, the student, people,* and so on), avoid sudden shifts to the first person (*I, we*) or to the second person (*you*). Similarly, avoid sudden shifts from third- or first-person singular to third- or first-person plural.

Poor

Most *average citizens* think *they* are in favor of a clean environment, but *you* may change *your* mind when *you* find out what it will cost. (Shift from third person *average citizens* and *they* to second person *you, your.*)

The teenager resents the way *he* is being stereotyped. *We're* as different among *ourselves* as any other group in the population. *They* are tired of being viewed as a collection of finger-snapping freaks who say "cool" all the time. (Shift from third-person singular *teenager* and *he* to first-person plural *we* to third-person plural *they.*)

Improved

Most *average citizens* think *they* are in favor of a clean environment, but *they* may change *their* minds when *they* find out what it will cost.

Teenagers resent the way *they* are being stereotyped. *They* are as different among *themselves* as any other group in the population. *They* are tired of being viewed as a collection of finger-snapping freaks who say "cool" all the time.

Spelling. Poor spelling can seriously damage an otherwise fine paper. Faced with any significant number of spelling errors, readers cannot maintain their original confidence in the writer's thoughtfulness and skill.

sp

The one spelling rule every writer needs to know is very simple: *Use a dictionary*. Rules for spelling specific words and groups of words almost always have exceptions and are difficult to learn and remember. Good spellers, almost without exception, turn out to be people who read a great deal and who have the dictionary habit, not people who have memorized spelling rules. The most important spelling rule, then, as well as the quickest and easiest one, is use the dictionary.

Yet, it can sometimes be handy to have available a list of frequently misspelled words with trouble spots highlighted in italics. For quick reference, we include such a list.

1. accom*m*odate	35. *interest*	69. promin*e*nt
2. achi*e*vement	36. *its* (*it's*)	70. p*u*rsue
3. ac*q*uire	37. *led*	71. qui*e*t
4. al*l* right	38. *lose*	72. rec*ei*ve
5. am*o*ng	39. *losing*	73. rec*ei*ving
6. app*a*rent	40. marri*a*ge	74. recom*m*end
7. arg*u*ing	41. m*e*re	75. refer*r*ing
8. arg*um*ent	42. necessary	76. repetition
9. beli*e*f	43. occasion	77. r*h*ythm
10. beli*e*ve	44. occur*r*ed	78. sen*s*e
11. ben*e*ficial	45. occur*r*ence	79. separate
12. ben*e*fi*t*ed	46. occur*r*ing	80. separation
13. cat*e*gory	47. op*i*nion	81. shi*n*ing
14. co*m*ing	48. *opport*unity	82. simil*a*r
15. compar*a*tive	49. pa*i*d	83. stud*y*ing
16. cons*c*ious	50. *particular*	84. succ*ee*d
17. controversial	51. perform*a*nce	85. suc*c*ession
18. controversy	52. person*a*l	86. su*r*prise
19. d*e*fine	53. person*n*el	87. techni*q*ue
20. defin*i*tely	54. posses*s*ion	88. th*a*n
21. defin*i*tion	55. poss*i*ble	89. th*e*n
22. d*e*scribe	56. practic*a*l	90. th*ei*r
23. d*e*scription	57. prec*e*de	91. th*e*re
24. disas*t*rous	58. prejudice	92. th*ey're*
25. *e*ffect	59. prepar*e*	93. thorough
26. embar*r*ass	60. preval*e*nt	94. transfer*r*ed
27. envir*o*nment	61. princip*al*	95. *to* (*too, two*)
28. exag*g*erate	62. princip*le*	96. un*n*ecessary
29. exist*e*nce	63. privi*l*ege	97. vill*ai*n
30. exist*e*nt	64. prob*a*bly	98. wom*a*n
31. experi*e*nce	65. proc*ee*d	99. *write*
32. expl*a*nation	66. proc*e*dure	100. wri*t*ing
33. fas*c*inate	67. prof*e*ssion	
34. h*ei*ght	68. prof*e*ssor	

Subject.   A word, phrase, or clause that names the person, place, thing, or idea that the sentence is about. (See also *Predicate*.)

> *Sal* went home.
>
> The president's *speech* was heard by 100,000 people.

Subject–verb agreement. A verb must agree with its subject in number and person. This rule has most practical meaning only in the present tense; in other tenses, the verb forms generally remain the same regardless of number or person. (The exception is in the past tense of *to be*; in that instance the verb forms do change: *I was, you were, he was, we were, they were.*)

In the present tense, the third-person singular verb usually differs from the others—most often because an *-s* or *-es* is added to the verb stem. A third-person singular verb is the verb that goes with the pronouns *he, she,* and *it* and with any singular noun.

to dream

	Singular	Plural
First person	I dream	we dream
Second person	you dream	you dream
Third person	he she it } dreams	they dream

The lovers *dream* of a long and happy future together.

The lover *dreams* of his sweetheart every night.

People often *dream* about falling from great heights.

Jennifer *dreams* about being buried alive.

Even with highly irregular verbs, the third-person singular in the present tense takes a special form (always with an *-s* at the end).

to be

	Singular	Plural
First person	I am	we are
Second person	you are	you are
Third person	he she it } is	they are

to have

	Singular	Plural
First person	I have	we have
Second person	you have	you have
Third person	he she it } has	they have

The clowns *are* happy.

Erica *is* sad.

The Joneses *have* a lovely new home.

Mr. Jones *has* a lot to learn.

The few cases in which a present-tense verb in the third-person singular has the same form as in the other persons come naturally to almost every writer and speaker: *he can, he may, he might,* and so on.

Special Cases:

- *Compound subjects.* If the subject is compound (joined by *and*), the verb is plural unless the two words function as a single unit—"Pork and beans *is* an easy dish to prepare," for example—or unless the two words refer to a single person, as in "My cook and bottle washer *has* left me" (one person performed both jobs).

Wrong	Right
Writing and reading *is* necessary for success in college.	Writing and reading *are* necessary for success in college.
The introduction and conclusion *does* not appear in an outline.	The introduction and conclusion *do* not appear in an outline.

- *Neither . . . nor, either . . . or, nor, or.* If two subjects are joined by any of these terms, the verb agrees with the closer subject.

Wrong	Right
Neither the students nor the teacher *are* correct.	Neither the students nor the teacher *is* correct.
Snowstorms or rain *cause* accidents.	Snowstorms or rain *causes* accidents.
Rain or snowstorms *causes* accidents.	Rain or snowstorms *cause* accidents.

- *Time, money, weight.* Words that state an amount (time, money, weight) have a singular verb when they are considered as a unit even if they are plural in form.

Wrong	Right
Two semesters *are* really a short time.	Two semesters *is* really a short time.
Five dollars *are* a modest fee for credit by examination.	Five dollars *is* a modest fee for credit by examination.

- *Titles.* Titles of songs, plays, movies, novels, or articles always have singular verbs, even if the titles are plural in form.

Wrong	Right
The Wings of the Dove were made into a movie.	*The Wings of the Dove was* made into a movie.
"The Novels of Early America" *were* published in *American Literature.*	"The Novels of Early America" *was* published in *American Literature.*

- *Collective nouns.* Collective nouns such as *family, audience, jury,* and *class* have singular verbs when they are considered as a unified group. If the individuals within the unit act separately, the verb will be plural.

Wrong	Right
The family *plan* a vacation.	The family *plans* a vacation.
The jury *is* divided on the verdict.	The jury *are* divided on the verdict.

| The audience *are* going to give this show a standing ovation. | The audience *is* going to give this show a standing ovation. |
| The audience *is* divided in their opinion of the show. | The audience *are* divided in their opinion of the show. |

- *Indefinite pronouns.* Indefinite pronouns such as *one, no one, someone, everyone, none, anyone, somebody, anybody, everybody, each, neither,* and *either* take singular verbs:

Wrong

None of the ideas *are* correct.
Each of the students *have* the time to study.
Either *are* a valid choice.

Right

None of the ideas *is* correct.
Each of the students *has* the time to study.
Either *is* a valid choice.

- *Intervening elements.*

  1. *Verb* separated by words:

     Wrong: Many state capitals—Carson City, Augusta, Jefferson City, Olympia—*is* only small towns.
     Right: Many state capitals—Carson City, Augusta, Jefferson City, Olympia—*are* only small towns.

     Here the plural *capitals*, not the singular *Olympia*, is the subject.

  2. *Verb* separated by phrases:

     Wrong: A crate of oranges *are* expensive.
     Right: A crate of oranges *is* expensive.

     Here *crate*, not *oranges*, is the subject.

     Wrong: Agreement of subjects with their verbs *are* important.
     Right: Agreement of subjects with their verbs *is* important.

     Here *agreement*, not *subjects* or *verbs*, is the subject.

  3. *Verb* separated by clauses:

     Wrong: Reading well, which is one of the necessary academic skills, *make* studying easier.
     Right: Reading well, which is one of the necessary academic skills, *makes* studying easier.

     Here *reading*, not *skills*, is the subject.

- *Reversed position.* If the subject comes after the verb, the verb must still agree with the subject.

  1. *There.* If a sentence begins with *there* and is followed by some form of *to be* (*is, are, was, were,* etc.), the number of *be* is determined by the subject. *There* is never the subject (except in a sentence like this one).

     Wrong: There *is* five students in this class.
     Right: There *are* five students in this class.

Here *students* is the subject, and it is plural. Therefore, the verb must be plural.

2. *Prepositional phrases.* Sometimes a writer begins a sentence with a prepositional phrase followed by a verb and then the subject. The verb must still agree with the subject.

Wrong:	Throughout a grammar book *appears* many helpful writing hints.
Right:	Throughout a grammar book *appear* many helpful writing hints.

Here *hints*, not *book*, is the subject.

sub

Subordination. The most important idea in a sentence should be in an independent clause. Lesser ideas, explanations, qualifying material, and illustrations should be in subordinate clauses or phrases.

Poor	**Improved**
John is a wonderful person. He is very shy. He is extremely kind to everybody.	Although very shy, John is a wonderful person who is extremely kind to everybody. (The main idea is that John is a wonderful person.)
	or
	Although he is a wonderful person who is extremely kind to everybody, John is very shy. (The main idea is that John is very shy.)
Professor Jones is terribly sarcastic. He is also a tough grader. It is true that he knows his subject. Most students dislike him, however.	Despite Professor Jones's knowledge of his subject, most students dislike him because of his terrible sarcasm and tough grading.

vb

Verb. A word that expresses an action, an occurrence, or a state of being. Verbs may be divided into three classes: *transitive verbs*, which require objects to complete their meaning (Mary *admires* him); *intransitive verbs*, which are complete in themselves (John *trembled*); and *linking verbs*, which join a subject to its complement (Phyllis *is* a beauty; Their actions *were* cowardly).

In sentences, a complete verb often consists of a *main verb* (marked in grammatical abbreviation as MV) and a *helping verb* (HV). Sometimes a complete verb is a single-word verb. Helping verbs, or auxiliaries, work along with principal parts or other verb forms (like present participles, the *-ing* form of a verb) to express appropriate action.

Helping Verbs

am	**can**	had	**might**	were
are	**could**	has	**must**	**will**
be	did	have	**shall**	**would**
been	do	is	**should**	
being	does	**may**	was	

The nine helping verbs in boldface print—*must, may, can, shall, will, might, could, would,* and *should*—constitute an important subgroup of helping verbs, called modals. Modals tell what the writer believes about the action and express probability, ability, or need or obligation. (She *may drive* the motorcycle; She *can drive* the motorcycle; She *must drive* the motorcycle.)

Verbs: principal parts. The form of most verbs changes according to which tense is being used, and to get the correct form a writer needs to know the principal parts of each verb. There are generally considered to be three principal parts: the *stem* or *infinitive* (the stem is the present tense form of the verb, and the infinitive is the stem preceded by *to*), the *past tense,* and the *past participle.* The past participle is the form used with helping verbs in perfect tenses (*I have seen, I had seen, I will have seen*) and in the passive voice (*I am seen, I was seen, I will be seen, I have been seen*), and in modal verb structures (*I can see, I should see, I may see*).

The principal parts of *regular verbs* are formed by adding *-ed* or *-d* to the stem: *rush, rushed, rushed; love, loved, loved; drag, dragged, dragged.* The past tense and past participle of regular verbs are always the same.

The principal parts of *irregular verbs* need to be learned separately—and even for the most experienced writer sometimes require checking in a dictionary or handbook. For quick reference, here is an alphabetical list of the principal parts of the most common irregular verbs.

Stem	Past tense	Past participle
arise	arose	arisen
be	was	been
bear	bore	borne, born
begin	began	begun
bind	bound	bound
blow	blew	blown
break	broke	broken
bring	brought	brought
burst	burst	burst
buy	bought	bought
catch	caught	caught
choose	chose	chosen
come	came	come
creep	crept	crept
deal	dealt	dealt
dig	dug	dug
dive	dived, dove	dived
do	did	done
draw	drew	drawn
drink	drank	drunk
drive	drove	driven
eat	ate	eaten

Stem	Past tense	Past participle
fall	fell	fallen
flee	fled	fled
fly	flew	flown
forbid	forbad, forbade	forbidden
freeze	froze	frozen
give	gave	given
go	went	gone
grow	grew	grown
hang	hung	hung
hang (execute)	hanged	hanged
know	knew	known
lay	laid	laid
lead	led	led
lend	lent	lent
lie	lay	lain
lose	lost	lost
mean	meant	meant
ride	rode	ridden
ring	rang	rung
rise	rose	risen
run	ran	run
see	saw	seen
seek	sought	sought
send	sent	sent
shake	shook	shaken
shine	shone, shined	shone, shined
shrink	shrank	shrunk
sing	sang	sung
sink	sank, sunk	sunk
sleep	slept	slept
sneak	sneaked	sneaked
speak	spoke	spoken
spin	spun	spun
spit	spat	spat
spread	spread	spread
steal	stole	stolen
stink	stank	stunk
swear	swore	sworn
swim	swam	swum
swing	swung	swung
take	took	taken
teach	taught	taught
tear	tore	torn
thrive	thrived, throve	thrived, thriven
throw	threw	thrown
wear	wore	worn
weep	wept	wept
write	wrote	written

Confusion of the past tense and past participle of irregular verbs is a frequent cause of writing errors. Remember that the past participle is the correct form after *has, have,* and *had.*

Wrong	**Right**
The mountaineers *had froze* to death.	The mountaineers *had frozen* to death.
The sprinter *has* just *broke* another track record.	The sprinter *has* just *broken* another track record.
We *seen* that movie when it first came out.	We *saw* that movie when it first came out.

Verbs: tenses. Most verbs can be expressed in any tense, and the many different tenses enable the writer to present fine shades of meaning with great accuracy.

There are six tenses. Most verbs can take either the *active voice* or the *passive voice* in any tense (see page 235). To make matters even more varied, *progressive constructions* can be used for all tenses of active verbs and some tenses of passive verbs.

to save

Tenses	**Active voice**	**Progressive**
Present	I save	I am saving
Past	I saved	I was saving
Future	I will (*or* shall) save	I will be saving
Present perfect	I have saved	I have been saving
Past perfect	I had saved	I had been saving
Future perfect	I will (*or* shall) have saved	I will have been saving

	Passive voice	
Present	I am saved	I am being saved
Past	I was saved	I was being saved
Future	I will (*or* shall) be saved	
Present perfect	I have been saved	
Past perfect	I had been saved	
Future perfect	I will (*or* shall) have been saved	

A. *Present tense.* The present tense indicates present action, of course, especially continuing or habitual action:

> I *save* ten dollars every week.
>
> I *eat* a good breakfast each morning.
>
> She *drives* carefully.

The present is also used to express permanent facts and general truths, and is usually the preferred tense for discussing literary actions:

> The speed of light *is* faster than the speed of sound.
>
> In *The Great Gatsby,* all the events *take* place during the 1920s.

The present can even be called upon to deal with future action.

Tomorrow she *drives* to the convention.

The *present progressive* indicates actions occurring—actions "in progress"—at the specific instant referred to.

I *am eating* a good breakfast, and I do not want to be interrupted.

She *is driving* too fast for these icy roads.

The same principle of action in progress at the time applies to all progressive tenses:

Past Progressive:	The criminal *was shaving* when the police arrested him.
Future Progressive:	At this time next week, I *will be surfing* in Hawaii.

B. *Past tense.* The past tense describes previous actions, generally actions over and done with:

The lifeguard *saved* two children last week.

She *drove* to Florida three years ago.

C. *Future tense.* The future tense describes actions after the present:

From now on, I *will save* fifteen dollars every week.

Marlene says that her in-laws *will drive* her to drink.

D. *Present perfect tense.* The present perfect tense (*have* or *has* plus the past participle) refers to past actions, generally of the fairly recent past, that still go on or have bearing on the present:

I *have saved* over one thousand dollars so far.

She *has driven* this short route to work many times.

The preceding sentences expressed in the simple past would suggest different meanings. "I saved over one thousand dollars" would suggest that the saving has now stopped. "She drove this short route to work many times" would suggest that some other route is now being used.

E. *Past perfect tense.* The past perfect tense (*had* plus the past participle) is employed for actions previous to the simple past—"more past than past."

The lifeguard saved two children last week and *had saved* three adults the week before.

She *had driven* to Florida three years ago, so she felt quite confident about making the trip again.

F. *Future perfect tense.* The future perfect tense (*will have* or *shall have* plus the past participle) expresses action that will be completed before some future time:

By this time next year, I *will have saved* two thousand dollars.

When she gets to Florida, she *will have driven* through three time zones.

The proper sequence of tenses within a sentence or series of sentences when different verbs refer to different time periods is an important consideration for all writers. The simple rule that verb tenses need to express precisely the intended period of time is not always simple to apply to one's own writing.

Improper sequence	Correct sequence
The witness *told* [past] the court that on the night of the crime he *saw* [past] the accused break the window of the liquor store.	The witness *told* [past] the court that on the night of the crime he *had seen* [past perfect] the accused break the window of the liquor store. (The past perfect *had seen* refers to events "more past than past.")
When I *will get* [future] to the lake, you *will* already *be* [future] there for two weeks.	When I *will get* [future] to the lake, you *will* already *have been* [future perfect] there for two weeks. (The future perfect *will have been* refers to events that will be completed before some future time.)

Voice. The quality of a verb that tells whether the subject *acts* or is *acted upon*. A verb is in the *active voice* when its subject does the acting, and in the *passive voice* when its subject is acted upon.

Active:	The Senate passed the new law.
Passive:	The new law was passed by the Senate.

Credits

Index

abbreviations, 197
abstract writing
  concrete writing *vs.*, 68–69
  in revising language, 68–70
  using comparisons to
    avoid, 70
  using specific details to
    avoid, 69
active verbs, 73–74, 233
active voice, 73–74, 233, 235
active writing
  determining your purpose/
    audience, 22–23
  overview, 20
  prewriting, 23–25
  sample student writing/first
    draft, 27–30
  strategy checklist, 30–31
  topic choosing, 20–22
  writing drafts, 26–30
addresses, and comma use, 207
ad hominem argument, logical
    fallacy, 144
adjective(s)
  –adverb confusion, 198–199
  comma usage with coordi-
    nating, 204–205
adverb(s)
  –adjective confusion,
    198–199
  misplaced modifiers and,
    215–216
advertisement(s)
  examining, 10–11
  sample, 10*f*
American Psychological
    Association (APA), 181
analogy
  definition of, 145
  logical fallacy type of
    argument by, 145–146
analysis
  causal, 125
  division as, 122, 123, 125
  overview, 123, 125
anecdote
  in conclusion writing, 58
  introduction strategies, 48
antecedents
  definition of, 199, 217–218
  pronoun agreement with
    compound, 219
  pronoun agreement with
    either/or and neither/nor
    joined, 219
  pronoun agreement with
    gender of, 217–218

pronoun agreement with
    number of, 217, 218–219
  pronoun reference to, 221
APA References list
  overview, 181, 183
  preparation, 184–185
  preparation tips, 185
  sample entries, 183–184
  sample list, 184–185
  as source list, 155
APA style documentation.
    See APA style source
    documentation for social
    sciences
APA style source documenta-
    tion for social sciences. *See
    also* APA References list
  MLA style documentation
    vs., 181, 182
  overview, 181
  parenthetical citations, 181–182
apostrophe usage
  in contractions, 199
  with plurals, 199, 200
  with possessive nouns/indef-
    inite pronouns, 199–201
appositive
  definition, 205
  nonrestrictive, 205, 206
  restrictive, 205–206
argument by analogy, logical
    fallacy, 145–146
argumentation paper writing
  developing debatable
    position, 147–148
  overview, 139, 147
  strategy checklist, 148–150
  tips for formal, 147
  topics, 150
  using logic in, 139
articles. *See* periodical articles
audience
  determining, 22–23
  process paper careful
    attention to, 114
  revising checklist, 63
  revising for, 62–63

"Banning of the Polygraph,
  The" (Kessler), 188–196
begging the question, logical
    fallacy, 145
block quotation. *See* quotation,
    block
body paragraph(s)
  development in paragraph
    coherence, 53, 55–57

development and paragraph
    unity, 53–55
  as element of structure, 63
  narrative paper writing
    sequencing of, 104
  revising, 63, 64–66
body paragraph writing
  overview, 49
  of topic sentences, 49–51
  transitions in, 51–53
  unity/coherence in develop-
    ment of, 53–57
books
  MLA Works Cited list
    citation for, 156
  source records for, 156
brackets usage in direct
    quotation, 201

Caldwell, Christopher, 16–19
capital letters usage, 201–202
card stacking, logical
    fallacy, 142
cartoon(s)
  reading, 11, 12
  sample, 12*f*
cases usage in thesis
    support, 37
causal analysis, 125
cause and effect paper
    writing
  as causal analysis, 125
  overview, 129
  strategy checklist, 130–131
  tips, 129–130
  topics, 131–132
chart
  reading, 11–12
  sample, 11*f*
chronological order
  in paragraph coherence, 55
  process paper maintaining
    of strict, 113
circular argument, logical
    fallacy, 145
citations. *See* parenthetical cita-
    tions; working citations list
classification. *See also* division
  in action, 122
  division *vs.*, 124–125
  overview, 122
  using, 123–124
classification paper writing
  overview, 125
  strategy checklist, 127
  tips, 126–127
  topics, 127

clause(s). *See also* dependent clauses; independent clauses; subordinate clauses
  cutting wordy, 72
  definition, 202
  predicate part of, 217
  subject–verb agreement and, 229
  wordiness source of cutting inadequate, 71
cliché, 79
collective nouns, 219, 228–229
colon usage, 202–203
comma
  semicolon usage in list/series using, 224
  usage, 203–207
comma splice, 207–208, 223. *See also* run-on sentence
comparison(s)
  concrete writing using, 70
  contrast *vs.*, 117
  definition of, 117
  in paragraph coherence, 56
  use to avoid abstract writing, 69
comparison–contrast paper writing
  overview, 117
  strategy checklist, 120
  tips, 117–118
  topics, 121
comparison–contrast patterns
  block method or subject-by-subject, 118
  combined, 119
  point-by-point or alternating, 119
compound subjects (of sentences), 219–220, 228
compound words, and hyphens, 213
conclusion
  as element of structure, 63
  narrative paper, 104
  non sequitur, 145
  process paper, 115
  revising, 63, 65, 66
conclusion writing
  by establishing new context for topic, 58–59
  by interpreting paper's ideas' significance, 57–58
  in paper writing, 57–59
  by presenting a quotation, 58
  by raising questions, 58
  by referring to paper's major ideas, 57
  by restating thesis in different words, 57
  strong, 57–59
  tips for strong, 59
  by using anecdote, 58

concrete writing
  abstract writing *vs.*, 68–69
  in revising language, 68–70
  using comparisons, 70
  using specific details, 69–70
conjunctions, 208
  subordinating, 212
connotation
  denotation and, 67
  importance of, 67
  in revising language, 67–68
contractions, and apostrophes, 199
contrast(s). *See also* comparison-contrast paper writing
  comma use and, 206
  comparison *vs.*, 117
  definition of, 117
conventions, and comma use, 206–207
coordinating adjectives, 204–205
correspondence, and comma use, 207

dangling modifiers, 214–215
dash usage, 208–209
data
  sample paragraphs using, 37
  statistics/cases/expert testimony as, 37
  thesis support using, 36
dates, and comma use, 206–207
deadwood
  cutting, 71–72
  as wordiness source, 71
deduction
  as logical thinking type, 140–141
  overview, 140
  as syllogism, 140–141
  using induction and, 141
definition
  extended, 133, 134–137
  extended *vs.* dictionary, 133
  formal, 134–136
  informal, 136–137
  overview, 133
  tips for writing one-sentence formal, 134–135
definition, words/terms needing
  abstractions, 134
  controversial terms, 134
  judgmental words, 134
  slang terms, 134
  specialized terms, 134
definition paper writing
  approaches sample, 136
  beginning with formal definition, 134
  formal, 135–136
  informal, 136–137
  strategy checklist, 137–138
  topics, 138

denotation
  connotation and, 67
  in revising language, 67
dependent clauses. *See also* subordinate clauses
  definition, 202
  sentence fragments and, 212–213
  subordinate clauses as, 212
descriptive paper writing
  overview, 97
  and revising strategy checklist, 99
  tips, 97–99
  topics, 99
details
  descriptive paper writing using organization/logical sequence of descriptive, 98
  thesis support using, 36–37
details, sensory
  concrete, 36
  thesis support using, 36
details, specific
  concrete writing using, 69–70
  descriptive paper writing using lively and, 98
  example paper writing using, 108
  narrative paper writing with, 102
  use to avoid abstract writing, 69
details, supporting
  formal outline, 40
  revising for appropriate, 61–62
  revising checklist, 61–62
dictionary
  definition *vs.* extended definition, 133
  use and spelling, 226
direct address, 206
direct question, 210
direct quotation. *See* quotation, direct
divided words, and hyphens, 213
division. *See also* classification
  in action, 122
  as analysis, 122, 123, 125
  classification *vs.*, 124–125
  overview, 122
  strategies review, 125
  using, 122–123
double negative, 209
Downes, Lawrence, 4–6
drafts. *See also* final draft; first draft; intermediate draft; rough draft writing tips
  research paper, 170
drawings, reading, 11

economy, and wordiness, 71–73
editing. *See also* revising and editing
  overview, 86

effect, 129. *See also* cause and effect paper writing
either/or, logical fallacy, 145
ellipsis, 161–162, 164, 209
end marks, 209–211
endnote, 172
enthymeme, 140
essay. *See also* paper
  considering writer's construction of, 3
  writing *vs.* research paper writing, 170
euphemisms, 80–81
example(s)
  good writing using, 107
  as illustration, 107
  overview, 107, 108
  in paragraphs, 107
  in sentences, 107
  thesis support using, 36
example paper writing
  overview, 107
  strategy checklist, 110–111
  tips, 108–110
  topics, 111
exclamation point usage, 211
extended definition
  dictionary *vs.*, 133
  formal, 134–136
  informal, 136–137

faulty parallelism, 74–75
final draft
  sample student, 94–96
  thesis, 61
first draft
  research paper, 170
  sample student, 27–30
  thesis, 61
first-person pronouns/verbs, 217
  subject–verb agreement with, 227
footnote, 171, 172
formal argument paper writing, 147
formal definition, 134–135
  paper writing, 135–136
  tips for writing one-sentence, 135
formal outline
  complex paper, 40–41
  overview/definition of, 39
  paper planning through, 39–45
formal outline, making
  by adding supporting details, 40
  definition of, 39
  by establishing main divisions, 39–40, 41
  formatting in, 40
  overview, 39
  thesis statement/purpose in, 39, 40
  thought blocks in, 39–40

writing sentence outline in, 40, 41–42
  writing topic outline in, 40
formal outline, preparation
  overview, 43–44, 168–169
  strategy checklist, 44–45
  tips, 44
  using notes in, 168
fragmentary sentences. *See* sentence fragments
fused sentence, 223. *See also* run-on sentence
future perfect tense, 234
future tense, 234

gender, pronoun agreement with antecedent in, 217–218
generalization
  hasty, 142
  over, 142–143
gerunds
  definition of, 221
  pronoun case and, 221
grammar essentials and common errors, 197–235
graph(s)
  reading, 11–12
  sample, 11*f*, 18*f*

"Hanging, A" (Orwell), 36–37
hasty generalization, logical fallacy, 142
helping verb (HV), 230–231
humor, in introduction writing, 49
hyphen usage, 213

ignoring the question, logical fallacy, 144
illustration
  example as, 107
  good writing using, 107
indefinite pronoun(s)
  agreement, 218
  apostrophe usage with possessives of, 199, 200
  subject–verb agreement with, 229
independent clauses
  colon usage with, 203
  comma usage with, 203–204
  definition, 202, 211
  reasons for missing, 211–212
  semicolon usage with, 223–224
  sentence fragments and, 211–212
  subordinate clauses/phrases *vs.*, 230
indirect question, 210
induction
  as logical thinking type, 139–140, 141
  overview, 139
  using deduction and, 141

infinitive, 213
informal definition, 136–137
  paper writing, 136–137
interjections, 206
intermediate draft
  learning from instructor's comments on, 89–91
  sample student, 87–91
  thesis, 61
interrupting elements, 204
intervening elements, 229
"Intimate Shopping: Should Everyone Know What You Bought Today?" (Caldwell), 17–19
intransitive verbs, 230
introduction
  as element of structure, 63
  narrative paper, 103–104
  process paper, 115
  revising, 63–64, 65
introduction strategies
  anecdote, 48
  dramatization, 48
  multiple paragraph, 47–48, 49
  one-paragraph, 47
introduction writing
  introduction strategies in, 47–48
  overview, 47
  paper divisions listing in, 47
  in paper writing, 47–49
  subject in, 47
  thesis statement in, 47
  tips, 49
introductory elements, 204
irregular verbs
  confusion of past tense and past participle of, 233
  principal parts of most common, 231–233
italics usage, 213–214

Kessler, Elizabeth, 188–196

language
  narrative paper writing using natural sounding, 102–103
  sexist, 83–85
language, revising. *See* revising language
library paper. *See* research paper
linking verbs, 230
logic
  argumentation paper use of, 139
  in thesis support, 36
logical fallacies
  avoiding, 141–146
  in thesis support, 36
logical fallacy type(s)
  ad hominem argument, 144
  argument by analogy, 145–146
  begging the question, 145
  card stacking, 142

logical fallacy
  type(s) (*continued*)
  circular argument, 145
  either/or, 145
  hasty generalization, 142
  ignoring the question, 144
  non sequitur, 143
  overgeneralization, 142–143
  post hoc, ergo propter hoc,
    141–142
  shifting burden of proof, 145
  slanting, 142
  straw man argument, 144
logical thinking type(s)
  deduction, 140–141
  induction, 139–140, 141

main verb (MV), 230
misplaced modifiers, 215–216
misreadings, comma use to
  prevent, 206
MLA. *See* Modern Language
  Association
*MLA Handbook for Writers of
  Research Papers,* 171, 172
MLA style documentation. *See*
  MLA style source documentation for humanities
MLA style research paper
  sample notes, 195
  sample paper, 187–196
  sample title page, 188
  sample Works Cited, 196
MLA style source documentation for humanities.
  See also MLA Works
  Cited list
  APA style documentation *vs.,*
    181, 182
  MLA Works Cited list, 172,
    174–181
  overview, 171
  parenthetical citations, 172–174
MLA Works Cited list
  citation for books, 156
  citation for periodical
    articles, 157
  citation for World Wide Web
    source, 158–159
  MLA style research paper
    sample, 196
  overview, 172, 174–175
  parenthetical documentation
    and, 172, 174
  preparation tips, 181
  sample entries, 175–181
  source list as, 155
modal verbs, 231
Modern Language Association
  (MLA), 171
modifiers
  dangling, 214–215
  misplaced, 215–216
  nonrestrictive, 205
  restrictive, 205

narrative, as story, 101
narrative paper writing
  overview, 101
  strategy checklist, 105
  tips, 102–104
  topics, 105
negative, double, 209
nonrestrictive appositive,
  205, 206
nonrestrictive elements, 205–206
nonrestrictive modifiers, 205
non sequitur, logical fallacy, 143
note(s)
  containing direct
    quotation, 163
  containing summary/
    paraphrase of original
    material, 163
  end, 172
  foot, 171, 172
  formal outline preparation
    and, 168
  MLA style research paper
    sample, 195
  research paper use of
    explanatory, 170–171
note taking, from source
    material
  overview, 161
  recording quotations in,
    161–162
  summarizing/paraphrasing
    in, 162–163
note taking while reading, 6
noun(s)
  antecedent, 199
  apostrophe usage with
    possessives of, 199–201
  capital letter usage with
    proper, 201–202
  definition of, 216
  pronoun agreement with
    collective, 219
  pronoun case and *we/us*
    followed by, 220
  singular, 200
  subject–verb agreement with
    collective, 228–229
number(s)
  comma use with, 207
  pronoun agreement with
    antecedent in, 217–218
  subject–verb agreement in, 227
  usage and rules, 216
numerals, usage and rules, 216

objective pronoun case, 219
objects (of sentences), 216
  pronoun case and com-
    pound, 219–220
  pronoun case and preposi-
    tion, 219–220
organization
  cause and effect paper, 130
  classification paper, 126–127
  comparison–contrast paper,
    118–119
  of descriptive details in
    descriptive paper writing, 98
  narrative paper, 103
  revising for better, 62
  revising checklist, 62
Orwell, George, 36–37
outline
  sentence, 40, 41–42
  topic, 40
outlining. *See also* formal
    outline; rough outline
  paper planning by, 39–45
overgeneralization, logical
    fallacy, 142–143

paper. *See also* essay
  formal outline for complex,
    40–41
paper planning. *See also* formal
    outline
  through formal outline, 39–45
  for successful paper, 39
paper writing. *See also* body
    paragraph writing;
    comparison–contrast paper
    writing; conclusion writing;
    descriptive paper writing;
    example paper writing;
    introduction writing; narra-
    tive paper writing; process
    paper writing; research
    paper writing
  body paragraph writing,
    49–57
  introduction writing, 47–49
  preparing formal outline for,
    168–169
  strong conclusion writing,
    57–59
paragraph(s). *See also* body
    paragraphs
  definition, 54
  examples in, 107
  introduction strategy of
    multiple, 47–48
  introduction strategy of
    zone, 47
  as transitions, 53
paragraph coherence
  chronological order in, 55
  comparison in, 56
  in developing body
    paragraphs, 53, 55–57
  overview, 55
  pronouns in, 57
  reason enumeration in, 56
  repetition in, 56
  space order in, 55–56
  tips for achieving, 57
paragraph unity
  in developing body
    paragraphs, 53–55
  example, 54

overview, 54
tips for achieving, 55
parallelism
correcting faulty, 74–75
definition of, 74, 216
paraphrase
definition of, 162
note containing original
material, 163
paraphrasing, from source
material
in note taking, 162–163
in papers, 163, 164, 165
recording quotations and,
162–163
summarizing and, 162–163
parentheses usage, 217
parenthetical citations
APA style, 181–182
MLA style, 172–174
overview, 172
parenthetical documentation
MLA examples, 172–174
MLA Works Cited list and,
172, 174
overview, 172
passive verbs, 73–74, 233
passive voice, 73–74, 233, 235
past participle of verbs
confusion of past tense
and, 233
of most common irregular
verbs, 231–233
as verb principal part,
231–233
past perfect tense, 234
past tense of verbs, 234
confusion of past participle
and, 233
of most common irregular
verbs, 231–233
as verb principal part, 231–233
peer review, revising through,
86–87
periodical articles
MLA Works Cited list citation for, 157
source records for, 157
period usage, 209–210
person (as form of pronouns
and verbs)
first/second/third, 217, 227
overview, 217
shifts in, 224, 225
subject–verb agreement in, 227
photograph(s)
examining, 9–10
sample, 9f
phrases. *See also* paraphrase
misplaced modifiers and, 215
subject–verb agreement and
prepositional, 230
subject–verb agreement and
verbs separated by, 229
subordinate, 230

plagiarism
avoiding, 166–168
common knowledge and, 166
direct quotations and, 166
example, 167–168
overview, 166
rules about, 166
plural(s)
apostrophe usage with,
199, 200
possessive, 200
possessive(s)
apostrophe usage with,
199–201
of indefinite pronouns,
199, 200
of nouns, 199–201
plural, 200
pronoun case, 219
post hoc, ergo propter hoc, logical
fallacy, 141–142
predicate, 217
preposition
definition of, 217
pronoun case and object
of, 220
prepositional phrases, 230
present perfect tense, 234
present tense, 233–234
prewriting
organizing ideas, 25
overview, 23–24
strategy checklist, 24–25
process paper writing
as "how-to" paper, 112
overview, 112
strategy checklist, 115–116
tips, 112–115
topics, 116
pronoun(s). *See also* indefinite
pronouns
antecedent, 199, 217–219
definition of, 217
first/second/third person, 217
in paragraph coherence, 57
reference to antecedents, 221
pronoun agreement
with antecedent in gender,
217–218
with antecedent in number,
217, 218–219
antecedents joined by either/
or and neither/nor, 219
collective noun, 219
compound antecedents, 219
indefinite, 218
pronoun case(s)
as/than and, 220
compound subjects/objects
and, 219–220
definition of, 219
forms of *to be* and, 220
gerunds and, 221
objective, 219
possessive, 219

preposition object and, 220
subjective, 219
we/us followed by noun
and, 220
proofreading
overview, 86, 91
strategy checklist for revising/
editing and, 92–94
tips for careful, 92
proper nouns, and capital letter
usage, 201–202
*Publication Manual of American
Psychological Association
(APA)*, 181
punctuation rules
for block quotations, 222
for direct quotations, 222
purpose
comparison–contrast
paper, 117
determining, 22, 23
formal outline, 39, 40
revising checklist, 63
revising for, 62–63

question(s)
begging the, 145
direct, 210
ignoring the, 144
indirect, 210
introduction writing with
challenging, 49
raising in conclusion
writing, 58
question mark usage, 210–211
quotation, block
punctuation rules for, 222
quotation marks and,
164, 222
quotation, direct
bracket usage in, 201
comma use with, 207
note containing, 163
plagiarism and, 166
punctuation rules for, 222
quotation marks usage
with, 222
usage in papers, 164–166
quotation marks
avoidance with words used
in special sense, 223
block quotations and, 164, 222
placement in quotations
recorded into notes, 161–162
usage, 164, 214, 221–223
usage with direct
quotations, 222
usage in quoting sources in
papers, 164
usage with titles, 214, 222
quotation recording in note
taking
overview, 161–162
quotation marks placement
in, 161–162

quotation recording in note
taking (*continued*)
source material summarizing/
paraphrasing and, 161–162
using ellipsis in, 161–162
using *sic* in, 161
quotations
colon usage with, 203
in conclusion writing, 58
in introduction writing, 49
quoting sources in papers
block format for, 164
overview, 163–164
quotation marks usage
in, 164
using ellipsis in, 164

reading critically
in action, 3–6
for best results, 2
strategy checklist, 6–7
tips, 2–3
why read?, 1–2
on your own, 16–19
reading visual image(s)
of cartoons, 11, 12
of charts, 11–12
of drawings, 11
examining advertisements,
10–11
examining photographs,
9–10
of graphs, 11–12
overview, 8
reading/evaluating Web
sites, 14–16
strategy checklist, 13
of tables, 11–12
tips, 8
reason enumeration, in
paragraph coherence, 56
regular verbs, 231
repetition
for clarity, 81
good and bad, 81–82
for impact, 81
in paragraph coherence, 56
repetition, undesirable
of meaning, 82
of same word, 82
of sounds, 82
repetition of meaning, pointless
avoiding, 72
as wordiness source, 71
research. *See* research paper
research essay. *See* research
paper
research paper. *See also* MLA-
style research paper
choosing subject for, 151
developing thesis of, 151–152
documenting sources for,
151–152

finding sources and developing working citations list
for, 153–159
overview, 151
preliminary reading for, 153
preliminary/rough outline
preparation, 153
research first steps strategy
checklist, 159–160
sample MLA-style, 187–196
using/evaluating Web sites
for, 153
research paper writing
APA-style source documen-
tation for social sciences,
181–185
essay writing *vs.*, 170
final copy, 171
final copy preparation tips,
185–186
first draft, 170
MLA-style source documen-
tation for humanities,
171–181
overview, 170–171
strategy checklist, 186–187
subsequent drafts, 170
using explanatory notes,
170–171
restrictive appositive, 205–206
restrictive modifiers, 205
revising
for appropriate supporting
details, 61–62
for audience, 62–63
for better organization, 62
body paragraphs, 63, 64–66
conclusion, 63, 65, 66
introduction, 63–64, 65
options for, 60
overview, 60
through peer review, 86–87
for purpose, 62–63
for sentence variety, 77–78
strategy checklist for descriptive paper writing and, 99
for suitable structure, 63–66
thesis, 60–61
for thought/content/
structure, 60
revising and editing
in action in sample student
writing, 86–96
for additional style problems,
79–85
improving style through,
71–78
strategy checklist for
proofreading and, 92–94
revising language
abstract writing in, 68–70
concrete writing in, 68–70
connotation in, 67–68

denotation in, 67
overview, 67
rough draft writing
strategy checklist, 30–31
tips, 26
rough outline
as preparation for formal
outline, 45
research paper preparation
of preliminary, 153
run-on sentence
comma splice, 207, 223
definition of, 223
as fused sentence, 223

second-person pronouns/
verbs, 217
subject–verb agreement
with, 227
semicolon usage, 223–224
sentence(s). *See also* run-on
sentence; topic sentence
writing
definition of, 224
examples in, 107
extended formal definition
writing, 134–135
objects of, 216, 219–220
proper sequence of verb
tenses in, 235
revising for variety in, 77–78
subjects of, 219–220, 226, 228
subordination and combining,
76–77
as transitions, 53
varying length of, 77
varying structure of, 77–78
sentence fragments
avoiding, 211–213
dependent clauses and,
212–213
independent clauses and,
211, 212
sexist language, 83
tips for avoiding and
correcting, 84–85
shifting burden of proof,
logical fallacy, 145
shifts
in person, 224, 225
in tense, 224–225
"Shy, Egg-Stealing Neighbor
You Didn't Know You
Had, The" (Downes), 4–6
sic, 161
slang, 83
terms needing definition, 134
slanting, logical fallacy, 142
source documentation. *See* APA
style source documentation
for social sciences; MLA
style source documentation
for humanities

source list. *See also* APA
References list; MLA
Works Cited list
APA References list as, 155
MLA Works Cited list as, 155
source records, 155–159
source material, selecting/
organizing/integrating
into paper
avoiding plagiarism in,
166–168
formal outline preparation
in, 168–169
note taking in, 161–163
overview, 161
quoting/paraphrasing
sources in, 163–166
strategy checklist, 169
source records
keeping, 155–159
using index cards for, 155
source records, for books
corresponding MLA Works
Cited list citation, 156
sample and information
included, 156
source records, for periodical
articles
corresponding MLA Works
Cited list citation, 157
sample and information
included, 157
source records, for World Wide
Web source
corresponding MLA Works
Cited list citation, 158–159
sample and information
included, 158
sources
documenting/crediting/
citing, 172
evaluating, 154–155
research paper documenta-
tion of, 151–152
research paper working
citations list and finding
of, 153–159
space order, in paragraph
coherence, 55–56
spammers, 14
spelling
dictionary use and, 226
importance of/rules, 225–226
words with frequent
incorrect, 226
statistics, thesis support
using, 37
stem/infinitive of verbs
of most common irregular
verbs, 231–233
as verb principal part,
231–233
story, as narrative, 101

straw man argument, logical
fallacy, 144
structure
body paragraphs as element
of, 63
conclusion as element of, 63
introduction as element of, 63
key elements of, 63
revising checklist, 65–66
revising for suitable, 63–66
style
revising and editing for additional problems in, 79–85
revising and editing to
improve, 71–78
subject
avoiding delay of, 73
-by-subject comparison-
contrast pattern, 118
delay as wordiness
source, 71
in introduction writing, 47
narrative paper writing
limiting of, 102
research paper choosing
of, 151
in thesis statement
development, 34
subjective pronoun case, 219
subjects (of sentences). *See also*
predicate
definition of, 226
pronoun case and com-
pound, 219–220
subject–verb agreement and
compound, 228
subject–verb agreement,
227–230
subordinate clauses. *See also*
dependent clauses
dependent clauses as, 212
independent clauses *vs.*, 230
subordinating conjunctions,
212–213
subordination, 230
combining sentences and,
76–77
faulty *vs.* proper, 76
summarizing, of source
material
in note taking, 162–163
paraphrasing and, 162–163
recording quotations and,
162–163
summary
definition of, 162
note containing original
material, 163
syllogism
deduction as, 140–141
enthymeme, 140
overview, 140
premises in, 140–141

tables
reading, 11–12
sample, 11
tense shifts, 224–225
term paper. *See* research
paper
testimony, thesis support using
expert, 37
thesis
building in introduction
writing, 49
classification paper, 126
definition of, 32
descriptive paper, 97–98
elements of good, 32–33
example paper, 108
final draft, 61
finding/supporting,
32–38
first draft, 61
intermediate draft, 61
narrative paper, 102
process paper, 114
restatement in conclusion
writing, 57
topic *vs.*, 32, 33, 35
understanding, 32
thesis development
overview, 34
research paper, 151–152
thesis evaluating tips, 32–33
thesis revising
improvement through,
60–61
options for, 60
strategy checklist, 61
thesis statement
formal outline, 39, 40
in introduction writing, 47
overview, 32, 33
thesis statement, development
tips, 34–35
thesis stating/supporting
strategy checklist, 38
thesis support
through details, 36–37
logic in, 36
logical fallacies in, 36
overview, 36
using data, 36
using examples, 36
using sensory details, 36
third-person pronouns/
verbs, 217
subject–verb agreement
with, 227
Thomas, Lewis, 54
thought blocks
in establishing formal
outline main divisions,
39–40
identifying in formal outline
preparation, 44

titles
abbreviations of, 197
comma use with, 207
quotation marks usage with, 214, 222
subject–verb agreement with, 228
topic, *vs.* thesis, 32, 33, 35
topic choosing
narrowing a topic in stages, 21–22
overview, 20
setting limits on topic, 20–21
topic sentence, in body paragraph writing, 49–51
topic sentence writing
implied, 50–51
overview, 49–50, 51
stated, 50
topic sentence placement in, 50
transition(s)
avoiding too many, 52–53
in body paragraph writing, 51–53
examples, 52
overview/definition of, 51
using sentences/paragraphs as, 53
transitions, common
concluding/summarizing, 52
giving examples/intensifying points, 52
indicating additions to previous ideas, 51
indicating cause and effect, 52
showing contrasts, 52
showing similarities, 52
showing space relations, 51
showing time relations, 51
transitive verbs, 230
trite expressions, 79–80, 81
trite ideas, 80
triteness, 79–80

underlining usage, 213–214

verb principal part(s)
irregular, 231–233
past participle, 231–233
past tense, 231–233
regular, 231
stem/infinitive, 231–233
verbs. *See also* subject–verb agreement
active voice of, 73–74, 233, 235
definition of, 230
first/second/third person, 217
helping, 230–231
infinitive, 213
intransitive, 230
linking, 230
main, 230
modal, 231
passive voice of, 73–74, 233, 235
transitive, 230
voice of, 235
verb tense(s)
active voice of, 233
future, 234
future perfect tense, 234
overview, 233
passive voice of, 233
past, 234
past perfect tense, 234
present, 233–234
present perfect tense, 234
progressive constructions of active/passive, 233
proper sequence in sentences, 235
visual images, reading. *See* reading visual images
voice, of verbs, 235. *See also* active voice; passive voice

Web site(s)
research paper use/evaluation of, 153
sample, 15
Web sites, reading/evaluating
examining a Web site, 15
overview, 14
strategy checklist, 16
tips for, 14–15
Web source
MLA Works Cited list citation for, 158–159
source records, 158
wordiness, economy and, 71–73
wordiness source(s)
deadwood, 71–72
delay of subject, 71, 73
inadequate clause cutting, 71, 72
pointless repetition of meaning, 71, 72
words
frequently misspelled, 226
hyphens and compound, 213
hyphens and divided, 213
used in special sense and quotation marks, 223
working citations list
overview, 154
research paper sources finding and development of, 153–159
Works Cited list. *See* MLA Works Cited list
writing. *See also* abstract writing; active writing; concrete writing; prewriting; rough draft writing tips; topic sentence writing
learning from instructor's comments on your, 89–91
writing, sample student
final draft, 94–96
first draft, 27–30
intermediate draft, 87–91
learning from instructor's comments on, 89–91
peer review of, 86–87
revising and editing, 86–96
revising thesis in, 61–65

yes and *no*, comma use with, 206